REEDS
MARINA GUIDE
2015

The source directory for all sail & power boat owners

© Adlard Coles Nautical 2014

Adlard Coles Nautical,
50 Bedford Square, London W1B 3DP
Tel: 0207 631 5600
Fax: 0207 631 5800
e-mail: info@reedsalmanacs.co.uk
www.reedsalmanacs.co.uk

Cover photo: Port Pendennis
Tel: 01326 211211
www.portpendennis.com

Section 1

The Marinas and Services Section has been fully updated for the 2014 season. These useful pages provide chartlets and facility details for some 194 marinas around the shores of the UK and Ireland, including the Channel Islands, the perfect complement to any Reeds Nautical Almanac.

Section 2

The Marine Supplies & Services section lists more than 1000 services at coastal and other locations around the British Isles. It provides a quick and easy reference to manufacturers and retailers of equipment, services and supplies both nationally and locally together with emergency services.

Advertisement Sales
Enquiries about advertising space should be addressed to:
Redactive Media Group,
17 Britton Street,
London, EC1M 5TP,
Tel: 0207 880 7553

Area Guide
Showing Coastal Divisions

Area 1 .....**South West England**... Isles of Scilly to Anvil Point

Area 2 .....**Central Southern England**...Anvil Point to Selsey Bill

Area 3 .....**South East England** .... Selsey Bill to North Foreland

Area 4 .....**East England** .... North Foreland to Great Yarmouth

Area 5 .....**North East England**... Great Yarmouth to Berwick-upon-Tweed

Area 6 .....**South East Scotland**.. Eyemouth to Rattray Head

Area 7 .....**North East Scotland**.................Rattray Head to Cape Wrath including Orkney & Shetland Is

Area 8 .....**North West Scotland** ....Cape Wrath to Crinan Canal

Area 9 .....**South West Scotland**...Crinan Canal to Mull of Galloway

Area 10 ...**North West England**.......................... Isle of Man & N Wales, Mull of Galloway to Bardsey Is

Area 11 ...**South Wales & Bristol Channel**.. Bardsey Island to Land's End

Area 12 ...**South Ireland** ....Malahide, clockwise to Liscannor Bay

Area 13 ...**North Ireland**...Liscannor Bay, clockwise to Lambay Island

Area 14 ...**Channel Islands**.. Guernsey and Jersey

SOUTH WEST ENGLAND – Isles of Scilly to Anvil Point

Key to Marina Plans symbols

Symbol		Symbol	
	Bottled gas	P	Parking
	Chandler		Pub/Restaurant
	Disabled facilities		Pump out
	Electrical supply		Rigging service
	Electrical repairs		Sail repairs
	Engine repairs		Shipwright
	First Aid		Shop/Supermarket
	Fresh Water		Showers
D	Fuel - Diesel		Slipway
P	Fuel - Petrol	WC	Toilets
	Hardstanding/boatyard		Telephone
@	Internet Café		Trolleys
	Laundry facilities	V	Visitors berths
	Lift-out facilities		Wi-Fi

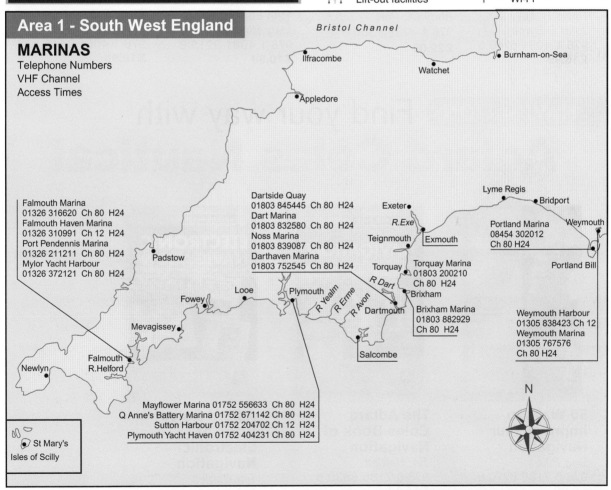

Area 1 - South West England

MARINAS
Telephone Numbers
VHF Channel
Access Times

Bristol Channel

Ilfracombe

Watchet

Burnham-on-Sea

Appledore

Falmouth Marina
01326 316620 Ch 80 H24
Falmouth Haven Marina
01326 310991 Ch 12 H24
Port Pendennis Marina
01326 211211 Ch 80 H24
Mylor Yacht Harbour
01326 372121 Ch 80 H24

Padstow

Dartside Quay
01803 845445 Ch 80 H24
Dart Marina
01803 832580 Ch 80 H24
Noss Marina
01803 839087 Ch 80 H24
Darthaven Marina
01803 752545 Ch 80 H24

Exeter
R.Exe
Teignmouth
Exmouth

Lyme Regis
Bridport

Portland Marina
08454 302012
Ch 80 H24

Weymouth

Portland Bill

Torquay
R Dart
Torquay Marina
01803 200210
Ch 80 H24
Brixham

Fowey
Looe
Plymouth
R Yealm
R Erme
R Avon
Dartmouth

Brixham Marina
01803 882929
Ch 80 H24

Weymouth Harbour
01305 838423 Ch 12
Weymouth Marina
01305 767576
Ch 80 H24

Mevagissey

Salcombe

Newlyn
Falmouth
R.Helford

Mayflower Marina 01752 556633 Ch 80 H24
Q Anne's Battery Marina 01752 671142 Ch 80 H24
Sutton Harbour 01752 204702 Ch 12 H24
Plymouth Yacht Haven 01752 404231 Ch 80 H24

St Mary's
Isles of Scilly

N

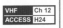

FALMOUTH MARINA

Falmouth Marina
North Parade, Falmouth, Cornwall, TR11 2TD
Tel: 01326 316620 Fax: 01326 313939
Email: falmouth@premiermarinas.com
www.premiermarinas.com

VHF	Ch 80
ACCESS	H24

Falmouth Marina lies tucked away in sheltered waters at the southern end of the Fal Estuary. Welcoming to both visiting and residential yachts, its comprehensive facilities include a restaurant, convenience store and hairdresser, while just a 20-minute walk away is Falmouth's town centre where you will find no shortage of shops and eating places. Comprising more than 70 sq miles of navigable water, the Fal Estuary is an intriguing cruising area full of hidden creeks and inlets.

FACILITIES AT A GLANCE

Key
a Marina office
b Waste oil and bin compound
c Under cover boat storage

FALMOUTH HAVEN MARINA

Falmouth Haven Marina
44 Arwenack Street
Tel: 01326 310991 Fax: 01326 211352
Email: welcome@falmouthhaven.co.uk

VHF	Ch 12
ACCESS	H24

Run by Falmouth Harbour Commissioners (FHC), Falmouth Haven Marina has become increasingly popular since its opening in 1982, enjoying close proximity to the amenities and entertainments of Falmouth town centre. Sheltered by a breakwater, the Haven caters for 100 boats and offers petrol and diesel supplies as well as good shower and laundry facilities.

Falmouth Harbour is considered by some to be the cruising capital of Cornwall and its deep water combined with easily navigable entrance – even in the severest conditions – makes it a favoured destination for visiting yachtsmen.

FACILITIES AT A GLANCE

PORT PENDENNIS MARINA

Port Pendennis Marina
Challenger Quay, Falmouth, Cornwall, TR11 3YL
Tel: 01326 211211 Fax: 01326 311116
www.portpendennis.com

VHF	Ch 80
ACCESS	H24

Easily identified by the tower of the National Maritime Museum, Port Pendennis Marina is a convenient arrival or departure point for trans-Atlantic or Mediterranean voyages. Lying adjacent to the town centre, Port Pendennis is divided into an outer marina, with full tidal access, and inner marina, accessible three hours either side of HW. Among its impressive array of marine services is Pendennis Shipyard, one of Britain's most prestigious yacht builders, while other amenities on site include car hire, tennis courts and a yachtsman's lounge, from where you can send faxes or e-mails. Within walking distance of the marina are beautiful sandy beaches, an indoor swimming pool complex and castle.

FACILITIES AT A GLANCE

MYLOR YACHT HARBOUR

Mylor Yacht Harbour Marina
Mylor, Falmouth, Cornwall, TR11 5UF
Tel: 01326 372121 Fax: 01326 372120
Email: enquiries@mylor.com

VHF	Ch M, 80
ACCESS	H24

Situated on the western shore of Carrick Roads in the beautiful Fal Estuary, Mylor Yacht Harbour has been improved and expanded in recent years, now comprising two substantial breakwaters, three inner pontoons and approximately 250 moorings. With 24 hour access, good shelter and excellent facilities, it ranks among the most popular marinas on the SW Coast of England.

Formerly the Navy's smallest dockyard, established in 1805, Mylor is today a thriving yachting centre as well as home to the world's only remaining sailing oyster fishing fleet. With Falmouth just 10 mins away, local attractions include the Eden Project in St Austell and the National Maritime Museum in Falmouth.

FACILITIES AT A GLANCE

Key
a Harbour cafe and shops
b Showers/toilets
c Kingsmoor Cottage and Castaways Wine Bar
d Marina office
e Rigging pontoon
f New public slipway
g Fueling pontoon
h Marine services and Harbour office
i Water taxi pick up
j Yacht club/laundry

MAYFLOWER MARINA

Mayflower International Marina
Ocean Quay, Richmond Walk, Plymouth, PL1 4LS
Tel: 01752 556633 Fax: 01752 606896
Email: info@mayflowermarina.co.uk

VHF Ch 80
ACCESS H24

Sitting on the famous Plymouth Hoe, with the Devon coast to the left and the Cornish coast to the right, Mayflower Marina is a friendly, well-run marina. Facilities include 24 hour access to fuel, gas and a launderette, full repair and maintenance services as well as an on site bar and brasserie. The marina is located only a short distance from Plymouth's town centre, where there are regular train services to and from several major towns and cities.

FACILITIES AT A GLANCE

Key
a Marina office
b Brokerage, chandlery
c Cafe
d Bar
e Brasserie
f Berth holders toilets and showers
g Ocean Court Flats

Northern approach

Southern approach

QUEEN ANNE'S BATTERY

Queen Anne's Battery
Plymouth, Devon, PL4 OLP
Tel: 01752 671142 Fax: 01752 266297
www.marinas.co.uk Email: qab@mdlmarinas.co.uk

VHF Ch 80
ACCESS H24

At the centre of Plymouth, Queen Anne's Battery has 235 resident berths, outstanding facilities for yachtsmen and motor cruisers alike, and a visitors' area with alongside pontoon berthing. Located just south of Sutton Harbour, all berths are well protected by a breakwater and double wavescreen.

As Plymouth Sound frequently provides the starting point for many prestigious international yacht races, the marina is often crowded with racers during the height of the season and its vibrant atmosphere can at times resemble a mini 'Cowes'.

FACILITIES AT A GLANCE

Key
a Toilets and showers
b Royal Western Yacht Club
c Marina office and provisions shop
d Bar/restaurant
e Cafe

MAYFLOWER · MARINA
· PLYMOUTH ·

www.mayflowermarina.co.uk VHF Channel 80
info@mayflowermarina.co.uk t: 01752 556633

Lat 50° 21.8 N   Long 004° 10.0 W

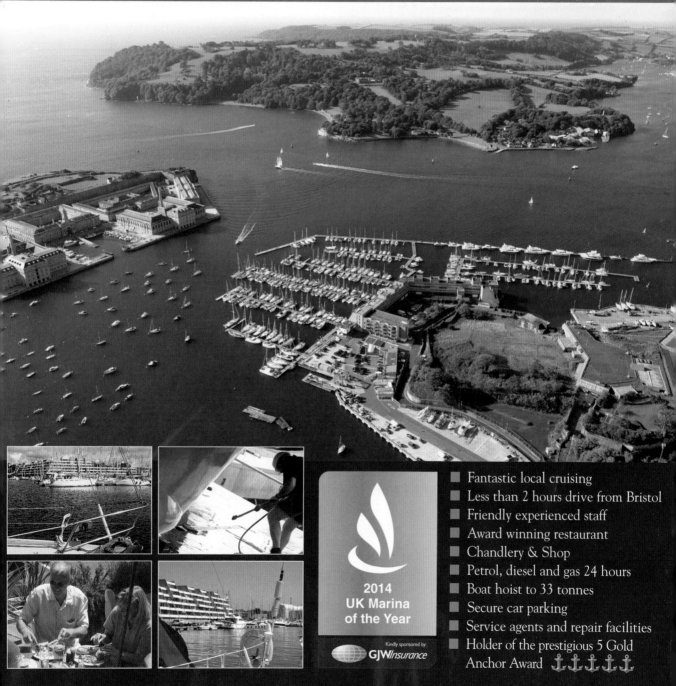

2014
**UK Marina
of the Year**

Kindly sponsored by:
GJWInsurance

- Fantastic local cruising
- Less than 2 hours drive from Bristol
- Friendly experienced staff
- Award winning restaurant
- Chandlery & Shop
- Petrol, diesel and gas 24 hours
- Boat hoist to 33 tonnes
- Secure car parking
- Service agents and repair facilities
- Holder of the prestigious 5 Gold Anchor Award ⚓⚓⚓⚓⚓

SUTTON HARBOUR

Sutton Harbour
The Jetty, Sutton Harbour, Plymouth, PL4 0DW
Tel: 01752 204702 Fax: 01752 204693
Email: marina@sutton-harbour.co.uk
www.suttonharbourmarina.com

VHF Ch 12
ACCESS H24

Sutton Harbour Marin
located in the heart of
Plymouth's historic
Barbican area and a sh
stroll from the city cer
offers 5-star facilities
in a sheltered location,
surrounded by boutiq
waterfront bars and restaurants. Offering 490 pontoon berths with a
minimum 3.5m depth, the harbour has 24-hr lock access on request
with free flow approx 3hrs either side of high tide. The marina
of choice for international yacht races such as
The Transat and Fastnet. Visitors are invited to
come and enjoy the unrivalled shelter, facilities,
atmosphere and location that Sutton harbour
offers.

FACILITIES AT A GLANCE

Key
a Fish market
b National Marine Aquarium
c Customs House
d The Cove
e Marina office
f Lock tower

PLYMOUTH YACHT HAVEN

Plymouth Yacht Haven Ltd
Shaw Way, Mount Batten, Plymouth, PL9 9XH
Tel: 01752 404231 Fax: 01752 484177
Email: plymouth@yachthavens.com www.yachthavens.com

VHF Ch 80
ACCESS H24

Situated at the mouth of the river
Plym, Plymouth Yacht Haven offers
good protection from the prevailing
winds and is within close proximity
of Plymouth Sound. This 450 berth
marina can accommodate vessels up to
45m in length and 7m draught.
Members of staff are on site 24/7 to
welcome you as a visitor and to serve diesel. 2008 saw the opening of
The Bridge Bar and Restaurant at the heart of the marina. Within easy
access are coastal walks, a golf course, and health centre with heated
swimming pool. The city of Plymouth and historic
Barbican are a short water-taxi ride away.

With a 75ton travel hoist, undercover storage,
and extensive range of marine services onsite,
Plymouth Yacht Haven has the perfect yard for any
maintenance required.

FACILITIES AT A GLANCE

Key
a Houses
b Berth holders car park
c Washdown area
d Shipwright, etc
e Snacks and takeaway
f Mountbatten Watersports Centre and bar/restaurant
g Main reception - toilets, showers, phones, launderette and disabled facilities
h The Bridge restaurant

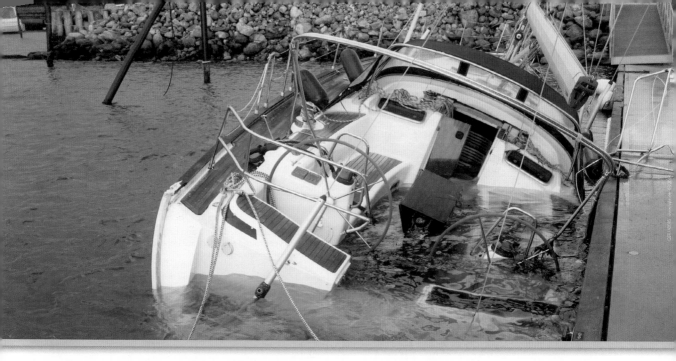

You would think that this must be covered... but is it? Check the small print!

Pantaenius offers...

 Wide range of **deductible-free** claims

 Engine damage due to breakdown of component*

 No hidden **fees** or **surcharges**

 Blue-water cruising

 Claims not excluded due to **wear and tear***

 12-months in-commission cover

 Worldwide support

 Racing – usually without additional terms

*See policy wording for full terms and conditions

Enjoy the great feeling of being in safe hands

PANTAENIUS
Sail & Motor Yacht Insurance

Germany · United Kingdom* · Monaco · Denmark · Austria · Spain · Sweden · USA** · Australia
Plymouth · Phone +44 17 52 22 36 56

pantaenius.co.uk

DARTHAVEN MARINA

Darthaven Marina
Brixham Road, Kingswear, Devon, TQ6 0SG
Tel: 01803 752242
Email: darthaven@darthaven.co.uk
www.darthaven.co.uk

| VHF | Ch 80 |
| ACCESS | H24 |

Darthaven Marina is a family run business situated in the village of Kingswear on the east side of the River Dart. Within half a mile from Start Bay and the mouth of the river, it is the first marina you come to from seaward and is accessible at all states of the tide. Darthaven prides itself on being more than just a marina, offering a high standard of marine services with both electronic and engineering experts plus wood and GRP repairs on site. A shop, post office and three pubs are within a walking distance of the marina, while a frequent ferry service takes passengers across the river to Dartmouth.

FACILITIES AT A GLANCE

Key
a Main office
   Chandlery
   Electricians
b Shipwrights
c Engineers
d Yacht taxi pontoon
e Berthing office
f Welding workshop

DART MARINA

Dart Marina
Sandquay Road, Dartmouth, Devon, TQ6 9PH
Tel: 01803 837161 Fax: 01803 835040
Email: yachtharbour@dartmarina.com
www.dartmarinayachtharbour.com

| VHF | Ch 80 |
| ACCESS | H24 |

Dart Marina Yacht Harbour, in one of the most stunning locations on the UK coastline, is a peaceful spot for simply sitting on deck relaxing and perfectly positioned for day sailing or more ambitious cruising. With visitor berths, 110 annual berths, all accessible at any tide, the Yacht Harbour is sought after for its intimate atmosphere and stylish setting.

Professional, knowledgeable and helpful, the marina team is on-site all year round and there are impeccable facilities including showers, bathrooms and laundry.

In Dartmouth there are restaurants, bistros, cafes, delis, independent shops, galleries, a cinema, chandlers, antique and lifestyle shops in abundance.

FACILITIES AT A GLANCE

NOSS MARINA

Noss Marina
Bridge Road, Kingswear, Devon, TQ6 0EA
Tel: 01803 839087 Fax: 01803 835620
Email: info@nossmarina.co.uk
www.nossmarina.co.uk

| VHF | Ch 80 |
| ACCESS | H24 |

Upstream of Dartmouth on the east shore of the River Dart is Noss Marina. Enjoying a peaceful rural setting, this marina is well suited to those who prefer a quieter atmosphere. Besides 180 fully serviced berths, 50 fore-and-aft moorings in the middle reaches of the river are also run by the marina, with mooring holders entitled to use all the facilities available to berth holders. During summer, a passenger ferry service runs regularly between Noss-on-Dart and Dartmouth, while a grocery service to your boat can be provided on request.

FACILITIES AT A GLANCE

Key
a Marina office
b Amenities

DARTSIDE QUAY

Dartside Quay
Galmpton Creek, Brixham, Devon, TQ5 0EH
Tel: 01803 845445 Fax: 01803 843558
Email: dartsidequay@mdlmarinas.co.uk www.marinas.co.uk

VHF | Ch 80
ACCESS | H24

Located at the head of Galmpton Creek, Dartside Quay lies three miles up river from Dartmouth.

In a sheltered position and with beautiful views across to Dittisham, it offers extensive boatyard facilities. The seven-acre dry boat storage area has space for over 300 boats and is serviced by a 65-ton hoist operating from a purpose-built dock, plus a 16-ton trailer hoist operating on a slipway.

There are also a number of summer mud moorings available and a well stocked chandlery, in fact if the item you want is not in stock we can order it in for you.

FACILITIES AT A GLANCE

Key
a Commercial unit
b Lower main quarry
c Middle quarry
d Top quarry
e Upper main quarry
f Cottage
g Battery, hazardous waste and oil disposal
h Admin/yard office and chandlery

BRIXHAM MARINA

Brixham Marina
Berry Head Road, Brixham
Devon, TQ5 9BW
Tel: 01803 882929 Fax: 01803 882737
www.marinas.co.uk Email: brixham@mdlmarinas.co.uk

VHF | Ch 80
ACCESS | H24

Home to one of Britain's largest fishing fleets, Brixham Harbour is located on the southern shore of Tor Bay, which is well sheltered from westerly winds and where tidal streams are weak. Brixham Marina, housed in a separate basin to the work boats, provides easy access in all weather conditions and at all states of the tide. A new boat lift dock has been installed with the state-of-the-art system capable of lifting boats of up to 50 tons and 60ft in length in just five minutes.

Local attractions include a walk out to Berry Head Nature Reserve and a visit to the replica of Sir Francis Drake's *Golden Hind*.

FACILITIES AT A GLANCE

Key
a Dock manager's office
b Information centre
c Boat sales and Sea School

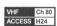

ADLARD COLES NAUTICAL
The Best Sailing Books

ANDY DU PORT
your first **channel**
CROSSING

Your First Channel Crossing

Andy Du Port

978 1 4081 0012 7

£16.99

Tel: 01256 302699
email: direct@macmillan.co.uk

TORQUAY MARINA

Torquay Marina
Torquay, Devon, TQ2 5EQ
Tel: 01803 200210 Fax: 01803 200225
Email: torquaymarina@mdlmarinas.co.uk www.marinas.co.uk

VHF | Ch 80
ACCESS | H24

Tucked away in the north east corner of Torbay, Torquay Marina is well sheltered from the prevailing SW'ly winds, providing safe entry in all conditions and at any state of the tide. Located in the centre of Torquay, the marina enjoys easy access to the town's numerous shops, bars and restaurants.

Torquay is ideally situated for either exploring Tor Bay itself, with its many delightful anchorages, or else for heading further west to experience several other scenic harbours such as Dartmouth and Salcombe. It also provides a good starting point for crossing to Brittany, Normandy or the Channel Islands.

FACILITIES AT A GLANCE

Key
a Dock manager's office
b Dockmaster offices
c Restaurant, cafe and newsagents

PORTLAND MARINA

Portland Marina
Osprey Quay, Portland, Dorset, DT5 1DX
Tel: 08454 302012 Fax: 08451 802012
www.deanreddyhoff.co.uk
Email: sales@portlandmarina.co.uk

⚓⚓⚓⚓

| VHF | Ch 80 |
| ACCESS | H24 |

Portland Marina is an ideal location for both annual berthing and weekend stopovers. The marina offers first class facilities including washrooms, on-site bar and restaurant, lift out and storage up to 320T, dry stacking up to 10m, 24-hour manned security, fuel berth, sewage pump out, extensive car parking and a full range of marine services including a chandlery.

The marina is within walking distance of local pubs and restaurants on Portland with Weymouth's bustling town centre and mainline railway station just a short bus or ferry ride away.

FACILITIES AT A GLANCE

Key
a Admin Office, washrooms, showers and laundry
b Bar and Restaurant
c Business/retail units
d Refuse and recycling bins
e Commercial units
f Dry stack storage building
g Sunseeker

Berthing guide
From low at hammerheads
Odds outside
Evens inside

WEYMOUTH HARBOUR

Harbour Office
13 Custom House Quay, Weymouth, Dorset, DT4 8BG
Tel: 01305 838423 Fax: 01305 767927
Email: b.office3@westdorset-weymouth.gov.uk
www.harbour.weymouth.gov.uk

| VHF | Ch 12 |
| ACCESS | H24 |

Weymouth Harbour, situated on the Jurassic Coast, lays NE of Portland in the protected waters of Weymouth Bay. Located in the heart of the old town and accessible at any state of tide, the Georgian harbour has numerous overnight berths. Pontoons on both quays have electricity and fresh water, as well as modern shower facilities. Restaurants and shops abound within walking distance and visitors are also welcome in the Royal Dorset YC and Weymouth SC, both situated on the quayside.

Vessels are advised to call *Weymouth Harbour* on Ch12 on approach, and vessels over 15m are recommended to give prior notification of intended arrival.

FACILITIES AT A GLANCE

Key
a Waiting pontoon for bridge
b Lifeboat
c Weymouth Sailing Club
d Royal Dorset Yacht Club

WEYMOUTH MARINA

Weymouth Marina
70 Commercial Road, Dorset, DT4 8NA
Tel: 01305 767576 Fax: 01305 767575
www.weymouth-marina.co.uk
Email: sales@weymouth-marina.co.uk

| VHF | Ch 80 |
| ACCESS | H24 |

With more than 280 permanent and visitors' berths, Weymouth is a modern, purpose-built marina ideally situated for yachtsmen cruising between the West Country and the Solent. It is also conveniently placed for sailing to France or the Channel Islands. Accessed via the town's historic lifting bridge, which opens every even hour 0800–2000 (plus 2100 Jun–Aug), the marina is dredged to 2.5m below chart datum. It provides easy access to the town centre, with its abundance of shops, pubs and restaurants, as well as to the traditional seafront where an impressive sandy beach is overlooked by an esplanade of hotels.

FACILITIES AT A GLANCE

ADLARD COLES NAUTICAL
The Best Sailing Books

Reeds iPad Almanac

Your invaluable Almanac data is available in segments, so that you can purchase just the parts that you need.

To Order Visit
www.reedsnauticalalmanac.co.uk

Key to Marina Plans symbols

Symbol	Description	Symbol	Description
	Bottled gas	P	Parking
	Chandler		Pub/Restaurant
	Disabled facilities		Pump out
	Electrical supply		Rigging service
	Electrical repairs		Sail repairs
	Engine repairs		Shipwright
	First Aid		Shop/Supermarket
	Fresh Water		Showers
	Fuel - Diesel		Slipway
	Fuel - Petrol	WC	Toilets
	Hardstanding/boatyard		Telephone
@	Internet Café		Trolleys
	Laundry facilities	V	Visitors berths
	Lift-out facilities		Wi-Fi

Area 2 - Central Southern England

MARINAS
Telephone Numbers
VHF Channel
Access Times

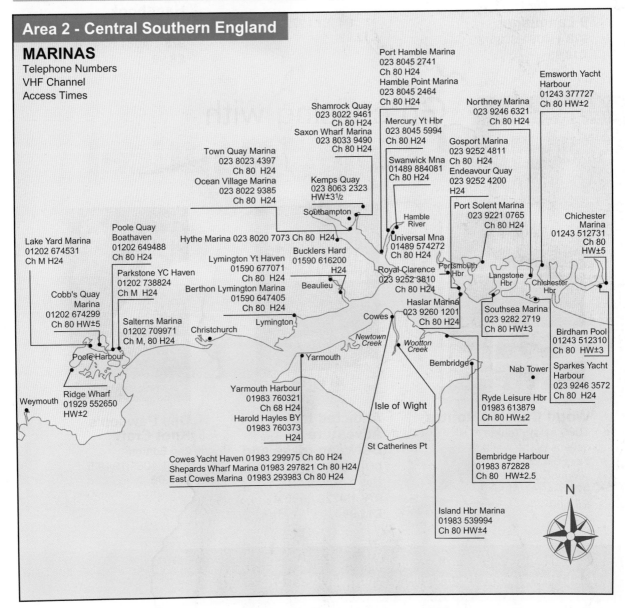

Port Hamble Marina
023 8045 2741
Ch 80 H24
Hamble Point Marina
023 8045 2464
Ch 80 H24

Emsworth Yacht Harbour
01243 377727
Ch 80 HW±2

Shamrock Quay
023 8022 9461
Ch 80 H24
Saxon Wharf Marina
023 8033 9490
Ch 80 H24

Mercury Yt Hbr
023 8045 5994
Ch 80 H24

Northney Marina
023 9246 6321
Ch 80 H24

Town Quay Marina
023 8023 4397
Ch 80 H24
Ocean Village Marina
023 8022 9385
Ch 80 H24

Kemps Quay
023 8063 2323
HW±3½

Swanwick Mna
01489 884081
Ch 80 H24

Gosport Marina
023 9252 4811
Ch 80 H24
Endeavour Quay
023 9252 4200
H24

Southampton

Hamble River

Port Solent Marina
023 9221 0765
Ch 80 H24

Chichester Marina
01243 512731
Ch 80 HW±5

Lake Yard Marina
01202 674531
Ch M H24

Poole Quay Boathaven
01202 649488
Ch 80 H24

Hythe Marina 023 8020 7073 Ch 80 H24

Bucklers Hard
01590 616200
H24

Universal Mna
01489 574272
Ch 80 H24

Portsmouth Hbr

Langstone Hbr

Chichester Hbr

Lymington Yt Haven
01590 677071
Ch 80 H24

Royal Clarence
023 9252 3810
Ch 80 H24

Parkstone YC Haven
01202 738824
Ch M H24

Berthon Lymington Marina
01590 647405
Ch 80 H24

Beaulieu

Haslar Marina
023 9260 1201
Ch 80 H24

Southsea Marina
023 9282 2719
Ch 80 HW±3

Cobb's Quay Marina
01202 674299
Ch 80 HW±5

Lymington

Cowes

Birdham Pool
01243 512310
Ch 80 HW±3

Salterns Marina
01202 709971
Ch M, 80 H24

Christchurch

Newtown Creek

Wootton Creek

Nab Tower

Sparkes Yacht Harbour
023 9246 3572
Ch 80 H24

Poole Harbour

Yarmouth

Bembridge

Weymouth

Ridge Wharf
01929 552650
HW±2

Isle of Wight

Ryde Leisure Hbr
01983 613879
Ch 80 HW±2

Yarmouth Harbour
01983 760321
Ch 68 H24
Harold Hayles BY
01983 760373
H24

St Catherines Pt

Bembridge Harbour
01983 872828
Ch 80 HW±2.5

Cowes Yacht Haven 01983 299975 Ch 80 H24
Shepards Wharf Marina 01983 297821 Ch 80 H24
East Cowes Marina 01983 293983 Ch 80 H24

Island Hbr Marina
01983 539994
Ch 80 HW±4

N

2

RIDGE WHARF YACHT CENTRE

Ridge Wharf Yacht Centre
Ridge, Wareham, Dorset, BH20 5BG
Tel: 01929 552650 Fax: 01929 554434
Email: office@ridgewharf.co.uk www.ridgewharf.co.uk

VHF	
ACCESS	HW±2

On the south bank of the River Frome, which acts as the boundary to the North of the Isle of Purbeck, is Ridge Wharf Yacht Centre. Access for a 1.5m draught is between one and two hours either side of HW, with berths drying out to soft mud. The Yacht Centre cannot be contacted on VHF, so it is best to phone up ahead of time to inquire about berthing availability.

A trip upstream to the ancient market town of Wareham is well worth while, although owners of deep-draughted yachts may prefer to go by dinghy. Tucked between the Rivers Frome and Trent, it is packed full of cafés, restaurants and shops.

FACILITIES AT A GLANCE

LAKE YARD MARINA

Lake Yard Marina
Lake Drive, Hamworthy, Poole, Dorset BH15 4DT
Tel: 01202 674531
Email: office@lakeyard.com www.lakeyard.com

VHF	Ch M
ACCESS	H24

Lake Yard is situated towards the NW end of Poole Harbour, just beyond the SHM No 73. The entrance can be easily identified by 2FR (vert) and 2FG (vert) lights. Enjoying 24 hour access, the marina has no designated visitors' berths, but will accommodate visiting yachtsmen if resident berth holders are away. Its on site facilities include full maintenance and repair services as well as hard standing and a 50 ton boat hoist, although for the nearest fuel go to Corralls (Tel 01202 674551), opposite the Town Quay. Lake Yard's Waterfront Club, offering spectacular views across the harbour, opens seven days a week for lunchtime and evening meals.

FACILITIES AT A GLANCE

COBB'S QUAY MARINA

Cobb's Quay Marina
Hamworthy, Poole, Dorset, BH15 4EL
Tel: 01202 674299 Fax: 01202 665217
Email: cobbsquay@mdlmarinas.co.uk www.marinas.co.uk

VHF	Ch 80
ACCESS	HW±5

Lying on the west side of Holes Bay in Poole Harbour, Cobb's Quay is accessed via lifting bridges at Poole Quay. With fully serviced pontoons for yachts up to 20m LOA, the marina can be entered five hours either side of high water and is normally able to accommodate visiting yachts. On site is the Cobb's Yacht Club, which welcomes visitors to its bar and restaurant.

Cobb's Quay Marina also offers a convenient 240 berth Dry Stack system for motorboats up to 10m. Offering increased security and lower maintenance costs, the service includes unlimited launching on demand seven days a week. For location, Poole is one of the largest natural harbours in the world and is considered by many to be among the finest.

FACILITIES AT A GLANCE

Key
a Dock manager's office
b Information point
c Yacht club
d Convenience store

POOLE QUAY BOAT HAVEN

Poole Quay Boat Haven
Poole Town Quay, Poole, Dorset, BH15 1HJ
Tel: 01202 649488 Fax: 01202 785619
Email: info@poolequayboathaven.co.uk

⚓⚓⚓⚓

VHF	Ch 80
ACCESS	H24

Once inside the Poole Harbour entrance small yachts heading for Poole Quay Boat Haven should use the Boat Channel running parallel south of the dredged Middle Ship Channel, which is primarily used by ferries sailing to and from the Hamworthy terminal. The marina can be accessed via the Little Channel and is easily identified by the large breakwater alongside the Quay. With deep water at all states of the tide the marina has berthing available for 125 yachts up to 35m, but due to its central location the marina can get busy so it is best to reserve a berth.

There is easy access to all of Poole Quay's facilities including restaurants, bars, Poole Pottery and the Waterfront Museum.

FACILITIES AT A GLANCE

Key
a Berthing office
b Showers/Toilets
c The Quay Hotel
d Fish landing area

Even nos - port side of pontoon
Odd nos - starboard side of pontoon

PORT OF POOLE MARINA

Port of Poole Marina
Poole Town Quay, Poole, Dorset, BH15 1HJ
Tel: 01202 649488 Fax: 01202 785619
Email: info@poolequayboathaven.co.uk

VHF	Ch 80
ACCESS	H24

Beware of the chain ferry operating at the entrance to Poole harbour. Once inside small yachts heading for the marina should use the Boat Channel running parallel south of the Middle Ship Channel. The marina is to the east of the main ferry terminals and can be identified by a large floating breakwater at the entrance.

The marina has all tides deep water and berthing for 60 allocated permanent vessels with overflow from Town Quay berthing on the breakwater, wich is also suitable for super yachts.

A water taxi is available during daylight hours to access the quay for restaurants and shops, also accessible with a 10–15min walk round the quays.

FACILITIES AT A GLANCE

Even nos - port side of pontoon
Odd nos - starboard side of pontoon
Numbering starts at hammerheads

NB All green lights are 2FG(vert)   2FR(vert)

PARKSTONE YACHT HAVEN

Parkstone Yacht Club
Pearce Avenue, Parkstone, Poole, Dorset, BH14 8EH
Tel: 01202 738824 Fax: 01202 716394
Email: office@parkstoneyc.co.uk

VHF | Ch M
ACCESS | H24

Situated on the north side of Poole Harbour between Salterns Marina and Poole Quay Boat Haven, Parkstone Yacht Haven can be entered at all states of the tides. Its approach channel has been dredged to 2.0m and is clearly marked by buoys. Run by the Parkstone Yacht Club, the Haven provides 200 deep water berths for members and visitors' berths. Other services include a new office facility with laundry and WCs, bar, restaurant, shower/changing rooms and wi-fi. With a busy sailing programme for over 2,500 members, the Yacht Club plays host to a variety of events including Poole Week, which is held towards the end of August. Please phone for availability.

FACILITIES AT A GLANCE

SALTERNS MARINA

Salterns Marina
40 Salterns Way, Lilliput, Poole
Dorset, BH14 8JR
Tel: 01202 709971 Fax: 01202 700398
Email: marina@salterns.co.uk www.salterns.co.uk

⚓⚓⚓⚓

VHF | Ch M, 80
ACCESS | H24

Holding the Five Gold Anchor award, Salterns Marina provides a service which is second to none. Located off the North Channel, it is approached from the No 31 SHM and benefits from deep water at all states of the tide. Facilities include 220 alongside pontoon berths as well as 75 swinging moorings with a free launch service. However, with very few designated visitors' berths, it is best to contact the marina ahead of time for availability.

Fuel, diesel and gas can all be obtained 24/7 and the well-stocked chandlery, incorporating a coffee shop, stays open seven days a week.

FACILITIES AT A GLANCE

Key
a Marina office
  Reception
  Chandlery
  Salterns Brokerage
  Coffee shop
  Toilets/Showers
  Marine Sales
  Laundry
  Sales offices

b Fuel pumps
  Yacht hoist
c Admin
d Dinghy racks
e Toilets & showers
f Salterns Hotel
g Boatyard workshop
h 45 tonne travel hoist
i Boatyard office
  Engine & boat sales

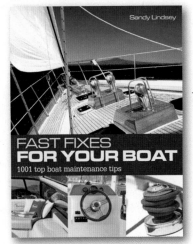
YARMOUTH HBR/HAROLD HAYLES BY

Yarmouth Harbour
Yarmouth, Isle of Wight, PO41 0NT
Tel: 01983 760321 Fax: 01983 761192
info@yarmouth-harbour.co.uk
www.yarmouth-harbour.co.uk

VHF | Ch 68
ACCESS | H24

Harold Hayles Ltd
The Quay, Yarmouth, Isle of Wight, PO41 0RS
Tel: 01983 760373 Fax: 01983 760666
Email: info@haroldhayles.co.uk
www.haroldhayles.co.uk

VHF |
ACCESS | H24

The most western harbour on the Isle of Wight, Yarmouth is not only a convenient passage stopover but a very desirable destination in its own right, with virtually all weather and tidal access, although strong N to NE'ly winds can produce a considerable swell. The HM launch patrols the harbour entrance and will direct visiting yachtsmen to a walkashore or standalone pontoon berth or pile. The pretty harbour and town offer plenty of fine restaurants and amenities.

Walkashore pontoon moorings are available from both Yarmouth Harbour and Harold Hayles Boatyard in the SW corner of the harbour. Pre-booking is preferred for both individuals or rallies.

FACILITIES AT A GLANCE

Key
a Royal Solent Yacht Club
b Harbour office
c Yarmouth Sailing Club
d Harold Hayles Boatyard

LYMINGTON YACHT HAVEN

Lymington Yacht Haven
King's Saltern Road, Lymington, S041 3QD
Tel: 01590 677071 Fax: 01590 678186
Email: lymington@yachthavens.com www.yachthavens.com

⚓⚓⚓⚓⚓

VHF	Ch 80
ACCESS	H24

The attractive old market town of Lymington lies at the western end of the Solent, just three miles from the Needles Channel. Despite the numerous ferries plying to and from the Isle of Wight, the river is well sheltered and navigable at all states of the tide, proving a popular destination with visiting yachtsmen. Access to the fuel berth is H24.

Lymington Yacht Haven is the first of the two marinas from seaward, situated on the port hand side. Offering easy access to the Solent, it is a 10-minute walk to the town centre and supermarkets. Bike and electric car hire are available through the marina office to explore the beautiful New Forest.

FACILITIES AT A GLANCE

Key
a Royal Lymington Yacht Club
b Lymington Town Sailing Club
c Owners store
d LYH office, brokerage, showers and laundry
e Haven Bar Bistro
f Yacht charter and sales
g Rigger
h Power boat sales
i Electronics

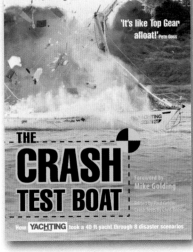
BERTHON LYMINGTON MARINA

Berthon Lymington Marina Ltd
The Shipyard, Lymington, Hampshire, SO41 3YL
Tel: 01590 647405 Fax: 01590 647446
www.berthon.co.uk Email: marina@berthon.co.uk

VHF	Ch 80
ACCESS	H24

Situated approximately half a mile up river of Lymington Yacht Haven, on the port hand side, is Lymington Marina. Easily accessible at all states of the tide, it offers between 60 to 70 visitors' berths, with probably the best washrooms in the Solent. Its close proximity to the town centre and first rate services mean that booking is essential on busy weekends. Lymington Marina's parent, Berthon Boat Co, has state of the art facilities and a highly skilled work force of 100+ to deal with any repair, maintenance or refit.

Lymington benefits from having the New Forest on its doorstep and the Solent Way footpath provides an invigorating walk to and from Hurst Castle.

FACILITIES AT A GLANCE

Key
a Dockmaster's office
b Berthon International
c Yacht maintenance & repair
d Building refit shed
e Anchor House
f Seaforth House
g Refueller

LYMINGTON HARBOUR

Lymington Harbour Commisioner
Bath Road, Lymington, S041 3SE
Tel: 01590 672014 Fax: 01590 671823
Email: harbouroffice@lymingtonharbour.co.uk

VHF	Ch ??
ACCESS	H24

Lymington Harbour Commission provides berths at Dan Bran Pontoon and Lymington Town Quay in addition to the river moorings.

Dan Bran is accessible at all states of the tide inside the wave screen. Power is available along its 650' length with use of the facilities at Lymington Town SC and walk ashore access to the town. It is sited between the marinas a short walk from Town Quay, and is an ideal for club rallies or events.

Town Quay provides shelter up river at the foot of the cobbles, which lead directly to the town centre. 25 boats (up to 2m draft) raft up to 5 deep on a walk ashore pontoon. 50 fore and aft moorings lie just off the quay.

FACILITIES AT A GLANCE

Key
a Royal Lymington Yacht Club
b Lymington Town Sailing Club
c Yacht charter and sales
d Power boat sales

BUCKLERS HARD MARINA

Bucklers Hard
Beaulieu, Brockenhurst, Hampshire, SO42 7XB
Tel: 01590 616200 Fax: 01590 616211
www.bucklershard.co.uk Email: river@beaulieu.co.uk

VHF
ACCESS H24

Meandering through the New Forest, the Beaulieu River is considered by many to be one of the most attractive harbours on the mainland side of the Solent. Two miles upstream from the mouth of the river lies Bucklers Hard, an historic 18th century village where shipwrights

skilfully constructed warships for Nelson's fleet. The Maritime Museum, showing the history of boat-building in the village, is open throughout the year.

The marina is manned 24/7 and offers deep water to visitors at all states of the tide, although the bar at the river's entrance should be avoided two hours either side of LW.

FACILITIES AT A GLANCE

COWES YACHT HAVEN

Cowes Yacht Haven
Vectis Yard, Cowes, Isle of Wight, PO31 7BD
Tel: 01983 299975 Fax: 01983 200332
www.cowesyachthaven.com
Email: berthing@cowesyachthaven.com

VHF Ch 80
ACCESS H24

Situated virtually at the centre of the Solent, Cowes is best known as Britain's premier yachting centre and offers all types of facilities to yachtsmen. Cowes Yacht Haven, operating 24 hours a day, has very few permanent moorings

and is dedicated to catering for visitors and events. At peak times it can become very crowded and for occasions such as Aberdeen Asset Management Cowes Week you need to book up in advance.

FACILITIES AT A GLANCE

2

SHEPARD'S WHARF MARINA

Shepard's Wharf Boatyard
Medina Road, Cowes, Isle of Wight, PO31 7HT
Tel: 01983 297821 Fax: 01983 294814
www.shephards.co.uk

| VHF | Ch 80 |
| ACCESS | H24 |

Just south of Cowes Yacht Haven, still on the starboard side, is Shepard's Wharf Marina and Dry Sailing Centre. Shepards operates on a first come first served basis except during Cowes Week and for organised rallies of six or more boats. All berths benefit from water and electricity with showers and wi-fi provided free of charge.

Onsite you will find the excellent Spanish restaurant Amabi, Solent Sail Company, Island Divers and Solent Yacht Brokers. For berthing availability, visiting yachtsmen should contact Shepard's Wharf Marina on VHF Ch 80. Fuel can be obtained from Cowes Harbour Fuels located 100m south of the chain ferry (Tel 01983 200716).

Shepard's Wharf is within easy walking distance of Cowes town centre (2min). Also worth visiting is the Sir Max Aitken Museum, Sir Max contributed enormously to ocean yacht racing and the museum is dedicated to his collection of nautical instruments, paintings and maritime artefacts.

FACILITIES AT A GLANCE

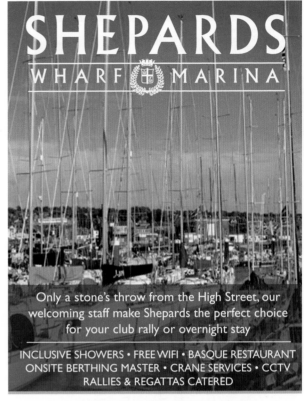

EAST COWES MARINA

East Cowes Marina
Britannia Way, East Cowes, Isle of Wight, PO32 6UB
Tel: 01983 293983 Fax: 01983 299276
www.eastcowesmarina.co.uk
Email: berths@eastcowesmarina.co.uk

| VHF | Ch 80 |
| ACCESS | H24 |

Accommodating around 235 residential yachts and 150 visiting boats at all states of the tide, East Cowes Marina is situated on the quiet and protected east bank of the Medina River, about a quarter mile above the chain ferry. A small convenience store is just five minutes walk away. The new centrally heated shower and toilet facilities ensure the visitor a warm welcome at any time of the year, as does the on-site pub and restaurant.

Several water taxis provide a return service to Cowes, ensuring a quick and easy way of getting to West Cowes.

FACILITIES AT A GLANCE

Key
a   Marina office
b   Showers, toilets & laundry
c   Pub and restaurant
d   RNLI, Inshore Lifeboat Centre
e   Clarence Boatyard
f   Commercial units

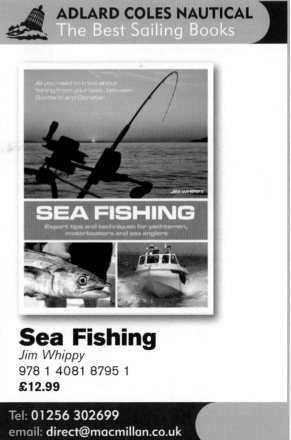

ISLAND HARBOUR MARINA

Island Harbour Marina
Mill Lane, Binfield, Newport, Isle of Wight, PO30 2LA
Tel: 01983 539994 Fax: 01983 523401
Email: info@island-harbour.co.uk

VHF Ch 80
ACCESS HW±4

Situated in beautiful rolling farmland about half a mile south of Folly Inn, Island Harbour Marina provides around 200 visitors' berths. Protected by a lock that is operated daily from 0800 – 2100 during the summer and from 0800 – 1730 during the winter, the marina is accessible for about three hours either side of HW for draughts of 1.5m.

Due to its secluded setting, the marina's on site chandlery also sells essential provisions and newspapers. A half hour walk along the river brings you to Newport, the capital and county town of the Isle of Wight.

FACILITIES AT A GLANCE

Key
a Control tower
b Bin store
c Chandlery
d Restaurant

HYTHE MARINA VILLAGE

Hythe Marina Village
Shamrock Way, Hythe, Southampton, SO45 6DY
Tel: 023 8020 7073 Fax: 023 8084 2424
Email: hythe@mdlmarinas.co.uk www.marinas.co.uk

VHF Ch 80
ACCESS H24

Situated on the western shores of Southampton Water, Hythe Marina Village is approached by a dredged channel leading to a lock basin. The lock gates are controlled 24 hours a day throughout the year, with a waiting pontoon to the south of the approach basin.

Hythe Marina Village incorporates full marine services as well as on-site restaurants and a selection of shops can be found in the town centre, a 5 minute walk away. Forming an integral part of the New Forest Waterside, Hythe is the perfect base from which to explore Hampshire's pretty inland villages and towns, or alternatively you can catch the ferry to Southampton's Town Quay.

FACILITIES AT A GLANCE

Key
a Restaurant and Bar
b Lock building
c Boat storage and Trailer park

TOWN QUAY

Associated British Ports
Town Quay, Southampton, SO14 2AQ
Tel: 02380 234397 Mobile: 07764 293588
Email: info@townquay.com www.townquay.com

VHF Ch 80
ACCESS H24

In the heart of Southampton, Town Quay is walking distance from the City's cultural quarter, West Quay Shopping Centre and a variety of restaurants, bars and theatres making the marina a vibrant place to stay all year round.

The marina is accessible at all states of the tide and the reception is open 24 hours a day with free drinks and wi-fi. Free cycle hire and use of a gas BBQ on the 'chill out' deck is available.

Located on the eastern shores of Southampton Water, Town Quay offers unrivalled views of Southampton's busy maritime activity and direct access to the world famous cruising and racing waters of the Solent.

FACILITIES AT A GLANCE

OCEAN VILLAGE MARINA

Ocean Village Marina
2 Channel Way, Southampton, SO14 3TG
Tel: 023 8022 9385 Fax: 023 8023 3515
Email: oceanvillage@mdlmarinas.co.uk www.marinas.co.uk

VHF Ch 80
ACCESS H24

The entrance to Ocean Village Marina lies on the port side of the River Itchen, just before the Itchen Bridge. With the capacity to accommodate large yachts and tall ships, the marina, accessible 24 hours a day, is a renowned home for international yacht races.

Situated at the heart of a waterside development incorporating shops, cinemas, restaurants and housing as well as The Royal Southampton Yacht Club, Ocean Village offers a vibrant atmosphere along with high quality service.

FACILITIES AT A GLANCE

Key
a Marina manager's office
b RSYC
c Dock office
d Harbour Lights Cinema
e Banana Wharf
f Pitcher and Piano

2

SHAMROCK QUAY

Shamrock Quay
William Street, Northam, Southampton, Hants, SO14 5QL
Tel: 023 8022 9461 Fax: 023 8021 3808
Email: shamrockquay@mdlmarinas.co.uk www.marinas.co.uk

VHF Ch 80
ACCESS H24

Shamrock Quay, lying upstream of the Itchen Bridge on the port hand side, offers excellent facilities to yachtsmen. It also benefits from being accessible and manned 24 hours a day. On-site there is a 75-ton travel hoist and a 47-ton boat mover, and for dining out there is a choice of restaurants and bars.

The city centre is about two miles away, where among the numerous attractions are the Medieval Merchant's House in French Street, the Southampton City Art Gallery and the SeaCity Museum in the Civic Centre.

FACILITIES AT A GLANCE

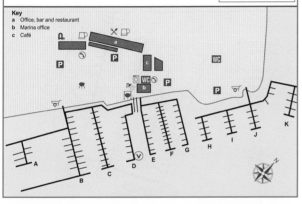

Key
a Office, bar and restaurant
b Marina office
c Café

KEMPS QUAY

Kemp's Shipyard Ltd
Quayside Road, Southampton, SO18 1BZ
Tel: 023 8063 2323 Fax: 023 8022 6002
Email: enquiries@kempsquay.com

VHF
ACCESS HW±3.5

At the head of the River Itchen on the starboard side is Kemps Quay, a family-run marina with a friendly, old-fashioned feel. Accessible only 3½ hrs either side of HW, it has a limited number of deep water berths, the rest being half tide, drying out to soft mud. Its restricted access is, however, reflected in the lower prices.

Although situated on the outskirts of Southampton, a short bus or taxi ride will soon get you to the city centre. Besides a nearby BP Garage selling bread and milk, the closest supermarkets can be found in Bitterne Shopping Centre, which is five minutes away by bus.

FACILITIES AT A GLANCE

SAXON WHARF

Saxon Wharf
Lower York Street, Northam
Southampton, SO14 5QF
Tel: 023 8033 9490 Fax: 023 8033 5215
Email: saxonwharf@mdlmarinas.co.uk www.marinas.co.uk

VHF Ch 80
ACCESS H24

Placed on the River Itchen in Southampton, Saxon Wharf is a marine service centre specifically designed for the superyacht market. With a 200-ton boat hoist and heavy duty pontoons, Saxon Wharf is the ideal location for large vessels in need of secure, quick turnaround lift-outs, repair work or even full-scale refits.

With a Dry Stack facility boasting the largest capacity forklift truck in the UK, Saxon Wharf can now dry stack boats of up to 13m LOA. There is also ample storage ashore and 24-hour security. Shamrock Quay, where there are bars and restaurants, is within 300 metres of this location.

FACILITIES AT A GLANCE

Key
a Office
b Security gate
c Southampton Yacht Services
d Offices

HAMBLE POINT MARINA

Hamble Point Marina
School Lane, Hamble, Southampton, SO31 4NB
Tel: 023 8045 2464 Fax: 023 8045 6440
Email: hamblepoint@mdlmarinas.co.uk www.marinas.co.uk

VHF Ch 80
ACCESS H24

Situated virtually opposite Warsash, this is the first marina you will come to on the western bank of the Hamble. Accommodating yachts and power boats up to 30m in length, it offers easy access to the Solent.

Boasting extensive facilities including 121 Dry Stack berths for motorboats up to 10 metres, the marina is within a 20-minute walk of Hamble Village, where services include a plethora of pubs and restaurants as well as a bank and a convenience store.

FACILITIES AT A GLANCE

Key
a Information
b First aid point
c Marina office
d Administration office
e Chandlery
f Sea Start
g Sailmakers

PORT HAMBLE MARINA

Port Hamble Marina
Satchell Lane, Hamble, Southampton, SO31 4QD
Tel: 023 8045 2741 Fax: 023 8045 5206
Email: porthamble@mdlmainas.co.uk www.marinas.co.uk

VHF Ch 80
ACCESS H24

Port Hamble Marina is situated on the River Hamble right in the heart of the South Coast's sailing scene. With thousands of visitors every year, this busy marina is popular with racing enthusiasts and cruising vessels looking for a vibrant atmosphere. The picturesque Hamble village, with its inviting pubs and restaurants, is only a few minutes walk away.

On site, Port Hamble also offers excellent facilities including the Banana Wharf bar and restaurant, which provides the perfect spot to meet, eat and drink by the water. Petrol and diesel is available seven days a week. Locally there are a number of companies on hand who cater for every boating need with all the services a boat owner requires to maintain their vessel.

FACILITIES AT A GLANCE

Key
a Dock manager's office
b Boat sales
c Royal Air Force YC
d Bar/restaurant

MERCURY YACHT HARBOUR

Mercury Yacht Harbour
Satchell Lane, Hamble, Southampton, SO31 4HQ
Tel: 023 8045 5994 Fax: 023 8045 7369
Email: mercury@mdlmarinas.co.uk www.marinas.co.uk

VHF Ch 80
ACCESS H24

Mercury Yacht Harbour is the third marina from seaward on the western bank of the River Hamble, tucked away in a picturesque, wooded site adjacent to Badnam Creek. Enjoying deep water at all states of the tide, it accommodates yachts up to 24m LOA and boasts an extensive array of facilities.

The on-site chandlery stocks a plethora of essential items, and for a good meal look no further than The Waters Edge bar and restaurant whose balcony offers striking views over the water. Hamble Village is only a 20-minute walk away.

FACILITIES AT A GLANCE

Key
a Toilets and showers
b Launderette
c Chandlery
d Restaurant and bar
e Dockmaster,
    marina manager's office
f Waste disposal
g Recycling area

UNIVERSAL MARINA

Universal Marina
Crableck Lane, Sarisbury Green, Southampton, SO31 7ZN
Tel: 01489 574272 Fax: 01489 574273
Email: info@universalmarina.co.uk

VHF Ch 80
ACCESS H24

Universal Marina is one of the few remaining independent marinas offering south coast moorings. Universal Marina's unique location is unbeatable, tucked in between the oak trees on the East Bank of the Hamble where 68 acres of natural wildlife and marshlands surrounds the busy and friendly marina. Positioned only minutes off the M27, it is one of the most accessible marinas on the south coast. The 250 berth complex, features all the latest facilities required by the modern day boat owner, recently upgraded pontoons, power, water and wifi available to each berth. Visitors are welcome & although there are no dedicated visitor berths these are available by prior arrangement.

FACILITIES AT A GLANCE

Key
a Marina Office and Chandlery
b Bar & restaurant
c Showers, WC
d Laundry room and WC
e Workshops
f Boatyard

2

SWANWICK MARINA

Swanwick Marina
Swanwick, Southampton, Hampshire, SO31 1ZL
Tel: 01489 884081 Fax: 01489 579073
Email: swanwick@premiermarinas.com
www.premiermarinas.com

VHF	Ch 80
ACCESS	H24

Situated on the east bank of the River Hamble next to Bursledon Bridge, Swanwick Marina is accessible at all states of the tide and can accommodate yachts up to 20m LOA.

The marina's fully-licensed bar and bistro, The Boat House, over-looking the river, is open for breakfast, lunch and dinner all year round. Alternatively, just a short row or walk away is the celebrated Jolly Sailor pub in Bursledon on the west bank, made famous for being the local watering hole in the British television series *Howard's Way*.

FACILITIES AT A GLANCE

Key
a Marina office
b Pub/restaurant
c Chandlery
d Boat sales offices

RYDE LEISURE HARBOUR

Ryde Harbour
The Esplanade, Ryde, Isle of Wight, PO33 1JA
Tel: 01983 613879 Fax: 01983 613903
www.rydeharbour.com Email: ryde.harbour@iow.gov.uk

VHF	Ch 80
ACCESS	HW±2

Known as the 'gateway to the Island', Ryde, with its elegant houses and abundant shops, is among the Isle of Wight's most popular resorts. Its well-protected harbour is conveniently close to the exceptional beaches as well as to the town's restaurants and amusements.

Drying to 2.5m and therefore only accessible to yachts that can take the ground, the harbour accommodates 90 resident boats as well as up to 75 visiting yachts. Fin keel yachts may dry out on the harbour wall.

Ideal for family cruising, Ryde offers a wealth of activities, ranging from ten pin bowling and ice skating to crazy golf and tennis.

Ice rink and ten pin bowling complex

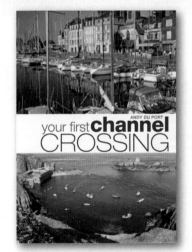
BEMBRIDGE HARBOUR

Bembridge Harbour
Harbour Office, The Duver, St Helens, Ryde
Isle of Wight, PO33 1YB
Tel: 01983 872828 Fax: 01983 872922
Email: chris@bembridgeharbour.co.uk
www.bembridgeharbour.co.uk

VHF	Ch 80
ACCESS	HW±2.5

Bembridge is a compact, pretty harbour whose entrance, although restricted by the tides (recommended entry for a 1.5m draught is 2½hrs before HW), is well sheltered in all but north north easterly gales. Offering excellent sailing clubs, beautiful beaches and fine restaurants, this Isle of Wight port is a first class haven with plenty of charm. With approximately 120 new visitors' berths on the Duver Marina pontoons, the marina at St Helen's Quay, at the western end of the harbour, is now allocated to annual berth holders only.

FACILITIES AT A GLANCE

Duver Marina

St Helen's

A – E

Bembridge Marina

Fisherman's Wharf

HASLAR MARINA

Haslar Marina
Haslar Road, Gosport, Hampshire, PO12 1NU
Tel: 023 9260 1201 Fax: 023 9260 2201
www.haslarmarina.co.uk Email: sales@haslarmarina.co.uk

VHF Ch 80
ACCESS H24

This modern, purpose-built marina lies to port on the western side of Portsmouth Harbour entrance and is easily recognised by its prominent lightship incorporating a bar and restaurant. Accessible at all states of the tide, Haslar's extensive facilities do not however include fuel, the nearest being at the Gosport Marina only a few cables north.

Within close proximity is the Royal Navy Submarine Museum and the Museum of Naval Firepower 'Explosion' both worth a visit.

FACILITIES AT A GLANCE

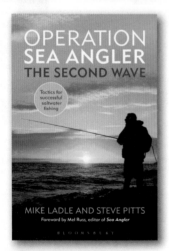

Key
a Admin. offices, security, toilets, showers, weather,
b Rubbish skips, security gate
c Bistro/bar and independent operators, trolleys
d Security, car park
e Superloo: toilets, showers, trolleys
f Bar, restaurant, toilets, shower, laundry
g Sealift
h Public slipway

Berth numbering
High numbers outermost. Even numbers on side of pontoon facing Portsmouth Harbour.

GOSPORT MARINA

Premier Gosport Marina
Mumby Road, Gosport, Hampshire, PO12 1AH
Tel: 023 9252 4811 Fax: 023 9258 9541
Email: gosport@premiermarinas.com
www.premiermarinas.com

VHF Ch 80
ACCESS H24

A few cables north of Haslar Marina, again on the port hand side, lies Gosport Marina. Boasting 519 fully-serviced, visitors' and 80 dry stack berths, its extensive range of facilities incorporates a fuel barge on its southern break-water as well as shower and laundry amenities. Numerous boatyard and engineering specialists are also located in and around the premises.

Within easy reach of the marina is Gosport town centre, offering a cosmopolitan selection of restaurants along with several supermarkets and shops.

FACILITIES AT A GLANCE

2

ENDEAVOUR QUAY

Endeavour Quay
Mumby Road, Gosport, Hampshire, PO12 1AH
Tel: 023 9258 4200 Email: enquiries@endeavourquay.co.uk
www.endeavourquay.co.uk

VHF
ACCESS H24

Endeavour Quay commands a prime location in Portsmouth Harbour on the Gosport waterfront with unrestricted access to its modern facilities by deep water. It is also a site of significant yacht building heritage being the birthplace of the famous yacht builders Camper & Nicholsons.

Now modernised, the marina provides a wide range of professional services from boat lifting (180 tons max) craneage, deep water berthing and outside/undercover storage. The open yard policy and the wide range of onsite marine related businesses makes Endeavour Quay an ideal location for emergency repairs to complex refit and specialist work for all types of vessels.

FACILITIES AT A GLANCE

ROYAL CLARENCE MARINA

Royal Clarence Marina, Royal Clarence Yard
Weevil Lane, Gosport, Hampshire PO12 1AX
Tel: 02392 523523 Fax: 02392 523523
Email: mikebraidley@castlemarinas.co.uk
www.royalclarencemarina.org

VHF   Ch 80
ACCESS H24

Royal Clarence Marina enjoys a unique setting, with the former Royal Navy victualling yard as its backdrop and views across to Gunwharf Quays on the opposite side of the harbour. The remarkably peaceful and calm marina lies within a deep water basin with 5.25m draught and offers berths up to 18m in length. RCM also has over 150m of alongside berthing making it the ideal location for rallies and other maritime events. Only five minutes from the entrance to Portsmouth Harbour, the marina is ideally located for cruising and racing in the Solent and beyond.

FACILITIES AT A GLANCE

PORT SOLENT MARINA

Port Solent Marina
South Lockside, Portsmouth, PO6 4TJ
Tel: 023 9221 0765 Fax: 023 9232 4241
www.premiermarinas.com
Email: portsolent@premiermarinas.com

⚓⚓⚓⚓⚓
VHF   Ch 80
ACCESS H24

Port Solent Marina is located to the north east of Portsmouth Harbour, not far from the historic Portchester Castle. Accessible via a 24-hour lock, this purpose built marina offers a full range of facilities. The Boardwalk comprises an array of shops and restaurants, while close by is a David Lloyd Health Centre and a large Odeon cinema.

No visit to Portsmouth Harbour is complete without a trip to the Historic Dockyard, home to Henry VIII's *Mary Rose*, Nelson's HMS *Victory* and the first iron battleship, HMS *Warrior*, built in 1860.

FACILITIES AT A GLANCE

Key a Laundry, berth holders showers, toilets and baby change
b Portsmouth Harbour YC
c Chandlery, marine engineers
d Under cover boat shed
e Berth holders showers, toilets and public toilets, baby change
f David Lloyd Health and Fitness Club
g The Boardwalk - bars/restaurants
h Odeon cinema
i Marina control and Port Solent reception
j Residential building

Bridgeheads 1 2 3

SOUTHSEA MARINA

Southsea Marina
Fort Cumberland Road, PO4 9RJ
Tel: 02392 822719 Fax: 02392 822220
Email: southsea@premiermarinas.com
www.premiermarinas.com

⚓⚓⚓
VHF   Ch 80
ACCESS HW±3

Southsea Marina is a small and friendly marina located on the western shore of Langstone Harbour, an expansive tidal bay situated between Hayling Island and Portsmouth. The channel is clearly marked by seven starboard and nine port hand markers. A tidal gate allows unrestricted movement in and out of the marina up to 3 hours either side of HW operates the entrance. The minimum depth in the marina entrance during this period is 1.6m and a waiting pontoon is available. There are excellent on site facilities including a bar, restaurant and chandlery.

FACILITIES AT A GLANCE

SPARKES MARINA

Sparkes Marina
38 Wittering Road, Hayling Island, Hampshire, PO11 9SR
Tel: 023 9246 3572 Fax: 023 9246 5741
Email: sparkes@mdlmarinas.co.uk www.sparkesmarina.co.uk

Just inside the entrance to Chichester Harbour, on the eastern shores of Hayling Island, lies Sparkes Marina. One of two marinas in Chichester to have full tidal access, its facilities include 24-hour showers and toilets, a laundry room, an office/reception, and the Piranha Bar & Restaurant.

In addition to its berthing and marina services, Sparkes has many skilled professionals on site, including specialists in engineering, outboard engines, glass fibre repairs, rigging, sails and covers, marine carpentry, electrical, boat management and valeting. There is storage ashore for over 200 boats and a 40 ton mobile crane (lifting capacity 15 tons).

FACILITIES AT A GLANCE

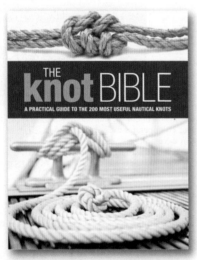

Key

a	P.T. Marine	c	Harbour office	e	Disabled toilets/showers	h	Sail Style
b	Piranha Bar/	d	Hayling Glass Fibre Repairs	f	Toilets/showers		
	Restaurant		Hayling Rigging Services	g	Laundry room		

NORTHNEY MARINA

Northney Marina
Northney Road, Hayling Island, Hampshire, PO11 0NH
Tel: 023 9246 6321 Fax: 023 9246 1467
Email: northney@mdlmarinas.co.uk
www.northneymarina.co.uk

Situated in Chichester Harbour, Northney Marina and its slipway are accessible at all states of the tide. The 228-berth marina is set on the northern shore of Hayling Island in the well marked Sweare Deep Channel, which branches off to port almost at the end of Emsworth Channel.

Offering excellent boatyard facilities, the marina incorporates a provisions store and laundry area as well as fantastic ablution facilities plus wi-fi and 24/7 staff cover. There is also an events area for rallies.

FACILITIES AT A GLANCE

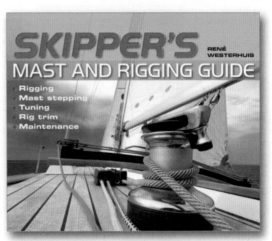

Key

a	Marina office and provisions store
b	Recycling facilities

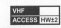

EMSWORTH YACHT HARBOUR

Emsworth Yacht Harbour Ltd
Thorney Road, Emsworth, Hants, PO10 8BP
Tel: 01243 377727 Fax: 01243 373432
Email: info@emsworth-marina.co.uk
www.emsworth-marina.co.uk

VHF
ACCESS HW±2

Accessible about one and a half to two hours either side of high water, Emsworth Yacht Harbour is a sheltered site, offering good facilities to yachtsmen.

Created in 1964 from a log pond, the marina is within easy walking distance of the pretty little town of Emsworth, which boasts at least 10 pubs, several high quality restaurants and two well-stocked convenience stores.

FACILITIES AT A GLANCE

Key
a Ground floor - toilets and showers
1st floor - harbour office
b Home Marine -
outboard engine repairs

CHICHESTER MARINA

Chichester Marina
Birdham, Chichester, West Sussex, PO20 7EJ
Tel: 01243 512731 Fax: 01243 513472
Email: chichester@premiermarinas.com
www.premiermarinas.com

VHF Ch 80
ACCESS HW±5

Chichester Marina, nestling in an enormous natural harbour, has more than 1,000 berths, making it one of the largest in the UK. Its approach channel can be easily identified by the CM SHM pile. The channel was dredged to 0.5m below CD in 2004, giving access of around five hours either side of HW at springs. Besides the wide ranging marine facilities, there are also a restaurant and small convenience store on site. Chichester, which is only about a five minute bus or taxi ride away, has several places of interest, the most notable being the cathedral.

FACILITIES AT A GLANCE

Key
a Brush washing facility
b Toilets, showers, baby change, telephone
c Trailer sailer storage
d BA Peters offices
e Launderette
f Toilets, showers, baby change, telephone, disabled facilities
g Restaurant/bar, chandlery, shop
h Reception car park
i CYC boat park
j Marina control building
k Security checkpoint

BIRDHAM POOL MARINA

Birdham Pool Marina
Birdham Pool, Chichester, Sussex
Tel: 01243 512310 Fax: 01243 513163
Email: mikebraidley@castlemarinas.co.uk

VHF Ch 80
ACCESS HW±3

Birdham Pool must be among Britain's most charming and rustic marinas. Its recently dredged channel allows access for up to four hours either side of HW via a lock. Any visiting yachtsman will not be disappointed by its unique and picturesque setting. The marina boasts a boatyard with skilled craftsmen offering a wide range of services as well as fuel. The channel is marked by green piles that should be left no more than 3m to starboard.

FACILITIES AT A GLANCE

Key to Marina Plans symbols

Bottled gas		P	Parking
Chandler			Pub/Restaurant
Disabled facilities			Pump out
Electrical supply			Rigging service
Electrical repairs			Sail repairs
Engine repairs			Shipwright
First Aid			Shop/Supermarket
Fresh Water			Showers
Fuel - Diesel			Slipway
Fuel - Petrol		WC	Toilets
Hardstanding/boatyard			Telephone
Internet Café	@		Trolleys
Laundry facilities		V	Visitors berths
Lift-out facilities			Wi-Fi

3

Area 3 - South East England

MARINAS
Telephone Numbers
VHF Channel
Access Times

N. Foreland

Margate

Ramsgate

Ramsgate Royal Harbour Marina
01843 572100
Ch 14, 80 H24

S. Foreland

Dover

Folkestone

Dover Marina
01304 241663
Ch 80 H24

Lady Bee Marina
01273 593801
Ch 14 H24

Brighton Marina
01273 819919
Ch M, 80 H24

Rye

Shoreham

Brighton

Harbour of Rye
01797 225225
Ch 14 HW±2

Littlehampton

Littlehampton Marina
01903 713553
Ch 80
HW-3 to +2.5
Hillyards
01903 713327
HW-3 to +2.5

Newhaven
Newhaven Marina
01273 513881
Ch 80 H24

Eastbourne

Sovereign Harbour Marina
01323 470099
Ch 17 H24

N

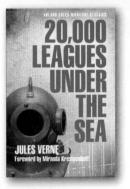

LITTLEHAMPTON MARINA

Littlehampton Marina
Ferry Road, Littlehampton, W Sussex
Tel: 01903 713553 Fax: 01903 732264
Email: sales@littlehamptonmarina.co.uk

VHF	Ch 80
ACCESS	HW-3 to +2.5

A typical English seaside town with funfair, promenade and fine sandy beaches, Littlehampton lies roughly midway between Brighton and Chichester at the mouth of the River Arun. It affords a convenient stopover for yachts either east or west bound, providing you have the right tidal conditions to cross the entrance bar with its charted depth of 0.7m. The marina lies about three cables above Town Quay and Fisherman's Quay, both of which are on the starboard side of the River Arun, and is accessed via a retractable footbridge that opens on request to the HM (note that you should contact him by 1630 the day before you require entry).

FACILITIES AT A GLANCE

Key
a Marina offices
b Cafe

THE SHIPYARD

The Shipyard
Rope Walk, Littlehampton, West Sussex, BN17 5DG
Tel: 01903 713327
Email: info@littlehamptonshipyard.co.uk

VHF	
ACCESS	HW-3 to +2.5

Formerly Hillyards, The Shipyard is a full service boatyard with moorings and storage for up to 50 boats. Based on the south coast within easy reach of London and the main yachting centres of the UK and Europe, The Shipyard provides a comprehensive range of marine services.

The buildings of the boatyard are on the River Arun, a short distance from the English Channel. They provide the ideal conditions to accommodate and service craft up to 36m in length and with a maximum draft 3.5m. There is also craning services for craft up to 40 tons and the facilities to slip vessels up to 27m. In addition there are secure facilities to accommodate vessels up to 54m in dry dock.

FACILITIES AT A GLANCE

LADY BEE MARINA

Lady Bee Marina
138-140 Albion Street, Southwick
West Sussex, BN42 4EG
Tel: 01273 593801 Fax: 01273 870349

VHF	Ch 14
ACCESS	H24

Shoreham, only five miles west of Brighton, is one of the South Coast's major commercial ports handling, among other products, steel, grain, tarmac and timber. On first impressions it may seem that Shoreham has little to offer the visiting yachtsman, but once through the lock and into the eastern arm of the River Adur, the quiet Lady Bee Marina, with its Spanish waterside restaurant, can make this harbour an interesting alternative to the lively atmosphere of Brighton Marina. Run by the Harbour Office, the marina meets all the usual requirements, although fuel is available in cans from Southwick garage or from Corral's diesel pump situated in the western arm.

FACILITIES AT A GLANCE

Key
a Sussex Yacht Club
b Riverside Boatyard

BRIGHTON MARINA

Brighton Marina
West Jetty, Brighton, East Sussex, BN2 5UP
Tel: 01273 819919 Fax: 01273 675082
Email: brighton@premiermarinas.com
www.premiermarinas.com

VHF	Ch M, 80
ACCESS	H24

Brighton Marina is the largest marina in the country and with its extensive range of shops, restaurants and facilities, is a popular and convenient stop-over for east and west-going passagemakers. Note, however, that it is not advisable to attempt entry in strong S to SE winds.

Only half a mile from the marina is the historic city of Brighton itself, renowned for being a cultural centre with a cosmopolitan atmosphere. Among its numerous attractions are the exotic Royal Pavilion, built for King George IV in the 1800s, and the Lanes, with its multitude of antiques shops.

FACILITIES AT A GLANCE

Key
a David Lloyd Heath & Fitness Club
b Bowling alley
c Casino/night club
d Multiplex cinema
e Yacht club
f Petrol station
g Mariners Quay
h Marina reception

3

NEWHAVEN MARINA

Newhaven Marina
The Yacht Harbour, Fort Road, Newhaven
East Sussex, BN9 9BY
Tel: 01273 513881 Fax: 01273 510493
Email: john.stirling@newhavenmarina.co.uk

VHF Ch 80
ACCESS H24

Some seven miles from Brighton, Newhaven lies at the mouth of the River Ouse. With its large fishing fleet and regular ferry services to Dieppe, the harbour has over the years become progressively commercial, therefore care is needed to keep clear of large vessels under manoeuvre. The marina lies approximately quarter of a mile from the harbour entrance on the west bank and was recently dredged to allow full tidal access except on LWS.

FACILITIES AT A GLANCE

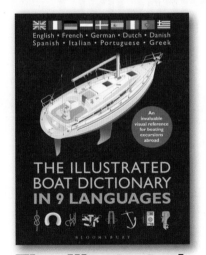

Coastguard

SOVEREIGN HARBOUR MARINA

Sovereign Harbour Marina
Pacific Drive, Eastbourne, East Sussex, BN23 5BJ
Tel: 01323 470099 Fax: 01323 470077
Email: sovereignharbour@premiermarinas.com
www.premiermarinas.com

VHF Ch 17
ACCESS H24

Opened in 1993 and taken over by Premier Marinas in 2007, Sovereign Harbour is situated to the eastern end of Eastbourne and is accessible at all states of the tide and weather except for in strong NE to SE'ly winds. Entered via a lock at all times of the day or night, the Five Gold Anchor Award marina is part of one of the largest waterfront complexes in the UK, enjoying close proximity to shops, restaurants and a multiplex cinema. A short bus or taxi ride takes you to Eastbourne, where you will find shops and eating places to suit all tastes and budgets.

FACILITIES AT A GLANCE

Key
a   The Waterfront, shops, restaurants, pubs and offices
b   Harbour office - weather information and visitor's information
c   Cinema
d   Retail park - supermarket and post office
e   Restaurant
f   Toilets, showers, launderette and disabled facilities
g   24 hr fuel pontoon (diesel, petrol and holding tank pump out)
h   Recycling centre
i   Boatyard, boatpark, marine engineers, riggers and electricians
NB   Berth numbering runs from low outer to high inner

ADLARD COLES NAUTICAL
The Best Sailing Books

English • French • German • Dutch • Danish
Spanish • Italian • Portuguese • Greek

An invaluable visual reference for boating excursions abroad

THE ILLUSTRATED BOAT DICTIONARY IN 9 LANGUAGES

BLOOMSBURY

The Illustrated Boat Dictionary in 9 Languages

978 1 4081 8785 2
£18.99

Tel: 01256 302699
email: direct@macmillan.co.uk

HARBOUR OF RYE

Harbour of Rye
New Lydd Road, Camber, E Sussex, TN31 7QS
Tel: 01797 225225
Email: rye.harbour@environment-agency.gov.uk
www.environment-agency.gov.uk/harbourofrye

VHF Ch 14
ACCESS HW±2

The Strand Quay moorings are located in the centre of the historic town of Rye with all of its amenities a short walk away. The town caters for a wide variety of interests with the nearby Rye Harbour Nature Reserve, a museum, numerous antique shops and plentiful pubs, bars and restaurants. Vessels, up to a length of 15 metres, wishing to berth in the soft mud in or near the town of Rye should time their arrival at the entrance for not later than one hour after high water. Larger vessels should make prior arrangements with the Harbour Master. Fresh water, electricity, shower and toilet facilities are available.

FACILITIES AT A GLANCE

DOVER MARINA

Dover Harbour Board
Harbour House, Dover, Kent, CT17 9TF
Tel: 01304 241663 Fax: 01304 242549
Email: marina@doverport.co.uk www.doverport.co.uk/marina

VHF	Ch 80
ACCESS	H24

Nestling under the famous White Cliffs, Dover sits between South Foreland to the NE and Folkestone to the SW. Boasting a maritime history stretching back as far as the Bronze Age, Dover is today one of Britain's busiest commercial ports, with a continuous stream of ferries and cruise liners plying to and from their European destinations. However, over the past years the harbour has made itself more attractive to the cruising yachtsman, with the marina, set well away from the busy ferry terminal, offering three sheltered berthing options in the Tidal Harbour, Granville Dock and Wellington Dock.

FACILITIES AT A GLANCE

Key
a Marina office
b Storage
c Waste oil disposal
d Scrubbing berth (tidal)

ROYAL HARBOUR MARINA

Royal Harbour Marina, Ramsgate
Harbour Office, Military Road, Ramsgate, Kent, CT11 9LQ
Tel: 01843 572100 Fax: 01843 590941
Email: portoframsgate@thanet.gov.uk
www.portoframsgate.co.uk

VHF	Ch 14, 80
ACCESS	H24

Steeped in maritime history, Ramsgate was awarded 'Royal' status in 1821 by George IV in recognition of the warm welcome he received when sailing from Ramsgate to Hanover with the Royal Squadron. Offering good shelter and modern facilities, the Royal Harbour comprises an outer marina accessible H24 and an inner marina, entered approximately HW±2. Permission to enter or leave the Royal Harbour must be obtained from Port Control on channel 14 and berthing instructions can be obtained from the Dockmaster on channel 80.

FACILITIES AT A GLANCE

Key
a Harbour office
b Port Control (VHF 14)
c Dock office
d Showers/toilets laundry
e RNLI
f Dockmasters office
g Fuel barge (VHF 14)
h Museum

EAST ENGLAND – North Foreland to Great Yarmouth

Key to Marina Plans symbols

🫗	Bottled gas	P	Parking
🪝	Chandler	✗	Pub/Restaurant
♿	Disabled facilities		Pump out
🔌	Electrical supply		Rigging service
	Electrical repairs		Sail repairs
🔧	Engine repairs	✗	Shipwright
➕	First Aid	🛒	Shop/Supermarket
	Fresh Water		Showers
D	Fuel - Diesel		Slipway
P	Fuel - Petrol	WC	Toilets
	Hardstanding/boatyard	☎	Telephone
@	Internet Café		Trolleys
▣	Laundry facilities	V	Visitors berths
	Lift-out facilities		Wi-Fi

4

Area 4 - East England

MARINAS
Telephone Numbers, VHF Channel, Access Times

Gallions Pt Marina
020 7476 7054
Ch M, 80 HW±5
South Dock Marina
020 7252 2244
Ch M HW-2½ to +1½
Poplar Dock Marina
020 7308 9930
Ch 13 HW±1
St Katharine Haven
020 7264 5312
Ch 80 HW-2 to +1½
Chelsea Harbour
020 7225 9157
Ch 80 HW±1½
Brentford Dock Marina
020 8232 8941 HW±2½
Penton Hook Marina
01932 568681
Ch 80 H24
Windsor Marina
01753 853911
Ch 80 H24
Bray Marina
01628 623654
Ch 80 H24

Suffolk Yacht Hbr 01473 659240 Ch 80 H24
Royal Harwich YC Marina 01473 780319 Ch 77 H24
Woolverstone Marina 01473 780206 Ch 80 H24
Fox's Marina 01473 689111 Ch 80 H24
Neptune Marina 01473 215204 Ch M, 80 H24
Ipswich Haven Marina 01473 236644 Ch M, 68, 80 H24

Burnham Yacht Harbour 01621 782150 Ch 80 H24
Essex Marina 01702 258531 Ch 80 H24
Bridgemarsh Marina 01621 740414 Ch 80 HW±4
Fambridge Yacht Haven 01621 740370 Ch M, 80 H24

Limehouse Marina
020 7308 9930
Ch 80 HW±3

Port Werburgh 01634 225107 Ch 80 HW±3

Chatham Maritime Marina
01634 899200

Gt Yarmouth

Lowestoft

Royal Norfolk & Suffolk YC
01520 566726 Ch 14, 80 H24
Lowestoft Haven Marina
01520 580300 Ch M, 80 H24
Lowestoft Cruising Club
07913 391950, H24

Southwold

Orford

Shotley Marina
01473 788982
Ch 80 H24

Ipswich

Harwich

Titchmarsh Marina   Walton Yacht Basin
01255 672185   01255 675873
Ch 80 HW±5   Ch 80 HW-¾ to +¼

Bradwell Marina 01621 776235 Ch M, 80 HW±4½
Blackwater Marina 01621 740264 Ch M HW±2
Tollesbury Marina 01621 869202 Ch 80 HW±2
Heybridge Basin 01621 853506 Ch 80 HW±1

R Thames

N. Foreland

Gillingham Marina
01634 280022
Ch 80 HW±4½

Ramsgate

N

GILLINGHAM MARINA

Gillingham Marina
173 Pier Road, Gillingham, Kent, ME7 1UB
Tel: 01634 280022 Fax: 01634 280164
Email: berthing@gillingham-marina.co.uk
www.gillingham-marina.co.uk

VHF Ch 80
ACCESS HW±4.5

Gillingham Marina comprises a locked basin, accessible four and a half hours either side of high water, and a tidal basin upstream which can be entered approximately two hours either side of high water. Deep water moorings in the river cater for yachts arriving at other times.

Visiting yachts are usually accommodated in the locked basin, although it is best to contact the marina ahead of time. Lying on the south bank of the River Medway, the marina is approximately eight miles from Sheerness, at the mouth of the river, and five miles downstream of Rochester Bridge. Facilities include a well-stocked chandlery, brokerage and an extensive workshop.

FACILITIES AT A GLANCE

Key
a Workshop
b Showers & toilets
c Shop
d Laundry
e Play area
f Reception & club
g Tender storage
h Lead in pontoon
i Petrol & diesel
j Leisure centre

PORT WERBURGH

Port Werburgh
Vicarage Lane, Hoo, Rochester, Kent, ME3 9TW
Tel: 01634 252107 Fax: 01634 253477
Email: jillswann@wanttoliveafloat.com

VHF Ch 80
ACCESS HW±3

Hoo Marina has been purchased by Residential Marine Ltd and is now incorporated into Port Werburgh. The port, some eight miles upriver from Sheerness, can be approached either straight across the mud flats at HW or via the creek, which has access HW±3 for shallow draught boats. The path of the creek is marked by withies, which must be kept to port.

The port accommodates residential and leisure boats from 20–200ft and has a lifting service available for craft up to 17 tons; a dry dock is available for larger boats. There are no workshop facilities but boat owners are encouraged to work on their own boats. Security is provided by H24 CCTV coverage.

All berths are supplied with water and electricity and the onsite amenity block has showers, toilets and a laundry room. There is a grocery store adjacent and shops in Hoo village approximately half a mile distant. There is a frequent bus service to nearby Rochester.

FACILITIES AT A GLANCE

CHATHAM MARITIME MARINA

Chatham Maritime Marina, The Lock Building,
Leviathan Way, Chatham Maritime, Chatham, Medway, ME4 4LP
Tel: 01634 899200 Fax: 01634 899201
Email: chatham@mdlmarinas.co.uk www.marinas.co.uk

VHF Ch 80
ACCESS H24

Chatham Maritime Marina
is situated on the banks of
the River Medway in Kent,
providing an ideal location
from which to explore the
surrounding area. There
are plenty of secluded
anchorages in the lower
reaches of the Medway
Estuary, while the river
is navigable for some 13
miles from its mouth at Sheerness right up to Rochester, and even
beyond for those yachts drawing less than 2m.
Only 45 minutes from London by road, the marina
is part of a multi-million pound leisure and retail
development, accommodating 358 boats following a
recent expansion.

FACILITIES AT A GLANCE

Key
a Fuel berth
b Pontoon access gate
c Crane pad
d Boat storage
e Facilities building
f Events berthing
g Waiting pontoon
h Lock control building
i Pump House No.5
j Pub, restaurant, hotel and
   convenience store

LIMEHOUSE MARINA

BWML Limehouse Marina
46 Goodhart Place, London, E14 8EG
Tel: 020 7308 9930 Fax: 020 7363 0428
Email: limehouse.marina@bwml.co.uk www.bwml.co.uk

VHF Ch 80
ACCESS HW±3

Limehouse Marina, situated
where the canal system
meets the Thames, is now
considered the 'Jewel in the
Crown' of the British inland
waterways network. With
complete access to 2,000 miles
of inland waterway systems
and with access to the Thames
at most stages of the tide
except around low water, the
marina provides a superb
location for river, canal and
sea-going pleasure craft alike. Boasting a wide
range of facilities and up to 90 berths, Limehouse
Marina is housed in the old Regent's Canal Dock.

FACILITIES AT A GLANCE

Key
a Cruising Association
b Chemical toilet disposal

4

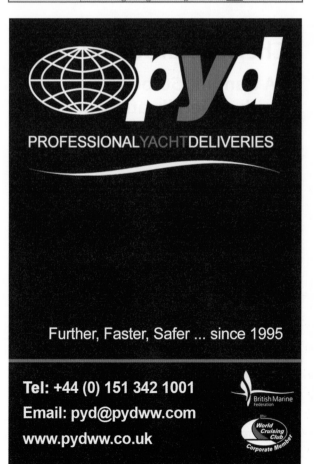
GALLIONS POINT MARINA

Gallions Point Marina, Gate 14, Royal Albert Basin
Woolwich Manor Way, North Woolwich
London, E16 2QY. Tel: 020 7476 7054 Fax: 020 7474 7056
Email: info@gallionspointmarina.co.uk
www.gallionspointmarina.co.uk

VHF Ch M, 80
ACCESS HW±5

Gallions Point
Marina lies about
500 metres down-
stream of the
Woolwich Ferry
on the north side
of Gallions Reach.
Accessed via a lock
at the entrance
to the Royal
Albert Basin, the
marina offers deep
water pontoon berths as well as hard standing.
Future plans to improve facilities include the
development of a bar/restaurant, a chandlery and
an RYA tuition school.

FACILITIES AT A GLANCE

Royal Albert Dock

Bascule Bridge

= Dock Edge Moorings

SOUTH DOCK MARINA

South Dock Marina
Rope Street, Off Plough Way
London, SE16 7SZ
Tel: 020 7252 2244 Fax: 020 7237 3806
Email: christopher.magro@southwark.gov.uk

VHF	Ch M
ACCESS	HW-2.5 to +1.5

South Dock Marina is housed in part of the old Surrey Dock complex on the south bank of the River Thames. Its locked entrance is immediately downstream of Greenland Pier, just a few miles down river of Tower Bridge. For yachts with a 2m draught, the lock can be entered HW-2½ to HW+1½ London Bridge, although if you arrive early there is a holding pontoon on the pier. The marina can be easily identified by the conspicuous arched rooftops of Baltic Quay, a luxury waterside apartment block. Once inside this secure, 200-berth marina, you can take full advantage of all its facilities as well as enjoy a range of restaurants and bars close by or visit historic maritime Greenwich.

FACILITIES AT A GLANCE

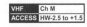

CHELSEA HARBOUR MARINA

Chelsea Harbour Marina
Estate Managements Office
C2-3 The Chambers, London, SW10 0XF
Tel: 07770 542783 Fax: 020 7352 7868
Email: harboumaster@chelsea-harbour.co.uk

VHF	
ACCESS	HW±1.5

Chelsea Harbour is widely thought of as one of London's most significant maritime sites. It is located in the heart of SW London, therefore enjoying easy access to the amenities of Chelsea and the West End. On site is the Chelsea Harbour Design Centre, where 80 showrooms exhibit the best in British and International interior design, offering superb waterside views along with excellent cuisine in the Wyndham Grand.

The harbour lies approximately 48 miles up river from Sea Reach No 1 buoy in the Thames Estuary and is accessed via the Thames Flood Barrier in Woolwich Reach. With its basin gate operating one and a half hours either side of HW (+ 20 minutes at London Bridge), the marina welcomes visiting yachtsmen.

FACILITIES AT A GLANCE

Key
a   Belvedere Tower
b   Harbour Yard
c   Wyndham Grand Hotel
d   Kings Quay
e   Chelsea Crescent
f   Thames Quay
    Showers, toilets & laundry

Key
a   Marina office
b   Conspic building

ST KATHARINE DOCKS

St Katharine's Marina Ltd
50 St Katharine's Way, London, E1W 1LA
Tel: 020 7264 5312 Fax: 020 7702 2252
Email: marina.reception@skdocks.co.uk
www.skdocks.co.uk

VHF	Ch 80
ACCESS	HW -2 to +1.5

St Katharine's Marina is a 160 berth full service marina located in central London next to Tower Bridge.

St Katharine Docks is a unique marina benefiting from waterside dining, boutique shops and excellent transport links to the West End. Visitors are welcomed all year round and the marina provides its own calendar of events details of which can be found on the website and social media pages.

The marina is ideally situated for visiting the Tower of London, Tower Bridge, *HMS Belfast* and the City of London all of which can be reached on foot. A short river bus service away is Greenwich and the Cutty Sark and to the west the Shard and London Eye.

FACILITIES AT A GLANCE

Key
a   Ivory House
b   Dickens Inn
c   Marina office
d   Tower Hotel

4

BRENTFORD DOCK MARINA

Brentford Dock Marina
2 Justin Close, Brentford, Middlesex, TW8 8QE
Tel: 020 8232 8941 Mob: 07970 143 987
E-mail: brentforddockmarina@gmail.com

VHF
ACCESS HW±2.5

Brentford Dock Marina is situated on the River Thames at the junction with the Grand Union Canal. Its hydraulic lock is accessible for up to two and a half hours either side of high water, although boats over 9.5m LOA enter on high water by prior arrangement. There is a grocery store on site. The main attractions within the area are the Royal Botanic Gardens at Kew and the Kew Bridge Steam Museum at Brentford.

FACILITIES AT A GLANCE

Key
a Shop
b Rubbish disposal
c Recycling bins
d Marina office and first aid
e Toilets, showers and slop out facilities

PENTON HOOK MARINA

Penton Hook Marina
Staines Road, Chertsey, Surrey, KT16 8PY
Tel: 01932 568681 Fax: 01932 567423
Email: pentonhook@mdlmarinas.co.uk
www.marinas.co.uk

VHF Ch 80
ACCESS H24

Penton Hook, the largest inland marina in Europe, is situated on what is considered to be one of the most attractive reaches of the River Thames; close to the vibrant town of Staines-on-Thames and about a mile downstream from Runnymede.

Providing unrestricted access to the River Thames through a deep water channel below Penton Hook Lock, the marina can accommodate ocean-going craft of up to 30m LOA and is ideally placed for a visit to Thorpe Park, reputedly one of the country's most popular family leisure attractions.

FACILITIES AT A GLANCE

Key
a Information point
b Dock manager's office
c Yacht club
d Repairs and under cover storage

WINDSOR MARINA

Windsor Marina
Maidenhead Road, Windsor
Berkshire, SL4 5TZ
Tel: 01753 853911
Email: windsor@mdlmarinas.co.uk www.marinas.co.uk

VHF Ch 80
ACCESS H24

Situated on the outskirts of Windsor town on the south bank of the River Thames, Windsor Marina enjoys a peaceful garden setting. On site is the Windsor Yacht Club and fuel (diesel and petrol), enabling you to fill up as and when you need.

A trip to the town of Windsor, comprising beautiful Georgian and Victorian buildings, would not be complete without a visit to Windsor Castle. With its construction inaugurated over 900 years ago by William the Conqueror, it is the oldest inhabited castle in the world and accommodates a priceless art and furniture collection.

FACILITIES AT A GLANCE

Key
a Boat sales & engineers
b Recycling bins
c Dock office
d Trimmers
e Yacht club

BRAY MARINA

Bray Marina
Monkey Island Lane, Bray
Berkshire, SL6 2EB
Tel: 01628 623654 Fax: 01628 773485
Email: bray@mdlmarinas.co.uk www.marinas.co.uk

VHF Ch 80
ACCESS H24

Bray Marina is situated in a country park setting among shady trees, providing berth holders with a tranquil mooring. From the marina there is direct access to the Thames and there are extensive well-maintained facilities available for all boat owners. The 400-berth marina boasts an active club, which holds social functions as well as boat training lessons and handling competitions, a small chandlery and engineering services.

Upstream is the National Trust property, Cliveden House, with its extensive gardens and woodlands. Cookham is home of the Queen's Swan Keeper, who can sometimes be seen in his traditional costume. Further on still is Hambledon Mill; from here the river is navigable as far as Lechlade.

FACILITIES AT A GLANCE

Key
a Boat storage
b Boat sales office
c Marina office, small chandlery, toilets, showers, repairs and engineering
d Battery, hazardous waste, oil and fuel disposal

BURNHAM YACHT HARBOUR MARINA

Burnham Yacht Harbour Marina Ltd
Burnham-on-Crouch, Essex, CM0 8BL
Tel: 01621 782150 Fax: 01621 785848
Email: admin@burnhamyachtharbour.co.uk

VHF	Ch 80
ACCESS	H24

Boasting four major yacht clubs, each with comprehensive racing programmes, Burnham-on-Crouch has come to be regarded by some as 'the Cowes of the East Coast'. At the western end of the town lies Burnham Yacht Harbour, dredged 2.2m below datum. Offering a variety of on site facilities, its entrance can be easily identified by a yellow pillar buoy with an 'X' topmark.

The historic town, with its 'weatherboard' and early brick buildings, elegant quayside and scenic riverside walks, exudes plenty of charm. Among its attractions are a sports centre, a railway museum and a two-screen cinema.

FACILITIES AT A GLANCE

Key
a Workshop
b Yacht sales
c Marina office
d Shower block
e The Swallowtail
f RNLI shore station
g Country park

ESSEX MARINA

Essex Marina
Wallasea Island, Essex, SS4 2HF
Tel: 01702 258531 Fax: 01702 258227
Email: info@essexmarina.co.uk
www.essexmarina.co.uk

VHF	Ch 80
ACCESS	H24

Surrounded by beautiful countryside, Essex Marina is situated in Wallasea Bay, about half a mile up river of Burnham on Crouch. Boasting 500 deep water berths, including 50 swinging moorings, the marina can be accessed at all states of the tide. On site are a 70 ton boat hoist, a chandlery and brokerage service as well as the Essex Marina Yacht Club.

Buses run frequently to Southend-on-Sea, just seven miles away, while a ferry service takes passengers across the river on weekends to Burnham, where you will find numerous shops and restaurants.

FACILITIES AT A GLANCE

Key
a Marina office & chandlery
b Essex Marina Yacht Club
c Brokerage & boat sales
d Licenced bar & restaurant

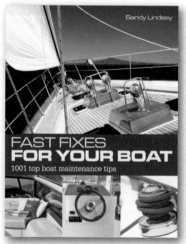

BRIDGEMARSH MARINA

Bridgemarsh Marine
Fairholme, Bridge Marsh Lane, Althorne, Essex
Tel: 01621 740414 Mobile: 07968 696815 Fax: 01621 742216

VHF | Ch 80
ACCESS | HW±4

On the north side of
Bridgemarsh Island, just
beyond Essex Marina on the
River Crouch, lies Althorne
Creek. Here Bridgemarsh
Marine accommodates over
100 boats berthed alongside
pontoons supplied with water
and electricity. A red beacon
marks the entrance to the

creek, with red can buoys identifying the approach channel into the
marina. Accessible four hours either side of high water, the marina
has an on site yard with two docks, a slipway and
crane. The village of Althorne is just a short walk
away, from where there are direct train services
(taking approximately one hour) to London.

FACILITIES AT A GLANCE

HEYBRIDGE BASIN

Heybridge Basin
Lock Hill, Heybridge Basin, Maldon, Essex, CM9 4RY
Tel: 01621 853506
Email: martin.maudsley@waterways.org.uk
www.essexwaterways.com

VHF | Ch 80
ACCESS | HW±1

Towards the head of the
River Blackwater, not
far from Maldon, lies
Heybridge Basin. Situated
at the lower end of the
14–mile long Chelmer and
Blackwater Navigation
Canal, it can be reached
via a lock about one
hour either side of HW

for a yacht drawing around 2m. If you arrive too early, there is good
holding ground in the river just outside the lock.
Incorporating as many as 200 berths, the basin has
a range of facilities, including shower and laundry
amenities. It is strongly recommendedthat you book
24 hours in advance for summer weekends.

FACILITIES AT A GLANCE

4

BRADWELL MARINA

Bradwell Marina, Port Flair Ltd, Waterside
Bradwell-on-Sea, Essex, CM0 7RB
Tel: 01621 776235 Fax: 01621 776393
Email: info@bradwellmarina.com
www.bradwellmarina.com

VHF | Ch M, 80
ACCESS | HW±4.5

Opened in 1984, Bradwell is a privately-
owned marina situated in the mouth
of the River Blackwater, serving as a
convenient base from which to explore
the Essex coastline or as a departure
point for cruising further afield to
Holland and Belgium.

    The yacht basin can be accessed
four and a half hours either side of HW
and offers plenty of protection from all
wind directions. With a total of 300 fully
serviced berths, generous space has
been allocated for manoeuvring between pontoons.
Overlooking the marina is Bradwell Club House,
incorporating a bar, restaurant, launderette and
ablution facilities.

FACILITIES AT A GLANCE

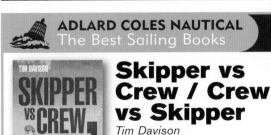

FAMBRIDGE YACHT HAVEN

Fambridge Yacht Haven
Church Road, North Fambridge, Essex, CM3 6LR
Tel: 01621 740370 Fax: 01621 742359
Email: fambridge@yachthavens.com www.yachthavens.com

VHF	Ch M, 80
ACCESS	H24

Just under a mile upstream of North Fambridge, Stow Creek branches off to the north of the River Crouch. The creek, marked with occasional starboard hand buoys and leading lights, leads to the entrance to Fambridge Yacht Haven, which enjoys an unspoilt, tranquil setting between saltings and farmland. Home to West Wick Yacht Club, the marina has 220 berths and can accommodate vessels up to 17m LOA.

The nearby village of North Fambridge features the Ferryboat Inn, a favourite haunt with the boating fraternity. Only six miles down river lies Burnham-on-Crouch, while the Essex and Kent coasts are within easy sailing distance.

FACILITIES AT A GLANCE

Key
a Marina reception
b Waste
c West Wick YC
d Boat Shed Essex
e Marina maintenance, workshop & stores
f Under cover storage

BLACKWATER MARINA

Blackwater Marina
Marine Parade, Maylandsea, Essex
Tel: 01621 740264
Email: info@blackwater-marina.co.uk

VHF	Ch M
ACCESS	HW±2

Blackwater Marina is a place where families in day boats mix with Smack owners and yacht crews; here seals, avocets and porpoises roam beneath the big, sheltering East Coast skies and here the area's rich heritage of working Thames Barges and Smacks remains part of daily life today.
But it isn't just classic sailing boats that thrive on the Blackwater. An eclectic mix of motor cruisers, open boats and modern yachts enjoy the advantages of a marina sheltered by its natural habitat, where the absence of harbour walls allows uninterrupted views of some of Britain's rarest wildlife and where the 21st century shoreside facilities are looked after by experienced professionals, who are often found sailing on their days off.

FACILITIES AT A GLANCE

Key
a Maylandsea Bay YC
b Harlow (Blackwater) Sailing Club
c Marina office

TOLLESBURY MARINA

Tollesbury Marina
The Yacht Harbour, Tollesbury, Essex, CM9 8SE
Tel: 01621 869202 Fax: 01621 868489
email: marina@woodrolfe.com www.woodrolfe.com

VHF	Ch 80
ACCESS	HW±2

Tollesbury Marina lies at the mouth of the River Blackwater in the heart of the Essex countryside. Within easy access from London and the Home Counties, it has been designed as a leisure centre for the whole family, with on-site activities comprising tennis courts and a covered heated swimming pool as well as a convivial bar and restaurant. Accommodating over 240 boats, the marina can be accessed two hours either side of HW and is ideally situated for those wishing to explore the River Crouch to the south and the Rivers Colne, Orwell and Deben to the north.

FACILITIES AT A GLANCE

Key
a Brokerage and Chandlery
b Workshop
c Covered Heated Pool and Tennis

TITCHMARSH MARINA

Titchmarsh Marina Ltd
Coles Lane, Walton on the Naze, Essex, CO14 8SL
Tel: 01255 672185 Fax: 01255 851901
Email: info@titchmarshmarina.co.uk
www.titchmarshmarina.co.uk

VHF	Ch 80
ACCESS	HW±5

Titchmarsh Marina sits on the south side of The Twizzle in the heart of the Walton Backwaters. As the area is designated as a 'wetland of international importance', the marina has been designed and developed to function as a natural harbour. The 420 berths are well sheltered by the high-grassed clay banks, offering good protection in all conditions. Access to Titchmarsh is over a sill, which has a depth of about 1m at LWS, but once inside the basin, the depth increases to around 2m. Among the excellent facilities on site are the well stocked Marinestore Chandlery and Harbour Lights Restaurant & Bar serving carvery meals daily.

FACILITIES AT A GLANCE
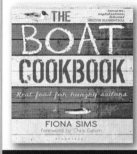

Key
a   Harbour master, chandlery (+ cycle hire) marine engineers, marine electronics
b   Hardstanding
c   Harbour Lights - restaurant and bar

4

WALTON YACHT BASIN

Walton and Frinton Yacht Trust
Mill Lane, Walton on the Naze, CO14 8PF
Managed by Bedwell & Co Tel: 01255 675873
Fax: 01255 677405 After hours Tel: 01255 672655

VHF	
ACCESS	HW-0.75, HW+0.25

Walton Yacht Basin lies at the head of Walton Creek, an area made famous in Arthur Ransome's *Swallows & Amazons* and *Secret Waters*. The creek can only be navigated two hours either side of HW, although yachts heading for the Yacht Basin should arrive on a rising tide as the entrance gate is kept shut once the tide turns in order to retain the water inside. Before entering the gate, moor up against the Club Quay to enquire about berthing availability.

A short walk away is the popular seaside town of Walton, full of shops, pubs and restaurants. Its focal point is the pier which, overlooking superb sandy beaches, offers various attractions including a ten-pin bowling alley. Slightly further out of town, the Naze affords pleasant coastal walks with striking panoramic views.

FACILITIES AT A GLANCE

SUFFOLK YACHT HARBOUR

Suffolk Yacht Harbour Ltd
Levington, Ipswich, Suffolk, IP10 0LN
Tel: 01473 659240 Fax: 01473 659632
Email: info@syharbour.co.uk
www.syharbour.co.uk

VHF	Ch 80
ACCESS	H24

A friendly, independently-run marina on the East Coast of England, Suffolk Yacht Harbour enjoys a beautiful rural setting on the River Orwell, yet is within easy access of Ipswich, Woodbridge and Felixstowe. With approximately 550 berths, the marina offers extensive facilities while the Haven Ports Yacht Club provides a bar and restaurant.

FACILITIES AT A GLANCE

SHOTLEY MARINA

Shotley Marina Ltd
Shotley Gate, Ipswich, Suffolk, IP9 1QJ
Tel: 01473 788982 Fax: 01473 788868
Email: sales@shotleymarina.co.uk
www.shotleymarina.co.uk www.eastcoastmarinas.co.uk

VHF	Ch 80
ACCESS	H24

Based in the well protected Harwich Harbour where the River Stour joins the River Orwell, Shotley Marina is only eight miles from the county town of Ipswich. Entered via a lock at all states of the tide, its first class facilities include extensive boat repair and maintenance services as well as a well-stocked chandlery and on site bar and restaurant. The marina is strategically placed for sailing up the Stour to Manningtree, up the Orwell to Pin Mill or exploring the Rivers Deben, Crouch and Blackwater as well as the Walton Backwaters.

FACILITIES AT A GLANCE

Key
a Shotley Marine Services
b Lock control
c Lock waiting pontoons
d Brokerage
e Mariners Bar and function rooms
f Baths, showers and toilets
g Launderette
h Shipwreck bar and restaurant
i Britannia Sailing School
j HMS Ganges Museum

"The East Coast's Premier Marina..."

shotleymarina.co.uk

Shotley Marina

The marina is situated where the rivers Stour and Orwell meet in Harwich Harbour. Access to this sheltered marina is via a hydraulically operated lock, manned continually throughout the year, 24 hours a day. The lockmaster listens on VHF CH80. The entrance to the lock is floodlit at night and the outer end of the access channel has lit piles. An "Inogon" guidance light system assists on entering the lock.

- **350 Ultra Modern Berths**
- **Safe & Secure Mooring**
- **24 Hour Access**
- **Specialist Boat Repairs**
- **Public House & Restaurant**
- **Water, Electricity, Modern Toilets, Showers, Laundry and Disabled Facilities**
- **Ships Stores**
- **WiFi Internet Access**

Shotley Marina Ltd. Shotley Gate, Ipswich, Suffolk IP9 1QJ
T: 01473 788982 F: 01473 788868 E: sales@shotleymarina.co.uk

ROYAL HARWICH YACHT CLUB MARINA

Royal Harwich Yacht Club Marina
Marina Road, Woolverstone, Suffolk, IP9 1BA
Tel: 01473 780319 Fax: 01473 780919
www.rhyc.demon.co.uk
Email: manager@royalharwich.co.uk

VHF	Ch 77
ACCESS	H24

This 54 berth marina is ideally situated at a mid point on the Orwell between Levington and Ipswich. The facility is owned and run by the Royal Harwich Yacht Club and enjoys a full catering and bar service in the Clubhouse. The marina benefits from full tidal access, and can accommodate yachts up to 14.5m on the hammerhead. Within the immediate surrounds, there are boat repair services, and a well stocked chandlery. The marina is situated a mile's walk from the world famous Pin Mill and is a favoured destination with visitors from Holland, Belgium and Germany. The marina welcomes racing yachts and cruisers, and is able to accommodate multiple bookings.

FACILITIES AT A GLANCE

RIVER ORWELL

A B

N

WC
RYHC

WOOLVERSTONE MARINA

Woolverstone Marina
Woolverstone, Ipswich, Suffolk, IP9 1AS
Tel: 01473 780206 Fax: 01473 780273
Email: woolverstone@mdlmarinas.co.uk www.marinas.co.uk

VHF	Ch 80
ACCESS	H24

Woolverstone Marina is set in 22 acres of glorious parkland on the picturesque River Orwell. Within easy reach of the sea and a multitude of scenic destinations, this is a great base to start cruising. Walton Backwaters and the River Deben are only a short distance away. If you prefer longer distance cruising then Belgium and Holland are directly across the North Sea.

Besides boat repair services, an on-site chandlery and excellent ablution facilities, the marina also incorporates a yacht brokerage and the Buttermans bar and restaurant, which overlooks the river and serves fine food using fresh local produce.

FACILITIES AT A GLANCE

Key
a Marina office, toilets, showers, launderette and boat sales
b Buttermans Bar Restaurant

G F E D C B A
b

Boat Storage   P

P   Boat Storage

Caravan Park   P

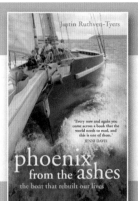
4

FOX'S MARINA

Fox's Marina & Boatyard
The Strand, Ipswich, Suffolk, IP2 8SA
Tel: 01473 689111 Fax: 01473 601737
Email: foxs@foxsmarina.com www.foxsmarina.com

VHF	Ch 80
ACCESS	H24

Located on the picturesque River Orwell, Fox's provides good shelter in all conditions and access at all states of tide with 100 pontoon berths and ashore storage for 200 vessels. A 70 tonne hoist is able to handle boats up to 80ft in length.

Fox's Marina & Boatyard offers a full range of in-house boatyard services and, with 10,000 sq ft of heated workshop space, are specialists in repairs and refits of sailing and motor yachts and commercial craft. Specific services include coppercoat and osmosis treatment, specialist GRP and gelcoat repairs, spray painting and varnishing, and custom stainless fabrication.

Also on-site, Fox's Marine & Country store, is the largest stockist of marine chandlery and equipment, sailing, leisure and country clothing in East Anglia.

FACILITIES AT A GLANCE

Key
a Chandlery
b Harbourmaster office
c Yacht Club

HAMILTON DOCK

Hamilton Dock, c/o Lowestoft Haven Marina
School Road, Lowestoft, Suffolk, NR33 9NB
Tel: 01502 580300 Fax: 01502 581851
Email: lowestofhaven@abports.co.uk
www.lowestofthavenmarina.co.uk

VHF	Ch M, 80
ACCESS	H24

Lowestoft Haven Marina's Hamilton Dock is based in an old fish dock in the outer harbour and offers easy access to the open sea making it an ideal overnight location, whilst its in town position means all the facilities of the town centre are at your doorstep.

The marina's 47 berths can accommodate vessels from 10–28m and is especially geared up for club bookings. It offers a full range of modern facilities and is complimented by the main marina at School Road for boatyard facilities.

FACILITIES AT A GLANCE

Key
a Toilets
b Fish Market

NEPTUNE MARINA

Neptune Marina Ltd
Neptune Quay, Ipswich, IP4 1QJ
Tel: 01473 215204 Fax: 01473 215206
Email: enquiries@neptune-marina.com

VHF	Ch M, 80
ACCESS	H±2.5

The Wet Dock at Ipswich, which was opened in 1850, became the largest in Europe and was in use right up until the 1930s. Now the dock incorporates Neptune Marina, situated at Neptune Quay on the Historic Waterfront, and ever increasing shoreside developments. This 26-acre dock is accessible through a 24-hr lock gate, with a waiting pontoon outside. The town centre is a 10 minute walk away, while Cardinal Park, a relatively new complex housing an 11-screen cinema and several eating places, is nearby. There are also a number of other excellent restaurants along the quayside and adjacent to the Marina. The Neptune Marina building occupies an imposing position in the NE corner of the dock with quality coffee shop and associated retail units.

FACILITIES AT A GLANCE

Key
a Old Custom House
b Conference centre
c Floating French restaurant
d Bistro
e Bellway apartments
f Neptune Marina office & facilities
g Marina storage yard

IPSWICH HAVEN MARINA

Ipswich Haven Marina
Associated British Ports
New Cut East, Ipswich, Suffolk, IP3 0EA
Tel: 01473 236644 Fax: 01473 236645
Email: ipswichhaven@abports.co.uk

VHF	Ch M, 68 & 80
ACCESS	H24

Lying at the heart of Ipswich, the Haven Marina enjoys close proximity to all the bustling shopping centres, restaurants, cinemas and museums that this County Town of Suffolk has to offer. The main railway station is only a 10-minute walk away, where there are regular connections to London, Cambridge and Norwich, all taking just over an hour to get to.

Within easy reach of Holland, Belgium and Germany, East Anglia is proving an increasingly popular cruising ground. The River Orwell, displaying breathtaking scenery, was voted one of the most beautiful rivers in Britain by the RYA.

FACILITIES AT A GLANCE

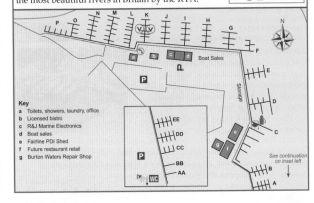

Key
a Toilets, showers, laundry, office
b Licensed bistro
c R&J Marine Electronics
d Boat sales
e Fairline PDI Shed
f Future restaurant retail
g Burton Waters Repair Shop

See continuation on inset left

ROYAL NORFOLK & SUFFOLK YACHT CLUB

Royal Norfolk and Suffolk Yacht Club
Royal Plain, Lowestoft, Suffolk, NR33 0AQ
Tel: 01502 566726 Fax: 01502 5521735
Email: admin@rnsyc.org.uk www.msyc.net

VHF	Ch 14, 80
ACCESS	H24

With its entrance at the inner end of the South Pier, opposite the Trawl Basin on the north bank, the Royal Norfolk and Suffolk Yacht Club marina occupies a sheltered position in Lowestoft Harbour. Lowestoft has always been an appealing destination to yachtsmen due to the fact that it can be accessed at any state of the tide, 24 hours a day. Note, however, that conditions just outside the entrance can get pretty lively when the wind is against tide. The clubhouse is enclosed in an impressive Grade 2 listed building overlooking the marina and its facilities include a bar and restaurant as well as a formal dining room with a full *à la carte* menu.

FACILITIES AT A GLANCE

RNSYC

Key
a Showers, toilets including disabled
b Restaurant
c Reception
d Sun lounge
e Bar
f Marina office

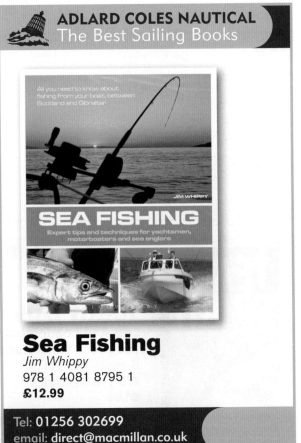

LOWESTOFT HAVEN MARINA

Lowestoft Haven Marina
School Road, Lowestoft, Suffolk, NR33 9NB
Tel: 01502 580300 Fax: 01502 581851
Email: lowestofthaven@abports.co.uk
www.lowestofthavenmarina.co.uk

⚓⚓⚓⚓⚓

VHF	Ch M, 80
ACCESS	H24

Lowestoft Haven Marina is based on Lake Lothing with easy access to both the open sea and the Norfolk Broads. The town centres of both Lowestoft and Oulton Broad are within a short distance of the marina.

The marina's 140 berths can accommodate vessels from 7–20m. Offering a full range of modern facilities the marina welcomes all visitors.

FACILITIES AT A GLANCE

Key
a   Boat storage
b   Marina office & Boat sales

4

LOWESTOFT CRUISING CLUB

Lowestoft Cruising Club
Off Harbour Road, Oulton Broad, Lowestoft, Suffolk, NR32 3LY
Tel: 07913 391950
www.lowestoftcruisingclub.co.uk

VHF	
ACCESS	H24

Lowestoft Cruising Club welcomes visitors and can offer a friendly atmosphere, some of the finest moorings and at very competitive rates. Whatever the weather, these moorings provide a calm, safe haven for visiting yachts and with the Mutford lock only 250 metres away, easy access onto the Norfolk and Suffolk Broads. Facilities include electricity and water, plus excellent showers, toilets and secure car parking. These moorings are the nearest ones to the railway stations (to Norwich and Ipswich), bus routes, shops, banks, pubs and restaurants in Oulton Broad.

FACILITIES AT A GLANCE

NORTH EAST ENGLAND - Great Yarmouth to Berwick-upon-Tweed

Key to Marina Plans symbols

Symbol		Symbol	
🔋	Bottled gas	P	Parking
	Chandler	✕	Pub/Restaurant
♿	Disabled facilities		Pump out
	Electrical supply		Rigging service
	Electrical repairs		Sail repairs
	Engine repairs	✕	Shipwright
✚	First Aid	🛒	Shop/Supermarket
	Fresh Water		Showers
D	Fuel - Diesel		Slipway
P	Fuel - Petrol	WC	Toilets
	Hardstanding/boatyard		Telephone
@	Internet Café		Trolleys
	Laundry facilities	V	Visitors berths
	Lift-out facilities		Wi-Fi

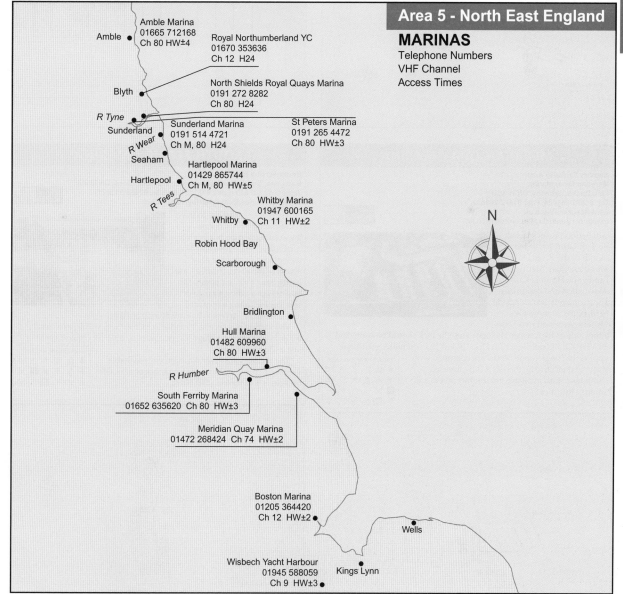

Area 5 - North East England

MARINAS
Telephone Numbers
VHF Channel
Access Times

Amble

Amble Marina
01665 712168
Ch 80 HW±4

Royal Northumberland YC
01670 353636
Ch 12 H24

Blyth

North Shields Royal Quays Marina
0191 272 8282
Ch 80 H24

R Tyne

Sunderland

Sunderland Marina
0191 514 4721
Ch M, 80 H24

St Peters Marina
0191 265 4472
Ch 80 HW±3

R Wear

Seaham

Hartlepool

Hartlepool Marina
01429 865744
Ch M, 80 HW±5

R Tees

Whitby Marina
01947 600165
Ch 11 HW±2

Whitby

Robin Hood Bay

Scarborough

Bridlington

Hull Marina
01482 609960
Ch 80 HW±3

R Humber

South Ferriby Marina
01652 635620 Ch 80 HW±3

Meridian Quay Marina
01472 268424 Ch 74 HW±2

Boston Marina
01205 364420
Ch 12 HW±2

Wells

Wisbech Yacht Harbour
01945 588059
Ch 9 HW±3

Kings Lynn

N

WISBECH YACHT HARBOUR

Wisbech Yacht Harbour
Harbour Master, Harbour Office, The Boathouse,
Harbour Square, Wisbech, Cambridgeshire PE13 3BH
Tel: 01945 588059 Fax: 01945 580589
Email: afoster@fenland.gov.uk www.fenland.gov.uk

VHF Ch 9
ACCESS HW±3

Regarded as the capital of the
English Fens, Wisbech is situated
about 25 miles north east of
Peterborough and is a market
town of considerable character and
historical significance. Rows
of elegant houses line the banks
of the River Nene, with the North
and South Brink still deemed two
of the finest Georgian streets in England.

Wisbech Yacht Harbour, linking Cambridgeshire with the sea, is
proving increasingly popular as a haven for small
craft, despite the busy commercial shipping. In
recent years the facilities have been developed and
improved upon and the HM is always on hand to
help with passage planning both up or downstream.

FACILITIES AT A GLANCE

BOSTON MARINA

Boston Marina
5/7 Witham Bank East, Boston, Lincs, PE21 9JU
Tel: 01205 364420 Fax: 01205 364420
Email: bostonmarina@5witham.fsnet www.bostonmarina.net

VHF Ch 12
ACCESS H±2

Boston Marina, located
near Boston Grand Sluice
in Lincolnshire, is an ideal
location for both seagoing
vessels and for river boats
wanting to explore the
heart of the Fens. The on
site facilities include a
fully-stocked chandlery
and brokerage service,
while nearby is the well-
established and recently
refurbished Witham bar and restaurant.

The old maritime port of Boston has numerous
modern-day and historical attractions, one of the
most notable being St Botolph's Church, better
known as the 'Boston Stump'.

FACILITIES AT A GLANCE

MERIDIAN QUAY MARINA

Humber Cruising Assn
Meridian Quay Marina
Fish Docks, Grimsby, DN31 3SD
Tel: 01472 268424 Fax: 01472 269832
www.hcagrimsby.co.uk
Email: berthmaster@hcagrimsby.co.uk

VHF Ch 74
ACCESS HW±2

Situated in the locked fish
dock of Grimsby, at the
mouth of the River Humber,
Meridian Quay Marina is
run by the Humber Cruising
Association and comprises
approximately 200 alongside
berths plus 30 more for
visitors. Accessed two hours
either side of high water via lock gates, the lock should be contacted
on VHF Ch 74 (call sign 'Fish Dock Island') as you make your final
approach. The pontoon berths are equipped with
water and electricity; there is a fully licensed
clubhouse. Also available are internet access and
laundry facilities.

FACILITIES AT A GLANCE

SOUTH FERRIBY MARINA

South Ferriby Marina
Red Lane, South Ferriby, Barton on Humber, Lincs, DN18 6JH
Tel: 01652 635620 (Lock 635219) Mobile: 07828 312071
Email: enquiries@southferribymarina.com

VHF Ch 74
ACCESS HW±3

Situated at the entrance to the
non-tidal River Ancholme
the existing marina has been
established since 1966 and is
well placed to provide easy
access to the River Humber and
North Sea. This is a family run
business providing a range of
services including a boatyard
and chandlery. Access is by way of lock at HW±3.

The marina has excellent road and rail services within easy reach,
while South Ferriby village has two pubs and a Post Office/Spar Shop
just a short walk away.

The picturesque River Ancholme is navigable
for about 17 miles; the maximum headroom under
bridges is 4.42 metres (14ft 6ins).

FACILITIES AT A GLANCE

HULL MARINA

Hull Marina
W 13, Kingston Street, Hull, HU1 2DQ
Tel: 01482 609960 Fax: 01482 224148
Email: carolyn.murray@bwml.co.uk
www.bwml.co.uk

VHF	Ch 80
ACCESS	HW±3

Situated on the River Humber, Hull Marina is literally a stone's throw from the bustling city centre with its array of arts and entertainments. Besides the numerous historic bars and cafés surrounding the marina, there are plenty of traditional taverns to be sampled in the Old Town, while also found here is the Street Life Museum, vividly depicting the history of the city.

Yachtsmen enter the marina via a tidal lock, operating HW±3, and should try to give 15 minutes' notice of arrival via VHF Ch 80; if arriving between 2100-0700 from Oct-Mar, 24 hrs notice is required. Hull is perfectly positioned for exploring the Trent, Ouse and the Yorkshire coast as well as across the North Sea to Holland or Belgium.

FACILITIES AT A GLANCE

Key
a Reception
b Boatshed
c Kildale Marine
d Lock control & lock keeper's cottage
NB Berth numbers low outer to high inner.

THE NORTH'S LARGEST CHANDLERY

KILDALE MARINE

The largest stock in the region.

Great technical knowledge.

Full rigging service.

Supplying everything for:
- Yachts
- Cruisers
- Dinghies
- Books & Charts
- Clothing & Footwear

MUSTO   **Gill**   **HENRI LLOYD**   **HARKEN**   **LOWRANCE**

spinlock   **Raymarine**   **ICOM**   **International.** yachtpaint.com

Kildalemarine.co.uk
01482 227464

Kildale Marine Ltd,
Hull Marina, Hull HU1 2DQ
Opening hours
6-days a week, closed Tuesday.

5

WHITBY MARINA

Whitby Marina
Whitby Harbour Office, Endeavour Wharf
Whitby, North Yorkshire YO21 1DN
Harbour Office: 01947 602354 Marina: 01947 600165
Email: port.services@scarborough.gov.uk

VHF | Ch 11
ACCESS | HW±2

The only natural harbour between the Tees and the Humber, Whitby lies some 20 miles north of Scarborough on the River Esk. The historic town is said to date back as far as the Roman times, although it is better known for its abbey, which was founded over 1,300 years ago by King Oswy of Northumberland. Another place of interest is the Captain Cook Memorial Museum, a tribute to Whitby's greatest seaman.

A swing bridge divides the harbour into upper and lower sections, with the marina being in the Upper Harbour. The bridge opens on request (VHF Ch 11) each half hour for two hours either side of high water.

FACILITIES AT A GLANCE

Key
a Marina office
b Waste oil bin

HARTLEPOOL MARINA

Hartlepool Marina
Lock Office, Slake Terrace, Hartlepool, TS24 0RU
Tel: 01429 865744
Email: enquiries@hartlepool-marina.com

VHF | Ch M, 80
ACCESS | HW±5

Hartlepool Marina is a modern boating facility on the NE coast. Nestling on the Tees Valley the multi award winning marina promotes up to 500 pontoon berths alongside a variety of reputable services all surrounded by an exciting array of on water activities, a cosmopolitan mix of bistros, bars, restaurants, shopping, hotels and entertainment options.

Beautiful cruising waters and golden sands to the North and South of the marina approach which is channel dredged to chart datum and accessible 5 hours either side of high water via a lock: vessels wishing to enter should contact the Marina Lock Office on VHF Ch 37/80 before arrival.

FACILITIES AT A GLANCE

Key
a Brittania House - amenity/cafe
b Neptune House - restaurant & bar
c Lock office and marina reception
d 220m complex with retail, restaurants and cafes
e Hartlepool Diving Club and HMS Abdiel sea cadet unit
f Fisherman's stores & landing area
g Office units
h Old West Quay Pub, restaurant and travel inn

SUNDERLAND MARINA

The Marine Activities Centre
Sunderland Marina, Sunderland, SR6 0PW
Tel: 0191 514 4721 Fax: 0191 514 1847
Email: mervyn.templeton@marineactivitiescentre.co.uk

VHF | Ch M, 80
ACCESS | H24

Sunderland Marina sits on bank of the River Wear and is easily accessible through the outer breakwater at all states of the tide. Among the extensive range of facilities on site are a newsagent, café, hairdresser and top quality Italian restaurant. Other pubs, restaurants, hotels and cafés are located nearby on the waterfront.

Both the Wear Boating Association and the Sunderland Yacht Club are also located in the vicinity and welcome yachtsmen to their respective bars and lounges.

FACILITIES AT A GLANCE

Key
a. Marina Reception
b. Marine News - Newsagent & Shop
c. Snow Goose - Café
d. Hairdresser
e. Trattoria Due - Italian Restaurant
f. Wear Boating Association
g. Hard stand compound
h. Refuse Compound

NORTH SHIELDS ROYAL QUAYS MARINA

North Shields Royal Quays Marina
Coble Dene Road, North Shields, NE29 6DU
Tel: 0191 272 8282 Fax: 0191 272 8288
www.quaymarinas.com
Email: royalquaysmarina@quaymarinas.com

VHF | Ch 80
ACCESS | H24

North Shields Royal Quays Marina enjoys close proximity to the entrance to the River Tyne, allowing easy access to and from the open sea as well as being ideally placed for cruising further up the Tyne. Just over an hour's motoring upstream brings you to the heart of the city of Newcastle, where you can tie up on a security controlled visitors' pontoon right outside the Pitcher and Piano Bar.

With a reputation for a high standard of service, the marina accommodates 300 pontoon berths, all of which are fully serviced. It is accessed via double sector lock gates which operate at all states of the tide and 24 hours a day.

FACILITIES AT A GLANCE

Key
a Marina office
   Toilets/showers
   Laundry
   Payphone
   Lock control
   Brokerage
b Refuse compound
c Chandlery & boat sales
d Access bridge & trolley park
e Boat sales and brokerage
f Bar/restaurant
g Waste oil disposal

ST PETERS MARINA

St Peters Marina, St Peters Basin
Newcastle upon Tyne, NE6 1HX
Tel: 0191 2654472 Fax: 0191 2762618
Email: info@stpetersmarina.co.uk
www.stpetersmarina.co.uk

VHF | Ch 80
ACCESS | HW±3

Nestling on the north bank of the River Tyne, some eight miles upstream of the river entrance, St Peters Marina is a fully serviced, 150-berth marina with the capacity to accommodate large vessels of up to 37m LOA. Situated on site is the Bascule Bar and Bistro, while a few minutes away is the centre of Newcastle. This city, along with its surrounding area, offers an array of interesting sites, among which are Hadrian's Wall, the award winning Gateshead Millennium Bridge and the Baltic Art Centre.

FACILITIES AT A GLANCE

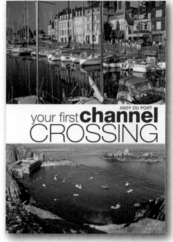

ROYAL NORTHUMBERLAND YACHT CLUB

Royal Northumberland Yacht Club
South Harbour, Blyth, Northumberland, NE24 3PB
Tel: 01670 353636

VHF Ch 12
ACCESS H24

The Royal Northumberland Yacht Club is based at Blyth, a well-sheltered port that is accessible at all states of the tide and in all weathers except for when there is a combination of low water and strong south-easterly winds. The yacht club is a private club with some 75 pontoon berths and a further 20 fore and aft moorings.

Visitors usually berth on the north side of the most northerly pontoon and are welcome to use the clubship, HY *Tyne* – a wooden lightship built in 1880 which incorporates a bar, showers and toilet facilities. The club also controls its own boatyard, providing under cover and outside storage space plus a 20 ton boat hoist.

FACILITIES AT A GLANCE

AMBLE MARINA

Amble Marina Ltd
Amble, Northumberland, NE65 0YP
Tel: 01665 712168
Email: marina@amble.co.uk   www.amble.co.uk

VHF Ch 80
ACCESS HW±4

Amble Marina is a small family run business offering peace, security and a countryside setting at the heart of the small town of Amble. It is located on the banks of the beautiful River Coquet and at the start of the Northumberland coast's area of outstanding natural beauty. Amble Marina has 250 fully serviced berths for residential and visiting yachts. Cafés, bars, restaurants and shops are all within a short walk.

From your berth watch the sun rise at the harbour entrance and set behind Warkworth Castle or walk on wide, empty beaches. There is so much to do or if you prefer simply enjoy the peace, tranquillity and friendliness at Amble Marina.

FACILITIES AT A GLANCE

You would think that this must be covered... but is it? Check the small print!

Pantaenius offers...

 Wide range of **deductible-free** claims

 Engine damage due to breakdown of component*

 No hidden **fees** or **surcharges**

 Blue-water cruising

 Claims not excluded due to **wear and tear***

 12-months in-commission cover

 Worldwide support

 Racing – usually without additional terms

*See policy wording for full terms and conditions

Enjoy the great feeling of being in safe hands

PANTAENIUS
Sail & Motor Yacht Insurance

Germany · United Kingdom* · Monaco · Denmark · Austria · Spain · Sweden · USA** · Australia
Plymouth · Phone +44 17 52 22 36 56

pantaenius.co.uk

Key to Marina Plans symbols

Symbol	Description	Symbol	Description
🛢	Bottled gas	P	Parking
⚓	Chandler	✗	Pub/Restaurant
♿	Disabled facilities		Pump out
🔌	Electrical supply		Rigging service
	Electrical repairs		Sail repairs
🔧	Engine repairs	✗	Shipwright
➕	First Aid	🛒	Shop/Supermarket
	Fresh Water		Showers
D	Fuel - Diesel		Slipway
P	Fuel - Petrol	WC	Toilets
	Hardstanding/boatyard	☎	Telephone
@	Internet Café		Trolleys
⊡	Laundry facilities	V	Visitors berths
	Lift-out facilities		Wi-Fi

6

Area 6 - South East Scotland

MARINAS
Telephone Numbers
VHF Channel
Access Times

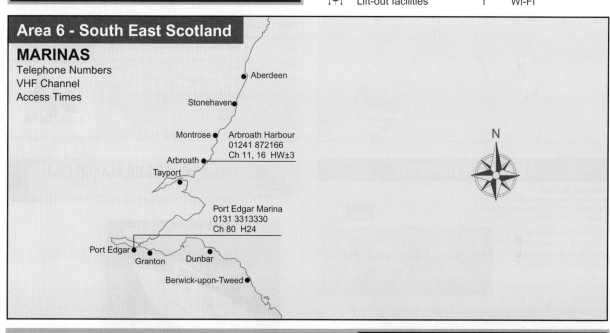

Aberdeen

Stonehaven

Montrose — Arbroath Harbour
01241 872166
Ch 11, 16 HW±3
Arbroath

Tayport

Port Edgar Marina
0131 3313330
Ch 80 H24

Port Edgar

Granton   Dunbar

Berwick-upon-Tweed

N

PORT EDGAR MARINA

Port Edgar Marina
Shore Road, South Queensferry
West Lothian, EH3 9SX
Tel: 0131 331 3330 Fax: 0131 331 4878
Email: enquiries@portedgarmarina.net

VHF	Ch 80
ACCESS	H24

Port Edgar is a large watersports centre and marina found on the south bank of the sheltered Firth of Forth. Situated in the village of South Queensferry, just west of the Forth Road Bridge, it is reached via a deep water channel just west of the suspension bridge.

The nearby village offers a sufficient range of shops and restaurants, while Port Edgar is only a 20-minute walk from Dalmeny Station from where trains run regularly into Edinburgh.

FACILITIES AT A GLANCE

Key
a   Changing rooms and toilets
b   Landing and trolleys
c   Port Edgar Yacht Club
d   Sail loft
e   Cafe
f   Marina office
g   Ferry Marine
h   Blue V
i   Bosuns Locker

Arbroath Harbour

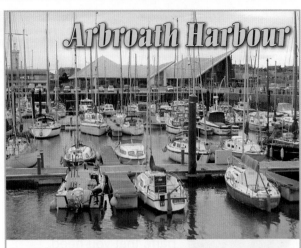

"Arbroath Harbour has 59 floating pontoon berths with security entrance which are serviced with electricity and fresh water to accommodate all types of leisure craft. Half height dock gates with a walkway are located between the inner and outer harbours, which open and close at half tide, maintaining a minimum of 2.5m of water in the inner harbour.

Other facilities in the harbour include free partking, toilets and showers, a crew room, fueling facilities, on site laundry facilities and boat builders' yard.

The town of Arbroath also offers a variety of social and sporting amenities to visiting crews and a number of quality pubs, restaurants, the famous twelfth century Abbey and Signal Tower Museum are located close to the harbour. The railway and bus stations are only 1km from the harbour with direct north and south connections."

Arbroath Harbour
Harbour Office . Arbroath . DD11 1PD

Harbour Master: Bruce Fleming
Tel: 01241 872166
Fax: 01241 878472
Email: harbourmaster@angus.gov.uk

Angus Council

ARBROATH HARBOUR

Arbroath Harbour
Harbour Office, Arbroath, DD11 1PD
Tel: 01241 872166 Fax: 01241 878472
Email: harbourmaster@angus.gov.uk

VHF	Ch 11
ACCESS	HW±3

Arbroath harbour has 59 floating pontoon berths with security entrance which are serviced with electricity and fresh water to accommodate all types of leisure craft. Half height

dock gates with walkway are located between the inner and outer harbours, which open and close at half tide, maintaining a minimum of 2.5m of water in the inner harbour.

The town of Arbroath offers a variety of social and sporting amenities to visiting crews and a number of quality pubs, restaurants, the famous twelfth century Abbey and Signal Tower Museum are located close to the harbour. Railway and bus stations are only 1km from the harbour with direct north and south connections.

FACILITIES AT A GLANCE

Key
a   Signal Tower Museum
b   Tourist Information
c   RNLI
d   Harbourmaster
e   Harbour gates & walkway

Yacht Havens

Marina
Dry Stack Marina

WE LOVE BOATING

the most helpful staff

9 Prime Marina Locations... *the perfect home for your boat*

Whether you're looking for an overnight visit, an annual berth or a safe winter haven, you'll find first-rate facilities and a warm welcome from our friendly, experienced team at whichever Yacht Havens location you choose.

Attractive berthing rates and flexible contracts to save you money, superb modern facilities for your enjoyment, free Wi-Fi at every berth for your convenience, and the freedom to exchange berths with other Yacht Havens.

We can provide you with the best boating experience across the UK, and now the Netherlands. Just ask us what we can do for you.

1 Largs Yacht Haven
Largs, Ayrshire
Tel: 01475 675333

2 Troon Yacht Haven
Troon, Ayrshire
Tel: 01292 315553

3 Neyland Yacht Haven
Neyland, Pembrokeshire
Tel: 01646 601601

4 Fambridge Yacht Haven
River Crouch, Essex
Tel: 01621 740370

5 Lymington Yacht Haven
Lymington, Hampshire
Tel: 01590 677071

6 Haven Quay
Lymington, Hampshire
Tel: 01590 677072

7 Plymouth Yacht Haven
Plymouth, Devon
Tel: 01752 404231

8 Yacht Haven Quay
Plymouth, Devon
Tel: 01752 481190

NEW!
9 Jachthaven Biesbosch
Drimmelen, Netherlands
Tel: +31(0)162 68 22 49

CALL US TODAY OR VISIT **www.yachthavens.com**

NORTH EAST SCOTLAND – Peterhead to Cape Wrath & Orkney & Shetland Is

Key to Marina Plans symbols

Bottled gas		Parking	
Chandler		Pub/Restaurant	
Disabled facilities		Pump out	
Electrical supply		Rigging service	
Electrical repairs		Sail repairs	
Engine repairs		Shipwright	
First Aid		Shop/Supermarket	
Fresh Water		Showers	
Fuel - Diesel		Slipway	
Fuel - Petrol		Toilets	
Hardstanding/boatyard		Telephone	
Internet Café		Trolleys	
Laundry facilities		Visitors berths	
Lift-out facilities		Wi-Fi	

Area 7 - North East Scotland

MARINAS
Telephone Numbers
VHF Channel
Access Times

Shetland Islands

7

Kirkwall Marina
07810 465835
Ch 14 H24

Stromness Marina
07810 465825
Ch 14 H24

Orkney Islands

Scrabster

Wick ● Wick Marina
01955 602030
Ch 14 H24

Helmsdale

Ullapool

Whitehills Marina
01261 861291
Ch 14 H4

Banff Harbour Marina
01261 815544
Ch 12 HW±4

Buckie Banff Macduff

Inverness Marina
07526 446348
Ch 12

Inverness

Findhorn

Peterhead ● Peterhead Bay Marina
01779 477868
Ch 14 H24

Caley Marina
01463 236539
Ch 74 H24

Burghead

Lossiemouth 01343 813066
Ch 12 HW±4

Seaport Marina
01463 725500
Ch 74 HW±4

Nairn Marina
01667 456008
Ch 10 HW±2

Hopeman

Mallaig

Aberdeen ●

N

PETERHEAD BAY MARINA

Peterhead Port Authority
Harbour Office, West Pier, Peterhead, AB42 1DW
Tel: 01779 477868/483600
Email: marina@peterheadport.co.uk
www.peterheadport.co.uk

| VHF | Ch 14 |
| ACCESS | H24 |

Based in the south west corner of Peterhead Bay Harbour, the marina provides one of the finest marine leisure facilities in the east of Scotland. In addition to the services on site, there are plenty of nautical businesses in the vicinity, ranging from ship chandlers and electrical servicing to boat repairs and surveying.

Due to its easterly location, Peterhead affords an ideal stopover for those yachts heading to or from Scandinavia as well as for vessels making for the Caledonian Canal.

FACILITIES AT A GLANCE

BANFF HARBOUR MARINA

Banff Harbour Marina
Harbour Office, Quayside, Banff, Aberdeenshire, AB45 1HQ
Tel: 01261 815544 Fax: 01261 815544
Email: james.henderson@aberdeenshire.gov.uk

| VHF | Ch 12 |
| ACCESS | HW±4 |

A former fishing and cargo port now used as a recreational harbour. Banff offers excellent facilities to both regular and visiting users. The marina now provides 92 berths, of which 76 are serviced pontoon berths and 16 unserviced, traditional moorings, in one of the safest harbours on the NE coast of Scotland.

The outer basin offers adequate berthing for visitors and a tidal area for regulars.

The harbour is tidal with a sandy bottom. Movement during low water neaps is no problem for the shallow drafted boat.

FACILITIES AT A GLANCE

Key
a Harbourmasters Office

NAIRN MARINA

Nairn Marina
Nairn Harbour, Nairnshire, Scotland
Tel: 01667 456008 Fax: 01667 452877
Email: nairn.harbourmaster@virgin.net

| VHF | Ch 10 |
| ACCESS | HW±2 |

Nairn is a small town on the coast of the Moray Firth. Formerly renowned both as a fishing port and as a holiday resort dating back to Victorian times, it boasts miles of award-winning, sandy beaches, famous castles such as Cawdor, Brodie and Castle Stuart, and two championship golf courses. Other recreational activities include horse riding or walking through spectacular countryside.

The marina lies at the mouth of the River Nairn, entry to which should be avoided in strong N to NE winds. The approach is made from the NW at or around high water as the entrance is badly silted and dries out.

FACILITIES AT A GLANCE

Key
a Restaurant
b Yacht Club
c Harbour office

WHITEHILLS MARINA

Whitehills Harbour Commissioners
Whitehills, Banffshire AB45 2NQ
Tel: 01261 861291
www.whitehillsharbour.co.uk
Email: harbourmaster@whitehillsharbour.co.uk

VHF	Ch 14
ACCESS	H24

Built in 1900, Whitehills is a Trust Harbour fully maintained and run by nine commissioners elected from the village. It was a thriving fishing port up until 1999, but due to changes in the fishing industry, was converted into a marina during 2000.

Three miles west of Banff Harbour the marina benefits from good tidal access – although there is just 1.5m at springs – comprising 38 serviced berths, with electricity, as well as eight non-serviced berths.

The nearby village of Whitehills boasts a selection of local stores and a couple of pubs. A coastal path leads from the marina to the top of the headland, affording striking views across the Moray Firth to the Caithness Hills.

FACILITIES AT A GLANCE

Key
a Harbour master
b Fish market
c Garage

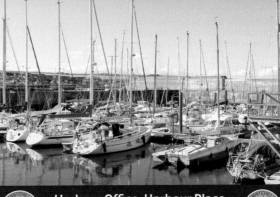
LOSSIEMOUTH MARINA

Marina Office
Lossiemouth, Moray, IV31 6PB
Tel: 01343 813066
Email: info@lossiemouthmarina.com

VHF	Ch 12
ACCESS	HW±4

Situated on the southern shore of the Moray Firth, Lossiemouth provides 95 serviced finger berths, 5 serviced dedicated visitor berths and 25 small boat berths. The Marina has full lift out facilities and a boat repair shed capable of handling 4 vessels at any one time with a marine engineer based on site.

The Marina is close to the town centre with a good range of shops and restaurants and also two championship golf courses. A regular bus service provides easy access to Elgin railway station (6 miles) and Inverness airport (35miles). Lossiemouth has miles of sandy beaches and is the ideal starting point for the Speyside Whisky trail.

FACILITIES AT A GLANCE

INVERNESS MARINA

Inverness Marina
Longman Drive, Inverness, IV1 1SU
Tel: 01463 220501
Email: info@invernessmarina.com
www.invernessmarina.com

VHF	Ch 12
ACCESS	H24

Inverness Marina is situated in the Inverness firth just one mile from the city centre and half a mile from the entrance to the Caledonian Canal. The marina has a minimum depth of 3m, 24hr access and 150 fully serviced berths. On site are a chandlery and services including rigging, engineering, electronics and boat repair.

Inverness is the capital of the highlands with transport networks including bus, train, and flights to the rest of the UK and Europe. Inverness is the gateway to the Highlands with best possible location as a base for touring with golf courses, historic sites and the Whisky Trail. The marina is a perfect base for cruising Orkney, Shetland and Scandinavia.

FACILITIES AT A GLANCE

SEAPORT MARINA

Seaport Marina
Muirtown Wharf, Inverness, IV3 5LE
Tel: 01463 725500 Fax: 01463 710942
Email: enquiries.scotland@britishwaterways.co.uk
www.scottishcanals.co.uk

VHF	Ch 74
ACCESS	HW±4

Seaport Marina is based at Muirtown Basin at the eastern entrance of the Caledonian Canal; a 60 mile coast-to-coast channel slicing through the majestic Great Glen. Only a 15 minute walk from the centre of Inverness, the Marina is an ideal base for visiting the Highlands.

There are shops and amenities nearby, as well as chandlers, boat repair services and a slipway. The marina also offers a variety of winter mooring packages and details of transit and short term licences, including the use of the Caledonian Canal can be found on the above website.

FACILITIES AT A GLANCE

Key
a Office, toilets, showers, laundry, disabled toilets
b Refuse disposal, waste oil disposal

CALEY MARINA

Caley Marina
Canal Road, Inverness, IV3 8NF
Tel: 01463 236539 Fax: 01463 238323
Email: info@caleymarina.com
www.caleymarina.com

VHF	Ch 74
ACCESS	H24

Caley Marina is a family run business based near Inverness. With the four flight Muirtown locks and the Kessock Bridge providing a dramatic backdrop, the marina runs alongside the Caledonian Canal which, opened in 1822, is regarded as one of the most spectacular waterways in Europe. Built as a short cut between the North Sea and the Atlantic Ocean, thus avoiding the potentially dangerous Pentland Firth on the north coast of Scotland, the canal is around 60 miles long and takes about three days to cruise from east to west. With the prevailing winds behind you, it takes slightly less time to cruise in the other direction.

FACILITIES AT A GLANCE

WICK MARINA

Wick Marina
Harbour Office, Wick, Caithness, KW1 5HA
Tel: 01955 602030 Fax: 01955 605936
Email: malcolm.bremner@wickharbour.co.uk

VHF	Ch 14, 16
ACCESS	H24

This is the most northerly marina on the British mainland and the last stop before the Orkney and Shetland Islands. Situated an easy five minutes walk from the town centre Wick Marina accommodates 70 fully serviced berths with all the support facilities expected in a modern marina including a boat lift.

This part of Scotland with its rugged coastline and rich history is easily accessible by air and a great starting point for cruising in the northern isles, Moray Firth, Caledonian Canal and Scandinavia, a comfortable 280-mile sail.

FACILITIES AT A GLANCE

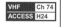

KIRKWALL MARINA

Kirkwall Marina
Harbour Street, Kirkwall, Orkney, KW15
Tel: 07810 465835 Fax: 01856 871313
Email: info@orkneymarinas.co.uk www.orkneymarinas.co.uk

VHF Ch 14
ACCESS H24

The Orkney Isles, comprising 70 islands in total, provides some of the finest cruising grounds in Northern Europe. The Main Island, incorporating the ancient port of Kirkwall, is the largest, although 16 others have lively communities and are rich in archaeological sites as well as spectacular scenery and wildlife.

Kirkwall Marina, an all year facility, is located within the harbour and just yards from the visitor attractions of this ancient port. Local shops, hotels and restaurants are all within walking distance.

FACILITIES AT A GLANCE

STROMNESS MARINA

Stromness Marina
Stromness, Orkney, KW16
Tel: 07810 465825 Fax: 01856 871313
Email: info@orkneymarinas.co.uk
www.orkneymarinas.co.uk

VHF Ch 14
ACCESS H24

Stromness lies on the south-western tip of the Orkney Isles' Mainland. Sitting beneath the rocky ridge known as Brinkie's Brae, it is considered one of Orkney's major seaports, with sailors first attracted to the fine anchorage provided by the bay of Hamnavoe.

Stromness offers comprehensive facilities including a chandlery and repair services. Also on hand are an internet café, a fitness suite and swimming pool as well as car and bike hire.

FACILITIES AT A GLANCE

Key
a Terminal building, Harbour Master's office
b Cafe
c Rope centre

Key to Marina Plans symbols

♨	Bottled gas	P	Parking
♺	Chandler	✕	Pub/Restaurant
♿	Disabled facilities	⚓	Pump out
🔌	Electrical supply		Rigging service
🔧	Electrical repairs		Sail repairs
🔧	Engine repairs	✂	Shipwright
✚	First Aid	🛒	Shop/Supermarket
🚰	Fresh Water	⛲	Showers
D	Fuel - Diesel	◣	Slipway
P	Fuel - Petrol	WC	Toilets
🍖	Hardstanding/boatyard	☏	Telephone
@	Internet Café	⛟	Trolleys
⊡	Laundry facilities	Ⓥ	Visitors berths
🛋	Lift-out facilities	🛈	Wi-Fi

Area 8 - North West Scotland

MARINAS
Telephone Numbers
VHF Channel
Access Times

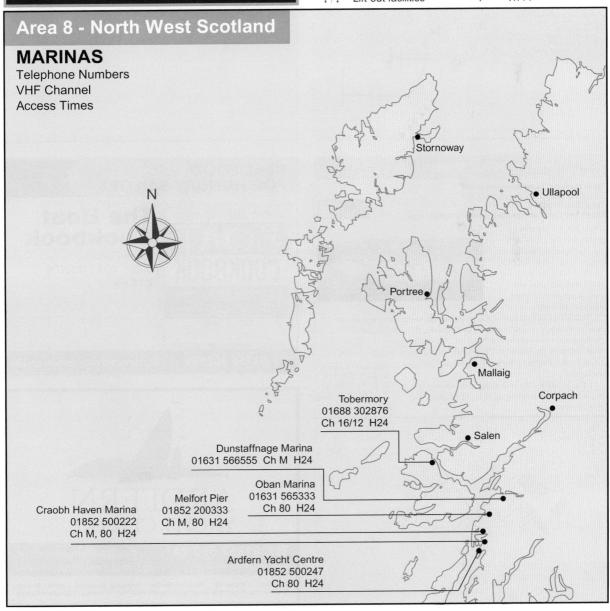

N

Stornoway

Ullapool

Portree

Mallaig

Corpach

Tobermory
01688 302876
Ch 16/12 H24

Salen

Dunstaffnage Marina
01631 566555 Ch M H24

Oban Marina
01631 565333
Ch 80 H24

Melfort Pier
01852 200333
Ch M, 80 H24

Craobh Haven Marina
01852 500222
Ch M, 80 H24

Ardfern Yacht Centre
01852 500247
Ch 80 H24

TOBERMORY

Tobermory Harbour Association
Taigh Solais, Tobermory, Isle of Mull, PA75 6NR
Mob: 07917 832497 Tel: 01688 302876
www.tobermoryharbour.co.uk
Email: jim.traynor@tobermoryharbour.co.uk

VHF	Ch 16/12
ACCESS	0800–2000

Tobermory Harbour pontoons are located in the west shore of Tobermory Bay with access directly to the town. The THA offers a full range of facilities and services afloat and ashore. The THA also offers swinging moorings for hire.

Tobermory is the iconic Scottish west coast destination, a natural historic harbour and protected anchorage. Tobermory offers an exceptional array of shops, bars and and restaurants, most offering fresh local shellfish and all within easy walking distance. Tobermory has transport links to and from all mainland ferries or destination tours throughout the Island of Mull.

FACILITIES AT A GLANCE

Key a Tobermory Harbour Association office
b Recycling
c Charter boats
d Large vessels
e Shallow draft vessels

DUNSTAFFNAGE MARINA

Dunstaffnage Marina Ltd
Dunbeg, by Oban, Argyll, PA37 1PX
Tel: 01631 566555 Fax: 01631 571044
Email: lizzy@dunstaffnage.sol.co.uk

VHF	Ch M
ACCESS	H24

Located just two to three miles north of Oban, Dunstaffnage Marina has recently been renovated to include an additional 36 fully serviced berths, a new breakwater providing shelter from NE'ly to E'ly winds and an increased amount of hard standing. Also on site is the Wide Mouthed Frog, offering a convivial bar, restaurant and accomodation with spectacular views of the 13th century Dunstaffnage Castle.

The marina is perfectly placed to explore Scotland's stunning west coast and Hebridean Islands. Only 10 miles NE up Loch Linnhe is Port Appin, while sailing 15 miles S, down the Firth of Lorne, brings you to Puldohran where you can walk to an ancient hostelry situated next to the C18 Bridge Over the Atlantic.

FACILITIES AT A GLANCE

OBAN MARINA

Oban Marina & Yacht Services Ltd
Isle of Kerrera, Oban, Argyll, PA34 4SX
Tel: 01631 565333
Email: info@obanmarina.com www.obanmarina.com

VHF	Ch 80
ACCESS	H24

Oban Marina is perfectly situated at the gateway to the Western Isles on the picturesque Isle of Kerrera. In sight of the town of Oban, it is a well serviced and popular marina offering access at all tides.

With 100 pontoons berths and 30 moorings, easily accessible diesel fuel berth, free wifi, shower block and laundry, this friendly, small marina offers visitors a warm welcome. A complimentary shuttle service runs hourly in the season to Oban where all the major facilities including restaurants, chandlery, banks and transport links are available.

For non-sailors, the re-furbished Boathouse is now available to rent, sleeping up to eight adults in five star comfort.

FACILITIES AT A GLANCE

Key
a Reception
b Showers/toilets
c Bar & grill
d Shed

MELFORT PIER AND HARBOUR

Melfort Pier and Harbour
Kilmelford, by Oban, Argyll
Tel: 01852 200333 Fax: 01852 200329
Email: melharbour@aol.com   www.mellowmelfort.com

VHF M, 80
ACCESS H24

Melfort Pier & Harbour is situated on the shores of Loch Melfort, one of the most peaceful lochs on the south west coast of Scotland. Overlooked by the Pass of Melfort and the Braes of Lorn, it lies approximately 18 miles north of Lochgilphead and 16 miles south of Oban. Its onsite facilities include showers, laundry, telephone, free Wi-Fi access and parking – pets welcome. Fuel, power and water are available at nearby Kilmelford Yacht Haven.

For those who want a few nights on dry land, Melfort Pier & Harbour offers lochside houses, each one equipped with a sauna, spa bath and balcony offering stunning views over the loch - available per night.

FACILITIES AT A GLANCE

CRAOBH HAVEN MARINA

Craobh Haven Marina
By Lochgilphead, Argyll, Scotland, PA31 8UA
Tel: 01852 500222 Fax: 01852 500252
Email: info@craobhmarina.co.uk
www.craobhmarina.co.uk

VHF Ch M, 80
ACCESS H24

Craobh Marina is idyllically situated in the heart of Scotland's most sought after cruising grounds. Not only does Craobh offer ready access to a wonderful choice of scenic cruising throughout the western isles, the marina is conveniently close to Glasgow and its international transport hub.

Craobh Marina has been developed from a near perfect natural harbour, offering secure and sheltered berthing for up to 250 vessels to 22m LOA and with a draft of 4m. With an unusually deep and wide entrance Craobh Marina provides shelter and a warm welcome for all types of craft.

FACILITIES AT A GLANCE

Key
a   Holiday cottages
b   Village store
c   Bar
d   Gift shop
e   Waste oil
f   Boat shed
g   Marina office

ARDFERN YACHT CENTRE

Ardfern Yacht Centre
Ardfern, by Lochgilphead, Argyll, PA31 8QN
Tel: 01852 500247 Fax: 01852 500624
www.ardfernyacht.co.uk Email: office@ardfernyacht.co.uk

VHF Ch 80
ACCESS H24

Developed around an old pier once frequented by steamers, Ardfern Yacht Centre lies at the head of Loch Craignish, one of Scotland's most sheltered and picturesque sea lochs. With several islands and protected anchorages nearby, Ardfern is an ideal place from which to cruise the west coast of Scotland and the Outer Hebrides.

The Yacht Centre comprises pontoon berths and swinging moorings as well as a workshop, boat storage and well-stocked chandlery, while a grocery store and eating places can be found in the village. Among the onshore activities available locally are horse riding, cycling, and walking.

FACILITIES AT A GLANCE

Key
a   Workshop
b   Showers, toilets and launderette
c   Chandlery and office

SOUTH WEST SCOTLAND – Crinan Canal to Mull of Galloway

Key to Marina Plans symbols

Bottled gas		Parking
Chandler		Pub/Restaurant
Disabled facilities		Pump out
Electrical supply		Rigging service
Electrical repairs		Sail repairs
Engine repairs		Shipwright
First Aid		Shop/Supermarket
Fresh Water		Showers
Fuel - Diesel		Slipway
Fuel - Petrol		Toilets
Hardstanding/boatyard		Telephone
Internet Café		Trolleys
Laundry facilities		Visitors berths
Lift-out facilities		Wi-Fi

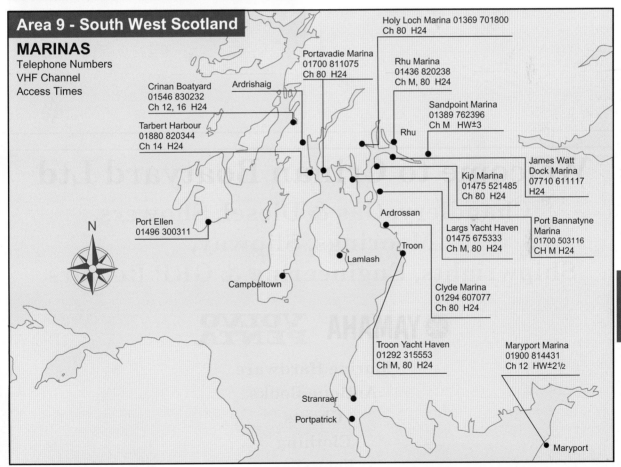

Area 9 - South West Scotland

MARINAS

Telephone Numbers
VHF Channel
Access Times

Holy Loch Marina 01369 701800
Ch 80 H24

Portavadie Marina
01700 811075
Ch 80 H24

Rhu Marina
01436 820238
Ch M, 80 H24

Crinan Boatyard
01546 830232
Ch 12, 16 H24

Ardrishaig

Sandpoint Marina
01389 762396
Ch M HW±3

Tarbert Harbour
01880 820344
Ch 14 H24

Rhu

James Watt
Dock Marina
07710 611117
H24

Kip Marina
01475 521485
Ch 80 H24

Port Ellen
01496 300311

Ardrossan

Port Bannatyne
Marina
01700 503116
CH M H24

Largs Yacht Haven
01475 675333
Ch M, 80 H24

Troon

Lamlash

Clyde Marina
01294 607077
Ch 80 H24

Campbeltown

Troon Yacht Haven
01292 315553
Ch M, 80 H24

Maryport Marina
01900 814431
Ch 12 HW±2½

Stranraer

Portpatrick

Maryport

N

9

PORT ELLEN MARINA

Port Ellen Marina
Port Ellen, Islay, Argyll, PA42 7DB
Tel: 01496 302458 Fax: 01496 300302
Email: bertie66@btinternet.com www.portellenmarina.com

VHF
ACCESS H24

A safe and relaxed marina for visitors to the *Malt Whisky Island*. There are seven classic distilleries and yet another still (private) to start production soon. If you are planning a cruise to the north then superb sailing will take you onward via Craighouse on Jura. Meeting guests or short term storage is trouble free with the excellent air and ferry services connecting to Glasgow. Once on Islay you will be tempted to extend your stay so be warned, check www.portellenmarina.com for the many reasons to visit, from golf to music.

FACILITIES AT A GLANCE

Key
a Bank
b Hotel

CRINAN BOATYARD

Crinan Boatyard Ltd
Crinan, Lochgilphead, Argyll, PA31 8SW
Tel: 01546 830232 Fax: 01546 830281
Email: info@crinanboatyard.co.uk
www.crinanboatyard.co.uk

VHF Ch 12, 16
ACCESS H24

Situated at the westerly entrance of the scenic Crinan Canal, Crinan Boatyard offers swinging moorings nightly or longer term, a fuelling/loading berth, a well stocked Chandlery, heads, showers, laundry and an experienced work force for repair work all on site. A hotel and coffee shop, just a short walk away at the Canal basin, great walking and the historic Kilmartin Glen close by are some of the attractions on shore.

The nearby town of Lochgilphead 7 miles away offers shopping and good travel links to Glasgow (85 miles) and its International Airport.

FACILITIES AT A GLANCE

TARBERT HARBOUR

Tarbert Harbour Authority
Harbour Office, Garval Road, Tarbert, Argyll, PA29 6TR
Tel: 01880 820344 Fax: 01880 820719
Email: tarbertharbour@btconnect.com

VHF	Ch 14
ACCESS	H24

Tarbert is situated on the west side of Loch Fyne, at 70km the longest sea loch in Scotland opening to the south into the Firth of Clyde.

The harbour is a natural amphi-theatre with an easily navigated narrow entrance at the east side opening onto Loch Fyne. Its eastern boundary is a line between Garbhaird Pt and Rubha Loisgte. The Harbour is accessible at all states of the tide and is one of Scotland's most sheltered harbours making it an excellent place to stay or leave a vessel unattended.

There are visiting berths for 65–100 sailing and motor yachts of varying sizes. Fresh water and electricity are available on the pontoons.

PORT BANNATYNE MARINA

Port Bannatyne Marina
Marine Road, Port Bannatyne, PA20 0LT
Tel: 01700 503116 Fax: 01700 503549
Email: portbannatynemarina@btconnect.com

VHF	Ch M
ACCESS	H24

Nestled in the bay at Port Bannatyne on the Isle of Bute, the marina is set in breathtakingly beautiful surroundings. The shore facilities include toilets and showers, lifting and winter storage and all boat repairs. Free wi-fi is available throughout the marina. Protected by a breakwater and accessible H24 the marina is dredged to –2.4m CD.

The village of Port Bannatyne offers a Post Office for essential groceries and three pubs. There are frequent bus services to both Rothesay and Ettrick Bay where a walk along a beautiful beach with amazing views can be completed with either a meal or tea and cake at the beach side restaurant.

PORTAVADIE MARINA

Portavadie Marina
Portavadie, Loch Fyne, Argyll, PA21 2DA
Tel: 01700 811075 Fax: 01700 811074
Email: info@portavadiemarina.com

VHF	Ch 80
ACCESS	H24

Portavadie Marina offers deep and sheltered berthing to residential and visiting boats in an area renowned for its superb cruising waters. Situated on the east side of Loch Fyne in close proximity to several islands and the famous Kyles of Bute, Portavadie is within easy sailing distance of the Crinan Canal, giving access to the Inner and Outer Hebrides. The marina has 230 berths 60 of which are reserved for visitors, plus comprehensive on shore facilities, including a choice of restaurants, bars and self catering accommodation. There is also a shop and small chandlery overlooking the marina, a dedicated fuel berth for petrol and diesel and bike hire.

This unspoiled area of Argyll which is less than two hours by road from Glasgow offers an ideal base for boat owners looking for a safe and secure haven.

Key
a   Reception, offices, conference room, open deck viewing platform
b   Bar & restaurant
c   WC, Showers & laundry
d   Luxury self-catering apartments

Berthing
A-H pontoons
Odd numbers on the north side
Even numbers on the south side
Numbers start at the inner end

Visitor S pontoon
Runs from S1 at the entrance to S60 at the access bridge

Visitor N pontoon
Runs from N1 at the north end to N19 at the access bridge

HOLY LOCH MARINA

Holy Loch Marina
Rankin's Brae, Sandbank, Dunoon, PA23 8FE
Tel: 01369 701800 Fax: 01369 704749
Email: info@holylochmarina.co.uk

VHF	Ch 80
ACCESS	H24

Holy Loch Marina, the marine gateway to Loch Lomond and the Trossachs National Park, lies on the south shore of the loch, roughly half a mile west of Lazaretto Point. Holy Loch is among the Clyde's most beautiful natural harbours and, besides being a peaceful location, offers an abundance of wildlife, places of local historical interest as well as excellent walking and cycling through the Argyll Forest Park. The marina can be entered in all weather conditions and is within easy sailing distance of Loch Long and Upper Firth.

Key
a   Office/Harbourmaster
b   Boat storage
c   Holy Loch Sailing Club
d   Pier

RHU MARINA

Rhu Marina
Rhu, Dunbartonshire, G84 8LH
Tel: 01436 820238 Fax: 01436 821039
Email: sbell@quaymarinas.com

VHF | Ch M, 80
ACCESS | H24

Located on the north shore of the Clyde Estuary, Rhu Marina is accessible at all states of the tide and can accommodate yachts up to 24m in length. It also operates 40 swinging moorings in the bay adjacent to the marina, with a ferry service provided.

Within easy walking distance of the marina is Rhu village, a conservation village incorporating a few shops, a pub and the beautiful Glenarn Gardens as well as the Royal Northern & Clyde Yacht Club. A mile or two to the east lies the holiday town of Helensburgh, renowned for its attractive architecture and elegant parks and gardens, while Glasgow city is just 25 miles away and can be easily reached by train.

FACILITIES AT A GLANCE

SANDPOINT MARINA

Sandpoint Marina Ltd
Sandpoint, Woodyard Road, Dumbarton, G82 4BG
Tel: 01389 762396 Fax: 01389 732605
Email: sales@sandpoint-marina.co.uk
www.sandpoint-marina.co.uk

VHF |
ACCESS | HW±3

Lying on the north bank of the Clyde estuary on the opposite side of the River Leven from Dumbarton Castle, Sandpoint Marina provides easy access to some of the most stunning cruising grounds in the United Kingdom. It is an independently run marina, offering a professional yet personal service to every boat owner. Among the facilities to hand are an on site chandlery, storage areas, a 40 ton travel hoist and 20 individual workshop units.

Within a 20-minute drive of Glasgow city centre, the marina is situated close to the shores of Loch Lomond, the largest fresh water loch in Britain.

FACILITIES AT A GLANCE

Key
a Marina office
b Workshops
c Undercover storage shed
d Chandler
e Undercover storage sheds

KIP MARINA

Kip Marina, The Yacht Harbour
Inverkip, Renfrewshire, Scotland, PA16 0AS
Tel: 01475 521485 Fax: 01475 521298
www.kipmarina.co.uk Email: enquire@kipmarina.co.uk

VHF	Ch 80
ACCESS	H24

Inverkip is a small village which lies on the south shores of the River Kip as it enters the Firth of Clyde. Once established for fishing, smuggling and, in the 17th century, witch-hunts, it became a seaside resort in the 1860s as a result of the installation of the railway. Today it is a yachting centre, boasting a state-of-the-art marina with over 600 berths and full boatyard facilities. With the capacity to accommodate yachts of up to 23m LOA, Kip Marina offers direct road and rail access to Glasgow and its international airport, therefore making it an ideal location for either a winter lay up or crew changeover.

FACILITIES AT A GLANCE

Key
a Boat sales, chandlery and reception
b Workshop and contractors
c Chartroom bar and restaurant

JAMES WATT DOCK MARINA

James Watt Dock Marina
East Hamilton Street
Greenock, Renfrewshire, PA15 2TD
Tel: 01475 729838
www.jwdmarina.co.uk Email: info@jwdmarina.co.uk

VHF	80
ACCESS	H24

Based in the historic James Watt Dock alongside the stunning Victorian Sugar Shed, this new marina opened in May 2011 and is the first step in establishing an exciting new River Clyde waterfront development only 23 miles from Glasgow and 15 miles from the airport. James Watt Dock will have all the usual amenities expected of a modern marina.

Within easy reach of Greenock's cinema, pool, ice rink, restaurants and shops, and with nearby transport connections, the marina will be a great location for both visitors and regular berthers.

FACILITIES AT A GLANCE

Key
a Marina office

LARGS YACHT HAVEN

Largs Yacht Haven Ltd
Irvine Road, Largs, Ayrshire, KA30 8EZ
Tel: 01475 675333 Fax: 01475 672245
Email: largs@yachthavens.com www.yachthavens.com

VHF	Ch M, 80
ACCESS	H24

Largs Yacht Haven offers a superb location among lochs and islands, with numerous fishing villages and harbours nearby. Sheltered cruising can be enjoyed in the inner Clyde, while the west coast and Ireland are only a day's sail away. With a stunning backdrop of the Scottish mountains, Largs incorporates 700 fully serviced berths and provides a range of on site facilities including chandlers, sailmakers, divers, engineers, shops, restaurants and club.

A 20-minute coastal walk brings you to the town of Largs, which has all the usual amenities as well as good road and rail connections to Glasgow.

FACILITIES AT A GLANCE

Key
a Reception
b Restaurant
c Largs Sailing Club
d Shops, offices, service companies
e Sail loft
f Boat repair shed
g Boat sales

9

CLYDE MARINA

Clyde Marina Ltd
The Harbour, Ardrossan, Ayrshire, KA22 8DB
Tel: 01294 607077 Fax: 01294 607076
www.clydemarina.com Email: info@clydemarina.com

| VHF | Ch 80 |
| ACCESS | H24 |

Situated on the Clyde Coast between Irvine and Largs, Clyde Marina is a modern bustling yacht harbour with boatyard, 50 Tonne hoist and active boat sales, set in a landscaped environment. A deep draft marina berthing vessels up to 30m LOA, draft up to 5m. Peviously accommodated vessels include tall ships and Whitbread 60s plus a variety of sail and power craft. Fully serviced pontoons plus all the yard facilities you would expect from a leading marina including boatyard and boatshed for repairs or storage. Good road and rail connections and only 30 minutes from Glasgow and Prestwick airports.

FACILITIES AT A GLANCE

TROON YACHT HAVEN

Troon Yacht Haven Ltd
The Harbour, Troon, Ayrshire, KA10 6DJ
Tel: 01292 315553 Fax: 01292 312836
Email: troon@yachthavens.com
www.yachthavens.com

| VHF | Ch 80, M |
| ACCESS | H24 |

Troon Yacht Haven, situated on the Southern Clyde Estuary, benefits from deep water at all states of the tide. Tucked away in the harbour of Troon, it is well sheltered and within easy access of the town centre.

There are plenty of cruising opportunities to be had from here, whether it be hopping across to the Isle of Arran, with its peaceful anchorages and mountain walks, sailing round the Mull or through the Crinan Canal to the Western Isles, or heading for the sheltered waters of the Clyde.

FACILITIES AT A GLANCE

Key
a Main building
  Toilets
  Showers
  Baths
  Laundry
b Marina office

MARYPORT MARINA

Maryport Development Ltd
Marine Road, Maryport, Cumbria, CA15 8AY
Tel: 01900 814431
www.maryportmarina.com
Email: enquires@maryportmarina.com

| VHF | Ch 12,16 |
| ACCESS | HW±2.5 |

Maryport Marina is located in the historic Senhouse Dock, which was originally built for sailing clippers in the late 19th century. The old stone harbour walls provide good shelter to the 190 berths from the prevailing south westerlies.

Maryport town centre and its shops, pubs and other amenities is within easy walking distance from the marina. Maryport a perfect location from which to explore the west coast of Scotland as well as the Isle of Man and the Galloway Coast. For those who wish to venture inland, then the Lake District is only seven miles away.

FACILITIES AT A GLANCE

Key
a Marina Office
b Boat repair facility
c Coastguard building
d Fish handling building
e Wet fish shop
f Aquarium, cafe
g Play area
h Amenity block

HARBOUR & MARINA

maryport

Maryport Marina is located in Cumbria, England with views of the Scottish coastline. The marina has excellent facilities for pontoon berthing and unlimited hard standing storage for those requiring winter repairs or storage.

Contact the marina for our special winter storage offers and annual berthing prices.

Tel: 01900814431 or enquiries@maryportmarina.com

9

marine road, maryport, cumbria CA15 8AY

NW ENGLAND, ISLE OF MAN & N WALES – Mull of Galloway to Bardsey Is

Key to Marina Plans symbols

Bottled gas		P	Parking
Chandler			Pub/Restaurant
Disabled facilities			Pump out
Electrical supply			Rigging service
Electrical repairs			Sail repairs
Engine repairs			Shipwright
First Aid			Shop/Supermarket
Fresh Water			Showers
Fuel - Diesel			Slipway
Fuel - Petrol		WC	Toilets
Hardstanding/boatyard			Telephone
@	Internet Café		Trolleys
Laundry facilities		V	Visitors berths
Lift-out facilities			Wi-Fi

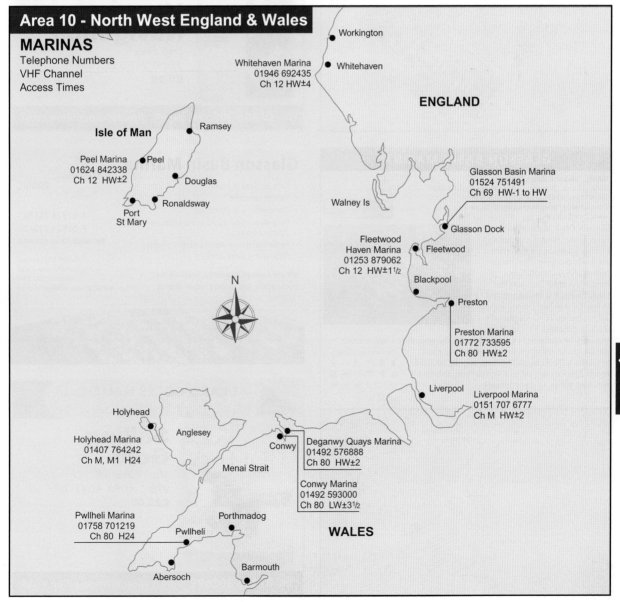

Area 10 - North West England & Wales

MARINAS
Telephone Numbers
VHF Channel
Access Times

Workington

Whitehaven Marina
01946 692435
Ch 12 HW±4

Whitehaven

ENGLAND

Isle of Man

Ramsey

Peel Marina
01624 842338
Ch 12 HW±2

Peel

Douglas

Walney Is

Glasson Basin Marina
01524 751491
Ch 69 HW-1 to HW

Ronaldsway

Port St Mary

Glasson Dock

Fleetwood Haven Marina
01253 879062
Ch 12 HW±1½

Fleetwood

Blackpool

N

Preston

Preston Marina
01772 733595
Ch 80 HW±2

Liverpool

Liverpool Marina
0151 707 6777
Ch M HW±2

Holyhead

Holyhead Marina
01407 764242
Ch M, M1 H24

Anglesey

Conwy

Deganwy Quays Marina
01492 576888
Ch 80 HW±2

Menai Strait

Conwy Marina
01492 593000
Ch 80 LW±3½

Pwllheli Marina
01758 701219
Ch 80 H24

Porthmadog

Pwllheli

WALES

Abersoch

Barmouth

10

WHITEHAVEN MARINA

Whitehaven Marina Ltd
Harbour Office, Bulwark Quay, Whitehaven, Cumbria, CA28 7HW
Tel: 01946 692435
Email: enquiries@whitehavenmarina.co.uk
www.whitehavenmarina.co.uk

VHF	Ch 12
ACCESS	HW±4

Whitehaven Marina can be found at the south-western entrance to the Solway Firth, providing a strategic departure point for those yachts heading for the Isle of Man, Ireland or Southern Scotland. The harbour is one of the more accessible ports of refuge in NW England, affording a safe entry in most weathers. The approach channel across the outer harbour is dredged to about 1.0m above chart datum, allowing entry into the inner harbour via a sea lock at around HW±4. Over 100 new walk ashore berths were installed in 2013.

Conveniently situated for visiting the Lake District, Whitehaven is an attractive Georgian town, renowned in the C18 for its rum and slave imports.

FACILITIES AT A GLANCE

GLASSON BASIN MARINA

BWML, Glasson Basin Marina
School Lane, Glasson Dock, Lancaster, LA2 0AW
Tel: 01524 751491 Fax: 01524 752626
Email: barnaby.hayward@bwml.co.uk
www.bwml.co.uk

VHF	Ch 69
ACCESS	HW-1 to HW

Glasson Dock Marina lies on the River Lune, west of Sunderland Point. Access is via the outer dock which opens 45 minutes before HW. Liverpool and thence via BWB lock into the inner basin. It is recommended to leave Lune No. 1 Buoy approx 1.5 hrs before HW. Contact the dock on Channel 69. The Marina can only be contacted by telephone. All the necessary requirements can be found either on site or within easy reach of Glasson Dock, including boat, rigging and sail repair services as well as a launderette, ablution facilities, shops and restaurants.

FACILITIES AT A GLANCE

Key
a Marina office
b Glasson Sailing Club
c Harbour House

Glasson Basin Marina

• Fully serviced pontoons
• Visitors welcome
• Comprehensive chandlery
• Fully serviced boatyard and workshops with 50 tonne hoist
• Professional workshop services including rigging and spray painting

We are a proud agent of Z Spars UK for yacht masts and rigging requirements

BWML

T: 01524 751491
F: 01524 752626
bwml.co.uk/ra-glasson

Glasson Basin Marina,
School Lane, Glasson Dock,
Lancaster LA2 0AW
barnaby.hayward@bwml.co.uk

PEEL MARINA

Peel Marina
The Harbour Office, East Quay, Peel, IM5 1AR
Tel: 01624 842338 Fax: 01624 843610
www.gov.im/harbours/
Email: enquiries@harbours.dot.gov.im

VHF Ch 12
ACCESS HW±2

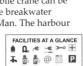

The Inner Harbour has recently been re-developed to provide a 120-berth marina in the southern end. Access is via a flap gate which opens approximately HW±2. A depth of 2·5m is retained at LW. Fresh water and electricity are provided on the pontoons, and a full range of facilities, including showers, laundry, chandlery, fuel and gas are available either in the marina or close by. There is no boat hoist but a mobile crane can be hired locally. Deepwater berths are available on the breakwater

Peel is the most active fishing port on the Isle of Man. The harbour is overlooked by its ancient castle, which also features the award-winning House of Manannan heritage centre. The town offers good shopping, banks, bars, a post office and chemist.

FACILITIES AT A GLANCE

East Quay

FLEETWOOD HAVEN MARINA

Fleetwood Haven Marina
c/o ABP, Port & Marina Office, Fleetwood, FY7 8BP
Tel: 01253 879062 Fax: 01253 879063
Email: fleetwoodhaven@abports.co.uk

VHF Ch 12
ACCESS HW±1.5

Fleetwood Haven Marina provides a good location from which to cruise Morecambe Bay and the Irish Sea. To the north west is the Isle of Man, the north is the Solway Firth and the Clyde Estuary, while to the south

west is Conwy, the Menai Straits and Holyhead.

Tucked away in a protected dock which dates to 1835, the marina has 420 full service berths and offers extensive facilities including a 75-tonne boat hoist, laundry and a first class shower/bathroom block.

Call Fleetwood Dock Radio on VHF Channel 12 (Tel 01253 872351) for permission to enter the dock channel.

FACILITIES AT A GLANCE

See inset of marina extension above

Fish Dock

PRESTON MARINA

Preston Marine Services Ltd
The Boathouse, Navigation Way, Preston, PR2 2YP
Tel: 01772 733595 Fax: 01772 731881
Email: info@prestonmarina.co.uk www.prestonmarina.co.uk

VHF Ch 80
ACCESS HW±2

Preston Marina forms part of the comprehensive Riversway Docklands development, meeting all the demands of modern day boat owners. With the docks' history dating back

over 100 years, today the marina comprises 40 acres of fully serviced pontoon berths sheltered behind the refurbished original lock gates.

Lying 15 miles up the River Ribble, which itself is an interesting cruising ground with an abundance of wildlife, Preston is well placed for sailing to parts of Scotland, Ireland or Wales. The Docklands development includes a wide choice of restaurants, shops and cinemas as well as being in easy reach of all the cultural and leisure facilities provided by a large town.

FACILITIES AT A GLANCE

Key
a Riverway control building
b Marina HQ
c Pub/restaurant

LIVERPOOL MARINA

Liverpool Marina
Coburg Wharf, Sefton Street, Liverpool, L3 4BP
Tel: 0151 707 6777 Fax: 0151 707 6770
Email: mail@liverpoolmarina.co.uk

VHF Ch M
ACCESS HW±2

Liverpool Marina is ideally situated for yachtsmen wishing to cruise the Irish Sea. Access is through a computerised lock that opens two and a half hours either side of high water between 0600 and 2200 daily. Once in the marina, you can enjoy the benefits of the facilities on offer,

including a first class club bar and restaurant.

Liverpool is now a thriving cosmopolitan city, with attractions ranging from numerous bars and restaurants to museums, art galleries and the Beatles Story.

FACILITIES AT A GLANCE

10

Brunswick Dock

Coburg Dock

Key
a Clubhouse bar,
   toilets and showers
b Fuel berth
c Hardstanding yard

CONWY MARINA

Conwy Marina
Conwy, LL32 8EP
Tel: 01492 593000 Fax: 01492 564828
Email: jroberts@quaymarinas.com
www.quaymarinas.com

VHF Ch 80
ACCESS LW±3.5

Situated in an area of outstanding natural beauty, with the Mountains of Snowdonia National Park providing a stunning backdrop, Conwy is the first purpose-built marina to be developed on the north coast of Wales. Enjoying a unique site next to the 13th century Conwy Castle, the third of Edward I's great castles, it provides a convenient base from which to explore the cruising grounds of the North Wales coast. The unspoilt coves of Anglesey and the beautiful Menai Straits prove a popular destination, while further afield are the Lleyn Peninsula and the Islands of Bardsey and Tudwells. The marina incorporates about 500 fully serviced berths which are accessible through a barrier gate between half tide and high water.

FACILITIES AT A GLANCE

DEGANWY QUAYS MARINA

Deganwy Quays Marina
Deganwy, Conwy, LL31 9DJ
Tel: 01492 576888 Fax: 01492 580066
Email: jjones@quaymarinas.com www.quaymarinas.com

VHF Ch 80
ACCESS HW±2

Deganwy Quays Marina is located in the centre of the north Wales coastline on the estuary of the Conwy River and sits between the river and the small town of Deganwy with the beautiful backdrop of the Vardre hills. The views from the Marina across the Conwy River are truly outstanding with the medieval walled town and Castle of Conwy outlined against the foothills of the Snowdonia National Park.

Deganwy Quays Marina opened in 2004 and has 165 fully serviced berths which are accessed via a tidal gate between half tide and high water.

FACILITIES AT A GLANCE

HOLYHEAD MARINA

Holyhead Marina Ltd
Newry Beach, Holyhead, Gwynedd, LL65 1YA
Tel: 01407 764242 Fax: 01407 769152
Email: info@holyheadmarina.co.uk

VHF	Ch M
ACCESS	H24

One of the few natural deep
water harbours on the Welsh
coast, Anglesey is conveniently
placed as a first port of call if
heading to North Wales from the
North, South or West. Its marina
at Holyhead, accessible at all
states of the tide, is sheltered
by Holyhead Mountain as
well as an enormous harbour
breakwater and extensive floating breakwaters, therefore offering
good protection from all directions.

Anglesey boasts numerous picturesque
anchorages and beaches in addition to striking
views over Snowdonia, while only a tide or two
away are the Isle of Man and Eire.

FACILITIES AT A GLANCE

Key
a Marina services
b Marina boatyard
c ILB
d Holyhead Sailing Club
e Lifeboat berth
f Fuel pontoon

Note:
DO NOT use visitors berths
in north easterly winds

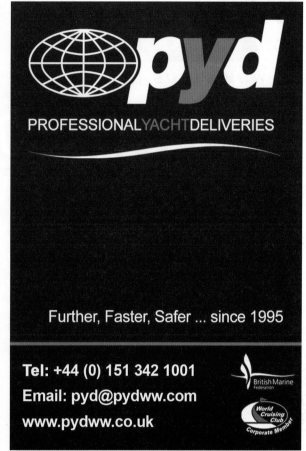
PWLLHELI MARINA

Pwllheli Marina
Glan Don, Pwllheli, North Wales, LL53 5YT
Tel: 01758 701219 Fax: 01758 701443
Email: hafanpwllheli@gwynedd.gov.uk

VHF	Ch 80
ACCESS	

Pwllheli is an old Welsh
market town providing the
gateway to the Llyn Peninsula,
which stretches out as far
as Bardsey Island to form
an 'Area of Outstanding
Natural Beauty'. Enjoying
the spectacular backdrop of
the Snowdonia Mountains,
Pwllheli's numerous attractions
include an open-air market every Wednesday, 'Neuadd Dwyfor', offering
a mix of live theatre and latest films, and beautiful
beaches.

Pwllheli Marina is situated on the south side of
the Llyn Peninsula. One of Wales' finest marinas and
sailing centres, it has over 400 pontoon berths and
excellent onshore facilities.

FACILITIES AT A GLANCE

Key
a Marina offices
   Toilets
   Showers
   Baby change
   Launderette
b Domestic refuse point
c Short stay boat park
d Pwllheli sailing club
e Chandlery
f Events pontoons

10

SOUTH WALES & BRISTOL CHANNEL – Bardsey Island to Land's End

Key to Marina Plans symbols

Bottled gas		P	Parking
Chandler			Pub/Restaurant
Disabled facilities			Pump out
Electrical supply			Rigging service
Electrical repairs			Sail repairs
Engine repairs			Shipwright
First Aid			Shop/Supermarket
Fresh Water			Showers
Fuel - Diesel			Slipway
Fuel - Petrol		WC	Toilets
Hardstanding/boatyard			Telephone
@ Internet Café			Trolleys
Laundry facilities		V	Visitors berths
Lift-out facilities			Wi-Fi

Area 11 - South Wales & Bristol Channel

MARINAS

Telephone Numbers
VHF Channel
Access Times

Barmouth

Aberdovey

Aberystwyth
01970 611422
Ch 80 HW±2 • Aberystwyth

WALES

Fishguard

Bristol Marina
0117 921 3198
Ch 80 HW-3 to HW

Sharpness Marina
01453 811476
Ch 13 HW-2 to HW

Milford Haven

Tenby

Burry Port

Swansea

Penarth Quay Marina
02920 705021
Ch 80 H24

Milford Marina
01646 696312
Ch 14, M H24

Swansea Marina
01792 470310
Ch 80 HW±4½

Barry • Cardiff

Bristol

Cardiff Marina
02920 396078
Ch 27 H24

Portishead Quay
Marina
01275 841941
Ch 80 HW±4

Neyland Yacht Haven
01646 601601
Ch M, 80 H24

Bristol Channel

Ilfracombe

Watchet

Burnham-on-Sea

Appledore

N

Padstow Harbour
01841 532239
Ch 12 HW±2

Padstow

Land's
End

Isles of
Scilly

Round Is

11

ABERYSTWYTH MARINA

Aberystwyth Marina, IMP Developments
Trefechan, Aberystwyth, Ceredigion, SY23 1AS
Tel: 01970 611422 Fax: 01970 624122
Email: enquiries@aberystwythmarina.com

VHF	Ch 80
ACCESS	HW±2

Aberystwyth is a picturesque university seaside town on the west coast of Wales. Its £9 million marina provides over 150 permanent pontoon berths and welcomes on average between 1,500 and 2,000 visiting yachts per year. Accessible two hours either side of high water, its facilities incorporate the usual marine services as well as an on-site pub and restaurant.

A short distance away are several pretty Welsh harbours, including Fishguard, Cardigan, Porthmadog and Abersoch, while the east coast of Ireland can be reached within a day's sail.

FACILITIES AT A GLANCE

Key
a Offices
b Offices
c Marina office
d Apartments
e Aberystwyth BC

MILFORD MARINA

Milford Marina
Milford Docks, Milford Haven, Pembrokeshire, SA73 3AF
Tel: 01646 696312 Fax: 01646 696314
Email: enquiries@milfordmarina.com www.milfordmarina.com

VHF	Ch 14
ACCESS	H24

Set within one of the deepest natural harbours in the world, Milford Marina is situated in a non-tidal basin within the UK's only coastal National Park, the ideal base for discovering the fabulous coastline in Pembrokeshire, Wales and Ireland. Continued investment has meant that the marina provides safe, secure and sheltered boat berths with a full range of shoreside facilities in the heart of SW Wales.

Accessed via an entrance lock (with waiting pontoons both inside and outside the lock), the marina is perfect for exploring the picturesque upper reaches of the River Cleddau or cruising out beyond St Ann's Head to the unspoilt islands of Skomer, Skokholm and Grassholm.

FACILITIES AT A GLANCE

Key
a Neil Hart Joinery
b Mustang Marine
c Neyland Marine Services
d Fish Processing
e Fish Markets
f Galley Café
g MPSC
h Servitec
i MITEC Building
j Seal Hospital
k Sail loft
l Charles Bar
m Norrad Electrics
n All Pets Vet Care
o Locks on Line
p Museum
q Marina Control
Martha's Vineyard
Dyfed Electronics
r Phoenix Bowl
s Windjammer Marine

NEYLAND YACHT HAVEN

Neyland Yacht Haven Ltd
Brunel Quay, Neyland, Pembrokeshire, SA73 1PY
Tel: 01646 601601 Fax: 01646 600713
Email: neyland@yachthavens.com www.yachthavens.com

VHF	Ch M, 80
ACCESS	H24

Approximately 10 miles from the entrance to Milford Haven lies Neyland Yacht Haven. Tucked away in a well protected inlet just before the Cleddau Bridge, this marina has 420 berths and can accommodate yachts up to 25m LOA with draughts of up to 2.5m. The marina is divided into two basins, with the lower one enjoying full tidal access, while entry to the upper one is restricted by a tidal sill. Visitor and annual berthing enquiries welcome.

Offering a comprehensive range of services, Neyland Yacht Haven is within a five minute walk of the town centre where the various shops and takeaways cater for most everyday needs. The Yacht Haven is a member of the TransEurope Group.

FACILITIES AT A GLANCE

Key
a   Marine services building
    Harbour's Master's office
    Public telephone
    Laundry
    Chandlery and café
    Restaurant and bar
b   Storage compound - refuse disposal
c   Upper Basin - showers and toilets
d   Refuse, recycling, battery disposal
e   Holding berth
    Showers and toilets
    Disabled persons toilets
f   Dale Sailing Co Ltd
    yacht repair yard
g   Tidal sill with depth gauge
h   Yacht club and slipway
i   Waste oil and used
    battery collection point
NB Berth numbering flows from low outer

Weather information collection point

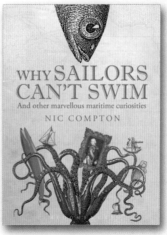
11

SWANSEA MARINA

Swansea Marina
Lockside, Maritime Quarter, Swansea, SA1 1WG
Tel: 01792 470310 Fax: 01792 463948
www.swansea.gov.uk/swanseamarina
Email: swanmar@swansea.gov.uk

VHF	Ch 80
ACCESS	HW±4.5

At the hub of the city's recently redeveloped and award winning Maritime Quarter, Swansea Marina can be accessed HW±4½ hrs via a lock. Surrounded by a plethora of shops, restaurants and marine businesses to cater for most yachtsmen's needs, the marina is in close proximity to the picturesque Gower coast, where there is no shortage of quiet sandy beaches off which to anchor. It also provides the perfect starting point for cruising to Ilfracombe, Lundy Island, the North Cornish coast or West Wales.

Within easy walking distance of the marina is the city centre, boasting a covered shopping centre and market. For those who prefer walking or cycling, take the long promenade to the Mumbles fishing village from where there are plenty of coastal walks.

FACILITIES AT A GLANCE

Key
a Leisure Centre
b Maritime Museum
c Pumphouse Restaurant
d Yacht Club
e Repair shed
f Mariott Hotel

PENARTH QUAYS MARINA

Penarth Quays Marina
Penarth, Vale of Glamorgan, CF64 1TQ
Tel: 02920 705021
Email: sjones@quaymarinas.com
www.quaymarinas.com

VHF	Ch 80
ACCESS	H24

Penarth Quays Marina has been established in the historic basins of Penarth Docks for over 20 years and is the premier boating facility in the region. The marina is Cardiff Bay's only 5 Gold Anchor marina and provides an ideal base for those using the Bay and the Bristol Channel. With 24hr access there is always water available for boating. Penarth and Cardiff boast an extensive range of leisure facilities, shops and restaurants making this marina an ideal base or destination. The marina has a blue flag and is a member of the TransEurope Group.

FACILITIES AT A GLANCE

Key
a Marina office
b Inner basin services building
c Boat shed
d Refuse compound
e Boat sales
f Restaurant

CARDIFF MARINA

Cardiff Marina
Watkiss Way, Cardiff, CF11 0SY
Tel: 02920 396078 Fax: 02920 345116
Email: info@themarinegroup.co.uk
www.themarinegroup.co.uk

VHF	Ch M
ACCESS	H24

Cardiff Marina provides safe, secure and sheltered moorings for motor boats and yachts on the River Ely in Cardiff Bay. Cardiff Bay is an attractive and approachable environment for all boat users with the Barrage allowing H24 access to the Bristol Channel. Its location ensures excellent transport links for easy access to Cardiff City Centre and the waterfront of Mermaid Quay.

Extensive boatyard services are available including a range of further marine services at Cardiff Marine Village.

Work is due to begin in spring 2014 on new marina facilities to include a new marina office, shower block, laundry and waterside bar.

FACILITIES AT A GLANCE

Key
a Marina Office
b Showers, toilets
c Workshop

SHARPNESS MARINA

Sharpness Marina
Berkeley, Gloucestershire GL13 9UN
Tel & fax: 01453 811476
Email: sharpnessmarine@gmx.com

VHF	Ch 13
ACCESS	HW-2

Sharpness is a small port on the River Severn lying at the entrance to the Gloucester and Sharpness Canal. At the time of its completion in 1827, the canal was the largest and deepest ship canal in the world. However, although once an important commercial waterway, it is now primarily used by pleasure boats. Yachts approaching the marina from seaward can do so via a lock two hours before high water, but note that the final arrival should be timed as late as possible to avoid strong tides in the entrance. From the lock, a passage under two swing bridges and a turn to port brings you to the marina, where pontoon berths are equipped with electricity and water supplies.

FACILITIES AT A GLANCE

BRISTOL MARINA

Bristol Marina Ltd
Hanover Place, Bristol, BS1 6TZ
Tel: 0117 921 3198 Fax: 0117 929 7672
Email: info@bristolmarina.co.uk

VHF	Ch 80
ACCESS	HW-3 to HW

Situated in the heart of the city, Bristol is a fully serviced marina providing over 100 pontoon berths for vessels up to 20m LOA. Among the facilities are a new fuelling berth and pump out station as well as an on site chandler and sailmaker. It is situated on the south side of the Floating Harbour, about eight miles from the mouth of the River Avon. Accessible from seaward via the Cumberland Basin, passing through both Entrance Lock and Junction Lock, it can be reached approximately three hours before HW.

Shops, restaurants, theatres and cinemas are all within easy reach of the marina, while local attractions include the SS *Great Britain*, designed by Isambard Kingdom Brunel, and the famous Clifton Suspension Bridge, which has an excellent visitors' centre depicting its fascinating story.

FACILITIES AT A GLANCE

Key
a Albion Boatyard
b Marina office

PORTISHEAD QUAYS MARINA

Portishead Quays Marina
Newfoundland Way, Portishead, North Somerset, BS20 7DF
Tel: 01275 841941 Fax: 01275 841942
Email: kberry@quaymarinas.com
www.quaymarinas.com

VHF	Ch 80
ACCESS	HW±3.5

Portishead Marina is a popular destination for cruising in the Bristol Channel. Providing an excellent link between the inland waterways at Bristol and Sharpness and offering access to the open water and marinas down channel. The entrance to the Marina is via a lock, with a minimum access of HW+/- 3.5hrs. Contact the Marina on VHF Ch 80 ahead of time for next available lock. The Marina provides 250 fully serviced berths and can accommodate vessels up to 40m LOA, draft up to 5.5m. The marina has a 35 tonnes boat hoist and the boatyard offers all the facilities you would expect from a Quay Marinas site.

FACILITIES AT A GLANCE

Key a Marina control building (reception, facilities & laundry)
     b Advance Marine Services & Chandlery
     c A&W Building & Coastguard
     d Boatyard facilities, fishing tackle supplies & café
     e Ray Williams Marine Engineer
     f Hall & Woodhouse pub (facilities & laundry)
     g Morrisons supermarket

PADSTOW HARBOUR

Padstow Harbour Commissioners
The Harbour Office, Padstow, Cornwall, PL28 8AQ
Tel: 01841 532239 Fax: 01841 533346
Email: padstowharbour@btconnect.com
www.padstow-harbour.co.uk

VHF	Ch 12, 16
ACCESS	HW±2

Padstow is a small commercial port with a rich history situated 1.5 miles from the sea within the estuary of the River Camel. The inner harbour is serviced by a tidal gate – part of the 1988–1990 flood defence scheme, which is open approximately two hours either side of high water. A minimum of 3m of water is maintained in the inner harbour at all times. Onshore facilities are excellent, please enquire at the Harbour Office.

This is a thriving fishing port, so perhaps it wasn't surprising that celebrity chefs like Rick Stein and Jamie Oliver would set up shop in the town. This is a great resting point for everything Cornish from surf and coastal walks to fish and chips and cream teas.

FACILITIES AT A GLANCE

Key a Residents' pontoons
     b Harbour office
     * Electricity and water points
     1-20 around harbour denote ladder numbers

11

SOUTH IRELAND – Malahide, clockwise to Liscannor Bay

Key to Marina Plans symbols

🜪	Bottled gas	P	Parking
♫	Chandler	✗	Pub/Restaurant
♿	Disabled facilities	♒	Pump out
⚡	Electrical supply	⚒	Rigging service
⚒	Electrical repairs	⚓	Sail repairs
🔧	Engine repairs	✂	Shipwright
✚	First Aid	🛒	Shop/Supermarket
⚓	Fresh Water	♨	Showers
D	Fuel - Diesel	◣	Slipway
P	Fuel - Petrol	WC	Toilets
✖	Hardstanding/boatyard	✆	Telephone
@	Internet Café	🛒	Trolleys
▣	Laundry facilities	V	Visitors berths
🜊	Lift-out facilities	ᛉ	Wi-Fi

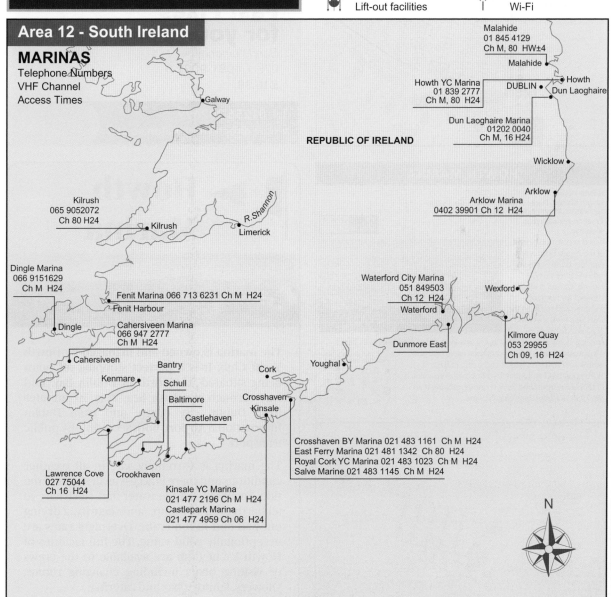

Area 12 - South Ireland

MARINAS
Telephone Numbers
VHF Channel
Access Times

Galway

REPUBLIC OF IRELAND

Kilrush
065 9052072
Ch 80 H24 — Kilrush

R.Shannon
Limerick

Dingle Marina
066 9151629
Ch M H24

Fenit Marina 066 713 6231 Ch M H24
Fenit Harbour

Dingle

Cahersiveen Marina
066 947 2777
Ch M H24

Cahersiveen

Bantry

Kenmare

Schull

Baltimore

Castlehaven

Lawrence Cove
027 75044
Ch 16 H24

Crookhaven

Kinsale YC Marina
021 477 2196 Ch M H24
Castlepark Marina
021 477 4959 Ch 06 H24

Cork

Youghal

Crosshaven
Kinsale

Crosshaven BY Marina 021 483 1161 Ch M H24
East Ferry Marina 021 481 1342 Ch 80 H24
Royal Cork YC Marina 021 483 1023 Ch M H24
Salve Marine 021 483 1145 Ch M H24

Dunmore East

Waterford City Marina
051 849503
Ch 12 H24
Waterford

Wexford

Kilmore Quay
053 29955
Ch 09, 16 H24

Malahide
01 845 4129
Ch M, 80 HW±4
Malahide

Howth YC Marina
01 839 2777
Ch M, 80 H24

DUBLIN
Howth
Dun Laoghaire

Dun Laoghaire Marina
01202 0040
Ch M, 16 H24

Wicklow

Arklow

Arklow Marina
0402 39901 Ch 12 H24

N

12

MALAHIDE MARINA

Malahide Marina
Malahide, Co. Dublin
Tel: +353 1 845 4129 Fax: +353 1 845 4255
Email: info@malahidemarina.net
www.malahidemarina.net

| VHF | Ch M, 80 |
| ACCESS | HW±4 |

Malahide Marina, situated just 10 minutes from Dublin Airport and 20 minutes north of Dublin's city centre, is a fully serviced marina accommodating up to 350 yachts. Capable of taking vessels of up to 75m in length, its first class facilities include a boatyard with hard standing for approximately 170 boats and a 30-ton mobile hoist. Its on site restaurant provides a large seating area in convivial surroundings. The village of Malahide has plenty to offer the visiting yachtsmen, with a wide variety of eating places, nearby golf courses and tennis courts as well as a historic castle and botanical gardens.

FACILITIES AT A GLANCE

Key
a Boat handling & storage area
b Refuelling bay
c Marina centre
d Boatyard
e Marina access bridge
f Restaurant
g Wash area

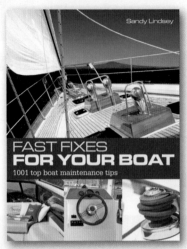
HOWTH MARINA

Howth Marina
Howth Marina, Harbour Road, Howth, Co. Dublin
Tel: +353 1 8392777 Fax: +353 1 8392430
Email: marina@hyc.ie
www.hyc.ie

| VHF | Ch M, 80 |
| ACCESS | H24 |

Based on the north coast of the rugged peninsula that forms the northern side of Dublin Bay, Howth Marina is ideally situated for north or south-bound traffic in the Irish Sea. Well sheltered in all winds, it can be entered at any state of the tide. Overlooking the marina is Howth Yacht Club, which has in recent years been expanded and is now said to be the largest yacht club in Ireland. With good road and rail links, Howth is in easy reach of Dublin's airport and ferry terminal, making it an obvious choice for crew changeovers.

FACILITIES AT A GLANCE

Key
a Harbour office
b RNLI boathouse
c Clubhouse
d Drying pad
e Waiting pontoons (A&B)

Howth Marina

The marina is owned and managed by Howth Yacht Club. It is a perfect stopping off point being situated just north of Dublin Bay, mid way through the Irish Sea; it is 30 minutes from Dublin city centre and from Dublin International Airport, both accessible by public transport.

The marina is extremely safe in all weather conditions and there is access at all stages of the tide. Facilities include water and electricity to all berths, diesel pump, and security, a drying out pad and 15 ton crane. Overnight rates are exceptionally good value. The full facilities of Howth Yacht Club are available to the crews of visiting boats including changing rooms, showers, laundry, bar and catering.

DUN LAOGHAIRE MARINA

Dun Laoghaire Marina
Harbour Road, Dun Laoghaire, Co Dublin, Eire
Tel: +353 1 202 0040 Fax: +353 1 202 0043
Email: info@dlmarina.com www.dlmarina.com

VHF	Ch M, 16
ACCESS	H24

Dun Laoghaire Marina – Gateway to Dublin and the first marina in the Republic of Ireland to be awarded five Gold anchors by THYA and also achieved the ICOMIA 'Clean Marina' accreditation – is the largest marina in Ireland. 24 hour access in all weather conditions. The town centre is located within 400m. Serviced berthing for 820 boats from 6m to 23m with visitors mainly on the hammerheads.

Larger vessels up to 30m and 80 tonne displacement can be accommodated alongside breakwater pontoons. Minimum draft is 3.6m LWS. With adjacent ferry terminal and rail station, Dublin 12kms and airport 35kms, the marina is an ideal location for crew change etc. Easy access to Dublin Bay, home to the biennial Dun Laoghaire Regatta.

FACILITIES AT A GLANCE

Key
a Royal Irish Yacht Club
b Marina office
c WC
d Royal St George Yacht Club
Berth numbering - odds to port, evens to starboard, increase inwards

ARKLOW MARINA

Arklow Marina
North Quay, Arklow, Co. Wicklow, Eire
Tel: +353 402 39901 Fax: +353 402 39902
Mobiles: 087 2375189 or 087 2588078
Email: technical@asl.ie
www.arklowmarina.com

VHF	Ch12
ACCESS	H24

Arklow is a popular fishing port and seaside town situated at the mouth of the River Avoca, 16 miles south of Wicklow and 11 miles north east of Gorey. The town is ideally placed for visiting the many beauty spots of County Wicklow including Glenmalure, Glendalough and Clara Lara, Avoca (Ballykissangel).

Arklow Marina is on the north bank of the river, just upstream of the commercial quays, with 42 berths in an inner harbour and 30 berths on pontoons outside the marina entrance. Vessels over 14m LOA should moor on the river pontoons.

FACILITIES AT A GLANCE

KILMORE QUAY

Kilmore Quay
Wexford, Ireland
Tel: +353 53 9129955 Fax: +353 53 9129915
Email: harbourmaster@wexfordcoco.ie www.wexford.ie

VHF	Ch 09, 16
ACCESS	H24

Located in the SE corner of Ireland, Kilmore Quay is a small rural fishing village situated approximately 14 miles from the town of Wexford and 12 miles from Rosslare ferry port.

Its 55-berthed marina, offering shelter from the elements as well as various on shore facilities, including diesel available 24/7, has become a regular port of call for many cruising yachtsmen. With several nearby areas of either historical or natural significance accessible using local bike hire, Kilmore is renowned for its 'green' approach to the environment.

FACILITIES AT A GLANCE

Key
a Harbour master's office - onshore facilities
b Lifeboat station
c Information board
d Stella Maris - community centre

WATERFORD CITY MARINA

Waterford City Marina
Waterford, Ireland
Tel: +353 87 238 4944 Fax: +353 51 849763
Email: jcodd@waterfordcity.ie

VHF	Ch 12
ACCESS	H24

Famous for its connections with Waterford Crystal, manufactured in the city centre, Waterford is the capital of the SE region of Ireland. As a major city, it benefits from good rail links with Dublin, and Limerick, a regional airport with daily flights to Britain and an extensive bus service to surrounding towns and villages. The marina is found on the banks of the River Suir, in the heart of this historic Viking city dating back to the ninth century. Yachtsmen can make the most of Waterford's wide range of shops, restaurants and bars without having to walk too far from their boats. With 150 fully serviced berths and first rate security, Waterford City Marina now provides shower, toilet and laundry facilities in its new reception building.

FACILITIES AT A GLANCE

12

CROSSHAVEN BOATYARD MARINA

Crosshaven Boatyard Marina
Crosshaven, Co Cork, Ireland
Tel: +353 214 831161 Fax: +353 214 831603
Email: info@crosshavenboatyard.com

VHF | Ch M
ACCESS | H24

One of three marinas at Crosshaven, Crosshaven Boatyard was founded in 1950 and originally made its name from the construction of some of the most world-renowned yachts, including *Gypsy Moth* and Denis Doyle's *Moonduster*. Nowadays, however, the yard has diversified to provide a wide range of services to both the marine leisure and professional industries. Situated on a safe and sheltered river only 12 miles from Cork City Centre, the marina boasts 100 fully-serviced berths along with the capacity to accommodate yachts up to 35m LOA with a 4m draught. In addition, it is ideally situated for cruising the stunning south west coast of Ireland.

FACILITIES AT A GLANCE

SALVE MARINE

Salve Marine
Crosshaven, Co Cork, Ireland
Tel: +353 214 831 145
Email: salvemarine@eircom.net

VHF | Ch M
ACCESS | H24

Crosshaven is a picturesque seaside resort providing a gateway to Ireland's south and south west coasts. Offering a variety of activities to suit all types, its rocky coves and quiet sandy beaches stretch from Graball to Church Bay and from Fennell's Bay to nearby Myrtleville. Besides a selection of craft shops selling locally produced arts and crafts, there are plenty of pubs, restaurants and takeaways to suit even the most discerning of tastes. Lying within a few hundred metres of the village centre is Salve Marine, accommodating yachts up to 43m LOA with draughts of up to 4m. Its comprehensive services range from engineering and welding facilities to hull and rigging repairs.

FACILITIES AT A GLANCE

ROYAL CORK YACHT CLUB

Royal Cork Yacht Club Marina
Crosshaven, Co Cork, Ireland
Tel: +353 21 483 1023 Fax: +353 21 483 2657
Email: mark@royalcork.com   www.royalcork.com

⚓⚓⚓⚓
VHF | Ch M
ACCESS | H24

Founded in 1720, the Royal Cork Yacht Club is one of the oldest and most prominent yacht clubs in the world. Organising, among many other events, the prestigious biennial Ford Cork Week, it boasts a number of World, European and national sailors among its membership.

The Yacht Club's marina is situated at Crosshaven, on the hillside at the mouth of the Owenabue River, just inside the entrance to Cork Harbour. The harbour is popular with yachtsmen as it is accessible and well sheltered in all weather conditions. It also benefits from the Gulf Stream producing a temperate climate practically all year round.

FACILITIES AT A GLANCE

Blue Flag
An Taisce

Berth numbering runs left to right in each bay, and lowest to highest in the direction of the arrows

Orange bay | Green bay | Blue bay | Red bay | Yellow bay | White bay

Dinghy Park

Royal Cork Yacht Club

EAST FERRY MARINA

East Ferry Marina
Cobh, Co Cork, Ireland
Tel: +353 21 481 1342 Fax: +353 21 481 1342

VHF | Ch 80
ACCESS | H24

East Ferry Marina lies on the east side of Great Island, one of three large islands in Cork Harbour which are now all joined by roads and bridges. Despite its remote, tranquil setting, it offers all the fundamental facilities including showers, water, fuel, electricity and that all important pub. The nearest town is Cobh, which is a good five mile walk away, albeit a pleasant one.

Formerly known as Queenstown, Cobh (pronounced 'cove') reverted back to its original Irish name in 1922 and is renowned for being the place from where thousands of Irish men and women set off to America to build a new life for themselves, particularly during the famine years of 1844–48.

FACILITIES AT A GLANCE

KINSALE YACHT CLUB MARINA

Kinsale Yacht Club Marina
Kinsale, Co Cork, Ireland
Tel: +353 21 4772196 Fax: +353 21 4774455
Email: kyc@iol.ie

VHF Ch M
ACCESS H24

Kinsale is a natural, virtually land-locked harbour on the estuary of the Bandon River, approximately 12 miles south west of Cork harbour entrance. Home to a thriving fishing fleet as well as frequented by commercial shipping, it boasts two fully serviced marinas, with the Kinsale Yacht Club

& Marina being the closest to the town. Visitors to this marina automatically become temporary members of the club and are therefore entitled to make full use of the facilities, which include a fully licensed bar and restaurant serving evening meals on Wednesdays, Thursdays and Saturdays. Fuel, water and repair services are also available.

FACILITIES AT A GLANCE

CASTLEPARK MARINA

Castlepark Marina Centre
Kinsale, Co Cork, Ireland
Tel: +353 21 4774959 Fax: +353 21 4773894
Email: tadgh@castleparkmarina.com

VHF Ch 16, 14
ACCESS H24

Situated on the south side of Kinsale Harbour, Castlepark is a small marina with deep water pontoon berths that are accessible at all states of the tide. Surrounded by rolling hills, it boasts its own beach as well as being in close proximity to the parklands of James Fort and a traditional

Irish pub. The attractive town of Kinsale, with its narrow streets and slate-clad houses, lies just 1.5 miles away by road or five minutes away by ferry. Known as Ireland's 'fine food centre', it incorporates a number of gourmet food shops and high quality restaurants as well as a wine museum.

FACILITIES AT A GLANCE

transeurope

LAWRENCE COVE MARINA

Lawrence Cove Marina
Lawrence Cove, Bere Island, Co Cork, Ireland
Tel: +353 27 75044 Fax: +353 27 75044
Email: lcm@iol.ie
www.lawrencecovemarina.com

VHF Ch 16
ACCESS H24

Lawrence Cove enjoys a peaceful location on an island at the entrance to Bantry Bay. Privately owned and run, it offers sheltered and secluded waters as well as excellent facilities and fully serviced pontoon berths. A few hundred yards from the marina you will find a shop,

pub and restaurant, while the mainland, with its various attractions, can be easily reached by ferry. Lawrence Cove lies at the heart of the wonderful cruising grounds of Ireland's south west coast and, just two hours from Cork airport, is an ideal place to leave your boat for long or short periods.

FACILITIES AT A GLANCE

CAHERSIVEEN MARINA

Cahersiveen Marina
The Pier, Cahersiveen, Co. Kerry, Ireland
Tel: +353 66 9472777 Fax: +353 66 9472993
Email: acard@eircom.net
www.cahersiveenmarina.ie

VHF Ch M
ACCESS H24

Situated two miles up Valentia River from Valentia Harbour, Cahersiveen Marina is well protected in all wind directions and is convenient for sailing to Valentia Island and Dingle Bay as well as for visiting some of the spectacular uninhabited islands in the surrounding area. Boasting a host of sheltered sandy beaches, the region is renowned for salt and fresh water fishing as well as being good for scuba diving.

Within easy walking distance of the marina lies the historic town of Cahersiveen, incorporating an array of convivial pubs and restaurants.

FACILITIES AT A GLANCE

12

DINGLE MARINA

Dingle Marina
Strand Street, Dingle, Co Kerry, Ireland
Tel: +353 87 232 5844 Fax: +353 69 5152546
Email:dingleharbour@agriculture.gov.ie
www.dinglemarina.com

VHF	Ch M
ACCESS	H24

Dingle is Ireland's most westerly marina, lying at the heart of the sheltered Dingle Harbour, and is easily reached both day and night via a well buoyed approach channel. The surrounding area is an interesting and unfrequented cruising ground, with several islands, bays and beaches for the yachtsman to explore.

The marina lies in the heart of the old market town, renowned for its hospitality and traditional Irish pub music. Besides enjoying the excellent seafood restaurants and 52 pubs, other recreational pastimes include horse riding, golf, climbing and diving.

FACILITIES AT A GLANCE

Key
a Marina centre building - cafe, dive centre, sailing and rowing centre, chandlery and showers
b Sea Life Centre
c Commercial berths - FVs & ferries
d Marina office

FENIT HARBOUR MARINA

Fenit Harbour & Marina
Fenit, Tralee, Co. Kerry, Republic of Ireland
Tel: +353 66 7136231 Fax: +353 66 7136473
Email: info@fenitharbour.com www.fenitharbour.com

VHF	Ch M
ACCESS	H24

Fenit Harbour Marina is tucked away in Tralee Bay, not far south of the Shannon Estuary. Besides offering a superb cruising ground, being within a day's sail of Dingle and Kilrush, the marina also provides a convenient base from which to visit inland attractions such as the picturesque tourist towns of Tralee and Killarney. This 120-berth marina accommodates boats up to 15m LOA and benefits from deep water at all states of the tide.

The small village of Fenit incorporates a grocery shop as well a several pubs and restaurants, while among the local activities are horse riding, swimming from one of the nearby sandy beaches and golfing.

FACILITIES AT A GLANCE

Key
a Warehouse
b Marina services, harbour office, lifeboat station

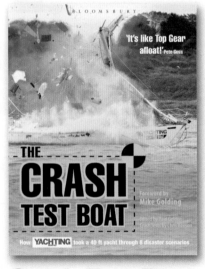

KILRUSH MARINA

Kilrush Marina Ltd
Kilrush, Co. Clare, Ireland
Tel: +353 65 9052072 Mobile: +353 86 2313870
Fax: +353 65 9051692 Email: hehirj@shannondevelopment.ie

VHF	Ch 80
ACCESS	H24

Kilrush Marina and boatyard is strategically placed for exploring the unspoilt west coast of Ireland, including Galway Bay, Dingle, W Cork and Kerry. It also provides a gateway to over 150 miles of cruising on Lough Derg, the R. Shannon and the Irish canal system. Accessed via lock gates, the marina lies at one end of the main street in Kilrush, the marina centre provides all the facilities for the visiting sailor. Kilrush is a vibrant market town with a long maritime history. A 15-minute ferry ride from the marina takes you to Scattery Is, once a 6th century monastic settlement but now only inhabited by wildlife. The Shannon Estuary is reputed for being the country's first marine Special Area of Conservation (SAC) and is home to Ireland's only known resident group of bottlenose dolphins.

FACILITIES AT A GLANCE

NORTH IRELAND – Liscannor Bay, clockwise to Lambay Island

Key to Marina Plans symbols

	Bottled gas	P	Parking
	Chandler		Pub/Restaurant
	Disabled facilities		Pump out
	Electrical supply		Rigging service
	Electrical repairs		Sail repairs
	Engine repairs		Shipwright
	First Aid		Shop/Supermarket
	Fresh Water		Showers
D	Fuel - Diesel		Slipway
P	Fuel - Petrol	WC	Toilets
	Hardstanding/boatyard		Telephone
@	Internet Café		Trolleys
	Laundry facilities	V	Visitors berths
	Lift-out facilities		Wi-Fi

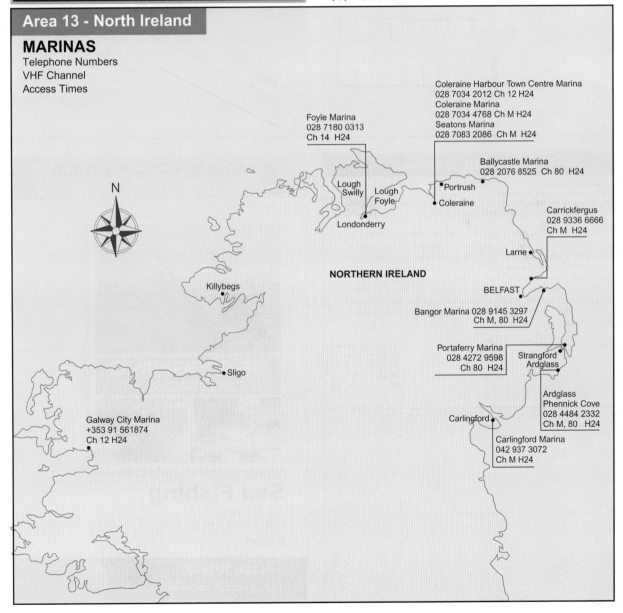

Area 13 - North Ireland

MARINAS
Telephone Numbers
VHF Channel
Access Times

N

Foyle Marina
028 7180 0313
Ch 14 H24

Coleraine Harbour Town Centre Marina
028 7034 2012 Ch 12 H24
Coleraine Marina
028 7034 4768 Ch M H24
Seatons Marina
028 7083 2086 Ch M H24

Ballycastle Marina
028 2076 8525 Ch 80 H24

Lough Swilly

Lough Foyle

Portrush

Coleraine

Londonderry

Carrickfergus
028 9336 6666
Ch M H24

Larne

NORTHERN IRELAND

Killybegs

BELFAST

Bangor Marina 028 9145 3297
Ch M, 80 H24

Portaferry Marina
028 4272 9598
Ch 80 H24

Strangford
Ardglass

Sligo

Ardglass
Phennick Cove
028 4484 2332
Ch M, 80   H24

Carlingford

Galway City Marina
+353 91 561874
Ch 12 H24

Carlingford Marina
042 937 3072
Ch M H24

GALWAY CITY MARINA

Galway City Marina
Galway Harbour Co, Harbour Office, Galway, Ireland
Tel: +353 91 561874 Fax: +353 91 563738
Email: info@galwayharbour.com

VHF	Ch 12
ACCESS	HW-2 to HW

The Galway harbour Company operates a small marina in the confines of Galway Harbour with an additional 60m of pontoon-walkway. Freshwater and electrical power is available at the pontoons. Power cars can be purchased from the harbour office during the days and also from a local pub 'Bar 8' on dock located on dock road. A number of visitors pontoons are available for hire during the summer and for winter layup. Sailors intending to call to Galway Harbour should first make contact with the Harbour office to determine if a berth is available — advisable as demand is high in this quiet and beautiful part of Ireland.

FACILITIES AT A GLANCE

FOYLE MARINA

Foyle Marina
Londonderry Port, Lisahally, L'Derry, BT47 6FL
Tel: 02871 860555 Fax: 02871 861656
www.londonderryport.com/leisure
Email: info@londonderryport.com

VHF	Ch 14
ACCESS	H24

Foyle Marina lies in the heart of the city, 17M from the mouth of Lough Foyle, is accessible at any state of the tide and is sheltered from all directions of wind. Approach is via well-marked navigation channel with a maintained depth of 8m.

The marina has recently undergone extensive improvements with over 680m of secure pontoon mooring now available. Foyle Marina now offers full facilities to visiting vessels. Toilets and showers on site, water and electricity at each berth. Vessels up to 130m LOA can be accommodated. Craft can berth either side of the pontoons in depths of 5–7m at LW.

The pontoons are within easy walking distance of the city centre where you will find restaurants, bars, cinemas, shopping and a host of tourist attractions.

FACILITIES AT A GLANCE

Key a Council offices
     b Appartments
     c Doctor's surgery

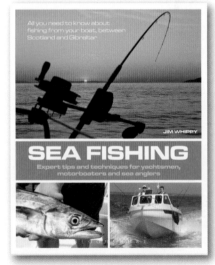

River Foyle

COLERAINE MARINA

Coleraine Marina
64 Portstewart Road, Coleraine,
Co Londonderry, BT52 1RR
Tel: 028 7034 4768 Email: rickiemac@talktalk.net

VHF	Ch M
ACCESS	H24

Coleraine Marina complex enjoys a superb location in sheltered waters just one mile north of the town of Coleraine and four and a half miles south of the River Bann Estuary and the open sea. Besides accommodating vessels up to 18m LOA, this modern marina with 105 berths offers hard standing, fuel, a chandlery and shower facilities.

Among one of the oldest known settlements in Ireland, Coleraine is renowned for its linen, whiskey and salmon. Its thriving commercial centre includes numerous shops, a four-screen cinema and a state-of-the-art leisure complex.

FACILITIES AT A GLANCE

Security Gate   Marina Office

COLERAINE HARBOUR MARINA

Coleraine Harbour Town Centre Marina
Coleraine Harbour Office, 4 Riverside Road, Coleraine, BT52 1XA
Tel: 028 7034 2012 Fax: 028 7034 2000
Email: info@coleraineharbour.com
www.coleraineharbour.com

VHF Ch 12
ACCESS H24

The Marina lies upstream from about five miles from the sea ideally situated in the centre of the town, just a few minutes stroll from a selection of shops, restaurants and bars.

In addition to the pontoon berths there is a 40 tonne Roodberg slipway launch/recovery trailer. Hard standing and covered storage are available.

Coleraine is an ideal base for exploring the many nearby attractions including the Old Bushmills Distillery and the Giants Causeway.

FACILITIES AT A GLANCE

Coleraine Harbour Town Centre Marina

- The Best Sheltered Pontoon Berthing on the Lower Bann
- Situated in the Centre of the Town
- Water/Electricity on Berths
- Diesel Pump
- 24 Hour Security
- 40 Tonne Slipway Trailer

- Hard Standing/Undercover Storage
- Special Rates for Lift Out of up to 24 Hours for Survey, Power Wash, Repairs.

info@coleraineharbour.com
www.coleraineharbour.com

SEATONS MARINA

Seatons Marina
Drumslade Rd, Coleraine, Londonderry, BT52 1SE
Tel: 028 7083 2086 Mobile 07718 883099
Email: jill@seatonsmarina.co.uk www.seatonsmarina.co.uk

VHF Ch M
ACCESS H24

Seatons Marina is a privately owned business on the north coast of Ireland, which was established by Eric Seaton in 1962. It lies on the east bank of the River Bann, approximately two miles downstream from Coleraine and three miles from the sea. Long term pontoon berths are available for yachts up to 11.5 with a maximum draft of 2.4m; fore and aft moorings are available for larger vessels. Lift out and mast stepping facilities are provided by a 12 tonne trailer hoist.

FACILITIES AT A GLANCE

BALLYCASTLE MARINA

Ballycastle Marina
Bayview Road, Ballycastle, Northern Ireland
Tel: 028 2076 8525/07803 505084 Fax: 028 2076 6215
Email: info@moyle-council.org

VHF Ch 80
ACCESS H24

Ballycastle is a traditional seaside town situated on Northern Ireland's North Antrim coast. The 74-berthed, sheltered marina provides a perfect base from which to explore the well known local attractions such as the Giant's Causeway world heritage site, the spectacular Nine Glens of Antrim, and Rathlin, the only inhabited island in Northern Ireland. The most northern coastal marina in Ireland, Ballycastle is accessible at all states of the tide, although yachts are required to contact the marina on VHF Ch 80 before entering the harbour. Along the seafront are a selection of restaurants, bars and shops, while the town centre is only about a five minute walk away.

FACILITIES AT A GLANCE

CARRICKFERGUS MARINA

Carrickferus Marina
3 Quayside, Carrickfergus, Co. Antrim, BT38 8BJ
Tel: 028 9336 6666 Fax: 028 9335 0505
Email: marinarec@carrickfergus.org
www.carrickfergus.org

VHF	Ch M
ACCESS	H24

Located on the north shore of
Belfast Lough, Carrickfergus
Marina and harbour incorporates
two sheltered areas suitable
for leisure craft. The harbour is
dominated by a magnificent 12th
century Norman Castle which,
recently renovated, includes
a film theatre, banqueting room and outdoor models depicting the
castle's chequered history.

With a wide range of services available to the
visitor, the marina is located 250m west of the
harbour and has become increasingly popular since
its opening in 1985. An interesting variety of shops
and restaurants along the waterfront caters for most
yachtsmen's needs.

FACILITIES AT A GLANCE

Key
a Development site
b Hotel/bar/restaurant
c Marina office
d Cinema/café/restaurant
e Retail superstore

BANGOR MARINA

Quay Marinas Limited
Bangor Marina, Bangor, Co. Down, BT20 5ED
Tel: 028 9145 3297 Fax: 028 9145 3450
Email: kbaird@quaymarinas.com
www.quaymarinas.com

VHF	Ch 11, 80
ACCESS	H24

Situated on the south shore of Belfast
Lough, Bangor is located close to
the Irish Sea cruising routes. The
Marina is right at the town's centre,
within walking distance of shops,
restaurants, hotels and bars. The
Tourist information centre is across
the road from marina reception
and there are numerous visitors'
attractions in the Borough. The Royal
Ulster Yacht Club and
the Ballyholme Yacht
Club are both nearby
and welcome visitors.

FACILITIES AT A GLANCE

Key
a Boat hoist - BJ Marine
b Boat yard - BJ Marine
c Bregenz House
d Chandlery/brokerage
   BJ Marine
e Dinghy berths
f Access bridge
g Lifeboat slipway
h Domestic waste facilities
i Waste oil tank
j Disabled berthing
NB Berth numbers low outer
to high inner, odd numbers on
right, even left

CARLINGFORD MARINA

Carlingford Marina
Co. Louth, Ireland
Tel: +353 (0)42 937 3072   Fax: +353 (0)42 937 3075
Email: info@carlingfordmarina.ie
www.carlingfordmarina.ie

VHF	Ch M
ACCESS	H24

Carlingford Lough is an eight-
mile sheltered haven between the
Cooley Mountains to
the south and the Mourne
Mountains to the north.
The marina is situated on the
southern shore, about four miles
from Haulbowline Lighthouse,
and can be easily reached via a
deep water shipping channel.
Among the most attractive
destinations in the Irish Sea, Carlingford is only
60 miles from the Isle of Man and within a day's
sail from Strangford Lough and Ardglass. Full
facilities in the marina include a first class bar and
restaurant offering superb views across the water.

FACILITIES AT A GLANCE

Key
a Bar and restaurant
b Toilets, showers and laundry
c Refuse
d Office
e Chandlery
f Marina office
g Waiting pontoon

ARDGLASS MARINA

Ardglass Marina
19 Quay Street, Ardglass, BT30 7SA
Tel & fax: 028 4484 2332
Email: ardglassmarina@tiscali.co.uk
www.ardglassmarina.co.uk

VHF	Ch M, 80
ACCESS	H24

Situated just south of
Strangford, Ardglass has the
capacity to accommodate
up to 22 yachts as well as
space for small craft. Despite
being relatively small
in size, the marina boasts an
extensive array of facilities,
either on site or close at hand.
Most of the necessary shops,
including grocery stores, a post office, chemist and off-licence, are
all within a five-minute walk from the marina.
Among the local onshore activities are golf,
mountain climbing in Newcastle, which is 18 miles
south, as well as scenic walks at Ardglass and
Delamont Park.

FACILITIES AT A GLANCE

Key
a Administration building
b Boat storage

Additional Facilities
Reception car park - 60 vehicles
Waste oil tanks
Local charts for Strangford Lough
Heavy duty battery charging
High pressure water washing
Internet and email access
Barbeque facilities
Car hire
Weather fax

PORTAFERRY MARINA

Portaferry Marina
1 Mill View, Portaferry, BT22 1LQ
Mobile: 07703 209780 Fax: 028 4272 9784
Email: info@portaferrymarina.co.uk

VHF	Ch 80
ACCESS	H24

Portaferry Marina lies on the east shore of the Narrows, the gateway to Strangford Lough on the north east coast of Ireland. A marine nature reserve of outstanding natural beauty, the Lough offers plenty of recreational activities.

The marina, which caters for draughts of up to 2.5m, is fairly small, accommodating around 30 yachts. The office is situated about 200m from the marina itself, where you will find ablution facilities along with a launderette.

Portaferry incorporates several pubs and restaurants as well as a few convenience stores, while one of its prime attractions is the Exploris Aquarium. Places of historic interest in the vicinity include Castleward, an 18th century mansion in Strangford, and Mount Stewart House & Garden in Newtownards.

FACILITIES AT A GLANCE

CHANNEL ISLANDS – Guernsey & Jersey

Key to Marina Plans symbols

	Bottled gas	P	Parking
	Chandler		Pub/Restaurant
	Disabled facilities		Pump out
	Electrical supply		Rigging service
	Electrical repairs		Sail repairs
	Engine repairs		Shipwright
	First Aid		Shop/Supermarket
	Fresh Water		Showers
	Fuel - Diesel		Slipway
	Fuel - Petrol	WC	Toilets
	Hardstanding/boatyard		Telephone
@	Internet Café		Trolleys
	Laundry facilities	V	Visitors berths
	Lift-out facilities		Wi-Fi

Area 14 - Channel Islands

MARINAS
Telephone Numbers
VHF Channel
Access Times

ALDERNEY

Beaucette Marina
01481 245000
Ch 80 HW±3

GUERNSEY

HERM

SARK

St Peter Port
Victoria Marina
01481 725987
Ch 12, Ch 80 HW±2½

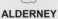Maître Ile

N

JERSEY

St Helier Marina
01534 447730
Ch 14 HW±3

BEAUCETTE MARINA

Beaucette Marina
Vale, Guernsey, GY3 5BQ
Tel: 01481 245000 Fax: 01481 247071
Mobile: 07781 102302
Email: info@beaucettemarina.com

VHF	Ch 80
ACCESS	HW±3

Situated on the north east tip of Guernsey, Beaucette enjoys a peaceful, rural setting in contrast to the more vibrant atmosphere of Victoria Marina. Now owned by a private individual and offering a high standard of service, the site was originally formed from an old quarry.

There is a general store close by, while the bustling town of St Peter Port is only 20 minutes away by bus.

FACILITIES AT A GLANCE

Key
a Harbour office
b Restaurant
c Showers/toilets
d Laundry & telephone
e Manager's cabin
f Boatyard

ST PETER PORT

Guernsey Harbours
PO Box 631, St Julian's Emplacement, St Peter Port
Tel: 01481 720229 Fax: 01481 714177
Email: guernsey.harbour@gov.gg

VHF	Ch 12, 80
ACCESS	HW±2.5

The harbour of St Peter Port comprises the Queen Elizabeth II Marina to the N and Victoria and Albert Marinas to the S, with visiting yachtsmen usually accommodated in Victoria Marina.

St Peter Port is the capital of Guernsey. Its regency architecture and picturesque cobbled streets filled with restaurants and boutiques help to make it one of the most attractive harbours in Europe. Among the places of interest are Hauteville House, home of the writer Victor Hugo, and Castle Cornet. There are regular bus services to all parts of the island for visitors to explore a rich heritage.

FACILITIES AT A GLANCE

Key
a Customs shed
b Tourist Information
c Royal Channel Islands Yacht Club
d Toilets, showers, launderette, shops, pub and restaurant
e Guernsey Yacht Club
f Ferry terminal

ST PETER PORT VICTORIA MARINA

Guernsey Harbours
PO Box 631, St Julian's Emplacement, St Peter Port
Tel: 01481 720229 Fax: 01481 714177
Email: guernsey.harbour@gov.gg

VHF	Ch 80
ACCESS	HW±2.5

Victoria Marina in St Peter Port accommodates some 300 visiting yachts. In the height of the season it gets extremely busy, but when full visitors can berth on 5 other pontoons in the Pool or pre-arrange a berth in the QE II or Albert marinas. There are no visitor moorings in the Pool. Depending on draught, the marina is accessible approximately two and a half hours either side of HW, with yachts crossing over a sill drying to 4.2m. The marina dory will direct you to a berth on arrival or else will instruct you to moor on one of the waiting pontoons just outside.

Guernsey is well placed for exploring the rest of the Channel Islands and nearby French ports.

FACILITIES AT A GLANCE

Key
a Toilets, showers, launderette and shops
b Royal Channel Islands Yacht Club
c Refuse skip
d Marina control, port office
e Dinghy/tender landing pontoon
f Pub/restaurant
g Tourist information

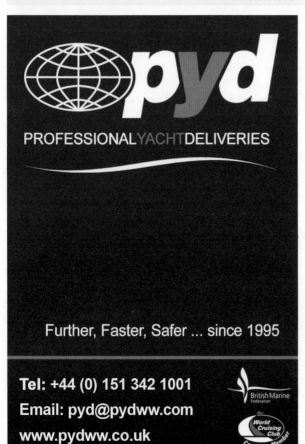
ST HELIER HARBOUR

St Helier Harbour
Maritime House, La Route du Port Elizabeth
St Helier, Jersey, JE1 1HB
Tel: 01534 447708
www.portofjersey.je Email: marinas@gov.je

VHF Ch 14
ACCESS HW±3

Jersey is the largest of the Channel Islands, attracting the most number of tourists per year. Although St Helier can get very crowded in the height of the summer, if you hire a car and head out to the north coast in particular you will soon find isolated bays and pretty little fishing villages.

All visiting craft are directed to St Helier Marina, which may be entered three hours either side of HW via a sill. There is a long holding pontoon to port of the entrance accessible at any state of the tide. La Collette Yacht Basin is not for visitors but Elizabeth Marina may accept larger craft by prior arrangement.

FACILITIES AT A GLANCE

Key
a   Marina office
b   Water/toilets/public phone
c   Tourism
d   Harbour office and Customs
e   Maritime house
f   Waiting pontoon
g   Passenger Terminal
h   Trailer park
i   Port control
j   Marina shop
k   Cafe
l   Self-service fuel

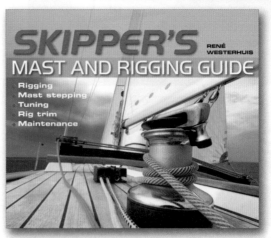

SECTION 2
MARINE SUPPLIES AND SERVICES GUIDE

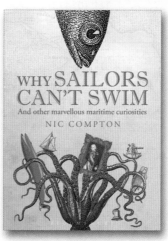

ADHESIVES

Casco Adhesives
Darwen   07710 546899

CC Marine Services Ltd
West Mersea   07751 734510

Industrial Self Adhesives Ltd
Nottingham   0115 9681895

Sika Ltd Garden City   01707 394444

Technix Rubber & Plastics Ltd
Southampton   01489 789944

Tiflex Liskeard   01579 320808

Trade Grade Products Ltd
Poole   01202 820177

UK Epoxy Resins
Burscough   01704 892364

Wessex Resins & Adhesives Ltd
Romsey   01794 521111

3M United Kingdom plc
Bracknell   01344 858315

ASSOCIATIONS/ AGENCIES

Cruising Association
London   020 7537 2828

**Fishermans Mutual Association
(Eyemouth) Ltd**
Eyemouth   01890 750373

Maritime and Coastguard Agency
Southampton   0870 6006505

Royal Institute of Navigation
London   020 7591 3130

Royal National Lifeboat Institution
Poole   01202 663000

**Royal Yachting Association
(RYA)** Southampton   0845 345 0400

BERTHS & MOORINGS

ABC Powermarine
Beaumaris   01248 811413

Aqua Bell Ltd Norwich   01603 713013

Ardfern Yacht Centre
Lochgilphead   01852 500247/500636

Ardmair Boat Centre
Ullapool   01854 612054

Arisaig Marine Ltd
Inverness-shire   01687 450224

Bristol Boat Ltd Bristol   01225 872032

British Waterways
Argyll   01546 603210

Burgh Castle Marine
Norfolk   01493 780331

Cambrian Marine Services Ltd
Cardiff   029 2034 3459

Chelsea Harbour Ltd
London   020 7225 9108

Clapson & Son (Shipbuilders) Ltd
Barton-on-Humber   01652 635620

Crinan Boatyard, Crinan 01546 830232

Dartside Quay Brixham   01803 845445

Douglas Marine
Preston   01772 812462

Dublin City Moorings
Dublin   +353 1 8183300

Emsworth Yacht Harbour
Emsworth   01243 377727

Exeter Ship Canal   01392 274306

HAFAN PWLLHELI
**Glan Don, Pwllheli, Gwynedd LL53
5YT**
Tel: (01758) 701219
Fax: (01758) 701443 VHF Ch80
Hafan Pwllheli has over 400 pontoon
berths and offers access at virtually all
states of the tide. Ashore, its modern
purpose-built facilities include luxury
toilets, showers, launderette, a secure
boat park for winter storage, 40-ton
travel hoist, mobile crane and plenty of
space for car parking. Open 24-hours a
day, 7 days a week.

Highway Marine
Sandwich   01304 613925

Iron Wharf Boatyard
Faversham   01795 537122

Jalsea Marine Services Ltd
Northwich   01606 77870

Jersey Harbours
St Helier   01534 447788

Jones (Boatbuilders), David
Chester   01244 390363

Lawrenny Yacht Station
Kilgetty   01646 651212

MacFarlane & Son
Glasgow   01360 870214

NEPTUNE MARINA LTD
**Neptune Quay, Ipswich, Suffolk
IP4 1AX**
Tel: (01473) 215204
Fax: (01473) 215206
**e-mail:
enquiries@neptune-marina.com
www.neptune-marina.com**
The quay to the heart of Ipswich! Call
Ipswich lock gates on Channel 68 and
Neptune Marina on Channel 80. Bring
your crew to the wonderful Ipswich
waterfront, with plenty of watering
holes and town centre activities. You
won't want to leave!

Orkney Marinas Ltd
Kirkwall   07810 465835

V Marine
Shoreham-by-Sea   01273 461491

Sutton Harbour Marina
Plymouth   01752 204186

Wicor Marine Fareham   01329 237112

Winters Marine Ltd
Salcombe   01548 843580

Yarmouth Marine Service
Yarmouth   01983 760521

Youngboats
Faversham   01795 536176

BOAT BUILDERS & REPAIRS

ABC Hayling Island   023 9246 1968

ABC Powermarine
Beaumaris   01248 811413

Advance Yacht Systems
Southampton   023 8033 7722

Aqua-Star Ltd
St Sampsons   01481 244550

Ardoran Marine
Oban   01631 566123

Baumbach Bros Boatbuilders
Hayle   01736 753228

Beacon Boatyard
Rochester   01634 841320

Bedwell & Co
Walton on the Naze   01255 675873

Blackwell, Craig
Co Meath   +353 87 677 9605

Boyd Boat Building
Falmouth   07885 436722

Boatcraft
Ardrossan   01294 603047

B+ St Peter Port   01481 726071

Brennan, John
Dun Laoghaire   +353 1 280 5308

Burghead Boat Centre
Findhorn   01309 690099

Carrick Marine Projects
Co Antrim   02893 355884

Chapman & Hewitt Boatbuilders
Wadebridge   01208 813487

Chicks Marine Ltd
Guernsey   01481 723716

Clarence Boatyard
East Cowes   01983 294243

Cooks Maritime Craftsmen - Poliglow
Lymington   01590 675521

Creekside Boatyard (Old Mill Creek)
Dartmouth   01803 832649

CTC Marine & Leisure
Middlesbrough   01642 372600

Davies Marine Services
Ramsgate   01843 586172

Dickie International
Bangor   01248 363400

Dickie International
Pwllheli   01758 701828

East Llanion Marine Ltd
Pembroke Dock   01646 686866

Emblem Enterprises
East Cowes   01983 294243

Fairlie Quay
Fairlie   01475 568267

Fairweather Marine
Fareham   01329 283500

Farrow & Chambers Yacht Builders
Humberston
            www.farrowand chambers.co.uk

Fast Tack Plymouth   01752 255171

Fergulsea Engineering
Ayr 01292 262978

Ferrypoint Boat Co
Youghal +353 24 94232

Floetree Ltd (Loch Lomond Marina)
Balloch 01389 752069

Freshwater Boatyard
Truro 01326 270443

Frogmore Boatyard
Kingsbridge 01548 531257

Furniss Boat Building
Falmouth 01326 311766

Gallichan Marine Ltd
Jersey 01534 746387

Garvel Clyde
Greenock 01475 725372

Goodchild Marine Services
Great Yarmouth 01493 782301

Gosport Boatyard
Gosport 023 9252 6534

Gweek Quay Boatyard
Helston 01326 221657

Halls
Walton on the Naze 01255 675596

Harris Pye Marine
Barry 01446 720066

Haven Boatyard
Lymington 01590 677073

Hayling Yacht Company
Hayling Island 023 9246 3592

Hoare Ltd, Bob
Poole 01202 736704

Holyhead Boatyard
Holyhead 01407 760111

Jackson Marine
Lowestoft 01502 539772

Jackson Yacht Services
Jersey 01534 743819

JEP Marine
Canterbury 01227 710102

JWS Marine Services
Southsea 023 9275 5155

Kimelford Yacht Haven
Oban 01852 200248

Kingfisher Marine
Weymouth 01305 766595

Kingfisher Ultraclean UK Ltd
Tarporley 0800 085 7039

King's Boatyard
Pin Mill 01473 780258

Kinsale Boatyard
Kinsale +353 21477 4774

Kippford Slipway Ltd
Dalbeattie 01556 620249

Lavis & Son, CH
Exmouth 01395 263095

Lawrenny Yacht Station
Lawrenny 01646 651212

Lencraft Boats Ltd
Dungarvan +353 58 682220

Mackay Boatbuilders
Arbroath 01241 872879

Marine Services
Norwich 01692 582239

Mashford Brothers
Torpoint 01752 822232

Mayor & Co Ltd, J
Preston 01772 812250

Mears, HJ Axmouth 01297 23344

Mill, Dan, Galway +353 86 337 9304

Miller Marine
Tyne & Wear 01207 542149

Morrison, A
Killyleagh 028 44828215

Moss (Boatbuilders), David
Thornton-Cleveleys 01253 893830

Multi Marine Composites Ltd
Torpoint 01752 823513

Newing, Roy E
Canterbury 01227 860345

Noble and Sons, Alexander
Girvan 01465 712223

Northney Marine Services
Hayling Island 023 9246 9246

Northshore Sport & Leisure
King's Lynn 01485 210236

O'Sullivans Marine Ltd
Tralee +353 66 7124957

Oyster Marine Ltd
Ipswich 01473 688888

Pachol, Terry
Brighton 01273 620192

Partington Marine Ltd, William
Pwllheli 01758 612808

Pasco's Boatyard
Truro 01326 270269

Penrhos Marine
Aberdovey 01654 767478

Penzance Marine Services
Penzance 01736 361081

PJ Bespoke Boat Fitters Ltd
Crewe 01270 812244

Preston Marine Services Ltd
Preston 01772 733595

Red Bay Boats Ltd
Cushendall 028 2177 1331

Reliance Marine
Wirral 0151 625 5219

Retreat Boatyard Ltd
Exeter 01392 874720/875934

Richardson Boatbuilders, Ian
Stromness 01856 850321

Richardson Yacht Services Ltd
Newport 01983 821095

Cordell Grove
Middlesbrough 01642 226226

Roberts Marine Ltd, S
Liverpool 0151 707 8300

Rothman Pantall & Co
Fareham 01329 280221

Rustler Yachts
Falmouth 01326 310210

Salterns Boatyard
Poole 01202 707391

Sea & Shore Ship Chandler
Dundee 01382 450666

SEAFIT MARINE SERVICES LTD
Falmouth Marina, North Parade,
Falmouth, Cornwall TR11 2TD
Tel: (01326) 313713
Fax: (01326) 313713
Mob: 07971 196175
Email: mary.townsend@homecall.
co.uk
For installation maintenance and repair
work - electrical, plumbing, hulls, rigs etc.

Seamark-Nunn & Co
Felixstowe 01394 275327

Seapower
Woolverstone 01473 780090

Slipway Cooperative Ltd
Bristol 0117 907 9938

Smith, GB, & Sons
Rock 01208 862815

Spicer Boatbuilder, Nick
Weymouth Marina 01305 767118

Storrar Marine Store
Newcastle upon Tyne 0191 266 1037

TT Marine Ashwell 01462 742449

Waterfront Marine
Bangor 01248 352513

Way, A&R, Boat Building
Tarbert, Loch Fyne 01546 606657

WestCoast Marine
Troon 01292 318121

Western Marine
Dublin +353 1 280 0321

Wigmore Wright Marine Services
Penarth 029 2070 9983

Williams, Peter
Fowey 01726 870987

WQI Ltd
Bournemouth 01202 771292

Yarmouth Marine Service
01983 760521

Youngboats
Faversham 01795 536176

BOATYARD SERVICES & SUPPLIES

A & P Ship Care
Ramsgate 01843 593140

ABC Marine
Hayling Island   023 9246 1968

Abersoch Boatyard Services Ltd
Abersoch   01758 713900

Amble Boat Co Ltd
Amble   01665 710267

Amsbrisbeg Ltd
Port Bannatyne   01700 831215

Ardmair Boat Centre
Ullapool   01854 612054

Ardmaleish Boat Building Co Rothesay
01700 502007

www.ardoran.co.uk
West coast Scotland. All marine
facilities.

Ardrishaig Boatyard
Lochgilphead   01546 603280

Arklow Slipway
Arklow   +353 402 33233

Baltic Wharf Boatyard
Totnes   01803 867922

Baltimore Boatyard
Baltimore   +353 28 20444

Bedwell and Co
Walton-on-the-Naze   01255 675873

Berthon Boat Co
Lymington   01590 673312

Birdham Shipyard
Chichester   01243 512310

BJ Marine Ltd Bangor   028 91271434

Blagdon, A
Plymouth   01752 561830

Boatcraft
Ardrossan   01294 603047

Boatworks + Ltd
St Peter Port   01481 726071

Brennan, John
Dun Laoghaire   +353 1 280 5308

Brighton Marina Boatyard
Brighton   01273 819919

Bristol Marina (Yard)
Bristol   0117 921 3198

Buckie Shipyard Ltd
Buckie   01542 831245

Bucklers Hard Boat Builders Ltd
Brockenhurst   01590 616214

C & J Marine Services
Newcastle Upon Tyne   0191 295 0072

Caley Marina Inverness   01463 236539

Cambrian Boat Centre
Swansea   01792 467263

Cambrian Marine Services Ltd
Cardiff   029 2034 3459

Cantell and Son Ltd
Newhaven   01273 514118

Canvey Yacht Builders Ltd
Canvey Island   01268 696094

Carroll's Ballyhack Boatyard
New Ross   +353 51 389164

Castlepoint Boatyard
Crosshaven   +353 21 4832154

Chabot, Gary
Newhaven   07702 006767

Chapman & Hewitt Boatbuilders
Wadebridge   01208 813487

Chippendale Craft Rye   01797 227707

Clapson & Son (Shipbuilders) Ltd
Barton on Humber   01652 635620

Clarence Boatyard
East Cowes   01983 294243

Coastal Marine Boatbuilders
(Berwick upon Tweed)
Eyemouth   01890 750328

Coastcraft Ltd
Cockenzie   01875 812150

Coates Marine Ltd
Whitby   01947 604486

Coombes, AA
Bembridge   01983 872296

Corpach Boatbuilding Company
Fort William   01397 772861

Craobh Marina
By Lochgilphead   01852 500222

Creekside Boatyard (Old Mill Creek)
Dartmouth   01803 832649

Crinan Boatyard
By Lochgilphead   01546 830232

Crosshaven Boatyard Co Ltd
Crosshaven   +353 21 831161

Dale Sailing Co Ltd
Neyland   01646 603110

Darthaven Marina
Kingswear   01803 752242

Dartside Quay Brixham   01803 845445

Dauntless Boatyard Ltd
Canvey Island   01268 793782

Davis's Boatyard Poole   01202 674349

Dinas Boat Yard Ltd
Y Felinheli   01248 671642

Dorset Yachts
Poole   01202 674531

Douglas Boatyard
Preston   01772 812462

Dover Yacht Co Dover   01304 201073

Dun Laoghaire Marina
Dun Laoghaire   +353 1 2020040

Elephant Boatyard
Southampton   023 8040 3268

Elton Boatbuilding Ltd
Kirkcudbright   01557 330177

Felixstowe Ferry Boatyard
Felixstowe   01394 282173

Ferguson Engineering
Wexford   +353 6568 66822133

Ferry Marine South
Queensferry   0131 331 1233

Findhorn Boatyard
Findhorn   01309 690099

Firmhelm Ltd Pwllheli   01758 612251

Fleming Engineering, J
Stornoway   01851 703488

Forrest Marine Ltd
Exeter   08452 308335

Fowey Boatyard
Fowey   01726 832194

Fox's Marina Ipswich   01473 689111

Frank Halls & Son
Walton on the Naze   01255 675596

Freeport Marine
Jersey   01534 888100

Furniss Boat Building
Falmouth   01326 311766

Garval Clyde
Greenock   01475 725372

Goodchild Marine Services
Great Yarmouth   01493 782301

Gosport Boatyard
Gosport   023 9252 6534

Gweek Quay Boatyard
Helston   01326 221657

Haines Boatyard
Chichester   01243 512228

Harbour Marine
Plymouth   01752 204691

Harbour Marine Services Ltd
Southwold   01502 724721

Harris Pye Marine
Barry   01446 720066

Hartlepool Marine Engineering
Hartlepool   01429 867883

Hayles, Harold
Yarmouth, IoW   01983 760373

Henderson, J Shiskine   01770 860259

Heron Marine
Whitstable   01227 361255

Hewitt, George
Binham   01328 830078

Holyhead Marina & Trinity Marine Ltd
Holyhead   01407 764242

Instow Marine Services
Bideford   01271 861081

Ipswich Haven Marina
Ipswich   01473 236644

Iron Wharf Boatyard
Faversham   01795 537122

Island Boat Services
Port of St Mary   01624 832073

Isle of Skye Yachts
Ardvasar   01471 844216

Jalsea Marine Services Ltd Weaver
Shipyard, Northwich   01606 77870

JBS Group
Peterhead   01779 475395

J B Timber Ltd
North Ferriby   01482 631765

Jersey Harbours Dept
St Helier   01534 885588

Kilnsale Boatyard
Kinsale   +353 21 4774774

Kilrush Marina & Boatyard – Ireland
+353 65 9052072

Kingfisher Ultraclean UK Ltd
Tarporley   01928 787878

Kinsale Boatyard
Kinsale   +353 21477 4774

KPB Beaucette   07781 152581

Lake Yard Poole   01202 674531

Lallow, C Isle of Wight   01983 292112

Latham's Boatyard
Poole   01202 748029

Leonard Marine, Peter
Newhaven   01273 515987

Lincombe Marine
Salcombe   01548 843580

Lomax Boatbuilders
Cliffony   +353 71 66124

Lymington Yacht Haven
Lymington   01590 677071

MacDougalls Marine Services
Isle of Mull   01681 700294

Macduff Shipyard Ltd
Macduff   01261 832234

Madog Boatyard
Porthmadog   01766 514205/513435

Mainbrayce Marine
Alderney   01481 822772

Malakoff and Moore
Lerwick   01595 695544

Mallaig Boat Building and Engineering
Mallaig   01687 462304

Maramarine
Helensburgh   01436 810971

Marindus Engineering
Kilmore Quay   +353 53 29794

Mariners Farm Boatyard
Gillingham   01634 233179

McGruar and Co Ltd
Helensburgh   01436 831313

Mill, Dan, Galway   +353 86 337 9304

Mitchell's Boatyard
Poole   01202 747857

Mooney Boats
Killybegs   +353 73 31152/31388

Moore & Son, J
St Austell   01726 842964

Morrison, A Killyleagh   028 44828215

Moss (Boatbuilders), David
Thornton-Cleveleys   01253 893830

Mustang Marine
Milford Haven   01646 696320

New Horizons Rhu   01436 821555

Noble and Sons, Alexander
Girvan   01465 712223

North Pier (Oban)
Oban   01631 562892

North Wales Boat Centre
Conwy   01492 580740

Northam Marine
Brightlingsea   01206 302003

Northshore Yacht Yard
Chichester   01243 512611

Oban Yachts and Marine Services
By Oban   01631 565333

Pearn and Co, Norman
Looe   01503 262244

Penrhos Marine
Aberdovey   01654 767478

**Penzance Dry Dock and Engineering
Co Ltd** Penzance   01736 363838

Philip & Son Dartmouth 01803 833351

Phillips, HJ Rye   01797 223234

Ponsharden Boatyard
Penryn   01326 372215

Powersail and Island Chandlers Ltd
East Cowes Marina   01983 299800

Priors Boatyard
Burnham-on-Crouch   01621 782160

R K Marine Ltd
Swanwick   01489 583572

Rat Island Sailboat Company (Yard) St
Mary's   01720 423399

Retreat Boatyard Ltd
Exeter   01392 874720/875934

Rice and Cole Ltd
Burnham-on-Crouch   01621 782063

Richardson Boatbuilders, Ian Stromness
01856 850321

Richardsons Boatbuilders
Binfield   01983 821095

Riverside Yard
Shoreham Beach   01273 592456

River Yar Boatyard
Yarmouth, IoW   01983 761000

Robertsons Boatyard
Woodbridge   01394 382305

Rossbrin Boatyard
Schull   +353 28 37352

Rossiter Yachts Ltd
Christchurch   01202 483250

Rossreagh Boatyard
Rathmullan   +353 74 9150182

Rudders Boatyard & Moorings
Milford Haven   01646 600288

Ryan & Roberts Marine Services
Askeaton   +353 61 392198

Rye Harbour Marina Rye
01797 227667

Rynn Engineering, Pat
Galway   +353 91 562568

Salterns Boatyard
Poole   01202 707391

Sandbanks Yacht Company
Poole   01202 611262

Scarborough Marine Engineering Ltd
Scarborough   01723 375199

Severn Valley Cruisers Ltd (Boatyard)
Stourport-on-Severn 01299 871165

Shepards Wharf Boatyard Ltd
Cowes   01983 297821

Shipshape
King's Lynn   01553 764058

Shotley Marina Ltd
Ipswich   01473 788982

Shotley Marine Services Ltd
Ipswich   01473 788913

Silvers Marina Ltd
Helensburgh   01436 831222

Skinners Boat Yard
Baltimore   +353 28 20114

Smith, GB, & Sons
Rock   01208 862815

Smith & Gibbs
Eastbourne   07802 582009

Sparkes Boatyard
Hayling Island   023 92463572

Spencer Sailing Services, Jim
Brightlingsea   01206 302911

Standard House Boatyard
Wells-next-the-Sea   01328 710593

Storrar Marine Store
Newcastle upon Tyne 0191 266 1037

Strand Shipyard Rye   01797 222070

Surry Boatyard
Shoreham-by-Sea   01273 461491

The Shipyard
Littlehampton   01903 713327

Titchmarsh Marina
Walton-on-the-Naze   01255 672185

Tollesbury Marina
Tollesbury   01621 869202

T J Rigging Conwy   07780 972411

Toms and Son Ltd, C
Fowey   01726 870232

Tony's Marine Service
Coleraine   028 7035 6422

Torquay Marina
Torquay   01803 200210

Trinity Marine & Holyhead Marina
Holyhead   01407 763855

Trouts Boatyard (River Exe)
Topsham   01392 873044

Upson and Co, RF
Aldeburgh   01728 453047

Versatility Workboats
Rye   01797 224422

Weir Quay Boatyard
Bere Alston   01822 840474

West Solent Boatbuilders
Lymington   01590 642080

Wicor Marine Fareham   01329 237112

Woodrolfe Boatyard
Maldon   01621 869202

Yarmouth Marine Services
Yarmouth, IoW   01983 760521

BOAT DELIVERIES & STORAGE

ABC Marine
Hayling Island   023 9246 1968

Abersoch Boatyard Services Ltd
Pwllheli   01758 713900

Ambrisbeg Ltd
Port Bannatyne   01700 502719

MARINE SUPPLIES AND SERVICES GUIDE

BOATYARD SERVICES & SUPPLIES – BOAT DELIVERIES & STORAGE

Arisaig Marine
Inverness-shire   01687 450224

Bedwell and Co
Walton-on-the-Naze   01255 675873

Berthon Boat Company
Lymington   01590 673312

Boat Shifters
          07733 344018/01326 210548

C & J Marine Services
Newcastle upon Tyne   0191 295 0072

Caley Marine
Inverness   01463 233437

Carrick Marine Projects
Co Antrim   02893 355884

Challenger Marine
Penryn   01326 377222

Coates Marine Ltd
Whitby   01947 604486

Convoi Exceptionnel Ltd
Hamble   023 8045 3045

**Creekside Boatyard (Old Mill
Creek)** Dartmouth   01803 832649

Crinan Boatyard Ltd
Crinan   01546 830232

Dale Sailing Co Ltd
Neyland   01646 603110

Dart Marina Ltd
Dartmouth   01803 833351

Dartside Quay
Brixham   01803 845445

Dauntless Boatyard Ltd
Canvey Island   01268 793782

Debbage Yachting
Ipswich   01473 601169

Douglas Marine Preston   01772
812462

East & Co, Robin
Kingsbridge   01548 531257

East Coast Offshore Yachting
                         01480 861381

Emsworth Yacht Harbour
Emsworth   01243 377727

Exeter Ship Canal   01392 274306

Exmouth Marina   01395 269314

Firmhelm Ltd Pwllheli 01758 612244

Forrest Marine Ltd
Exeter   08452 308335

Fowey Boatyard
Fowey   01726 832194

Freshwater Boatyard
Truro   01326 270443

Hafan Pwllheli Pwllheli 01758 701219

Houghton Boat Transport
Tewkesbury   07831 486710

Gweek Quay Boatyard
Helston   01326 221657

Iron Wharf Boatyard
Faversham   01795 537122

Jalsea Marine Services Ltd
Northwich   01606 77870

KG McColl
Oban   01852 200248

Latham's Boatyard
Poole   01202 748029

Lavis & Son, CH
Exmouth   01395 263095

Lincombe Boat Yard
Salcombe   01548 843580

MCL Transboat   08455 201900

Marine Resource Centre Ltd
Oban   01631 720291

Marine & General Engineers
Guernsey   01481 245808

Milford Marina
Milford Haven   01646 696312/3

Moonfleet Sailing
Poole   01202 682269

Southerly
Chichester   01243 512611

Pasco's Boatyard
Truro   01326 270269

Pearn and Co, Norman
Looe   01503 262244

Performance Yachting
Plymouth   01752 565023

Peters & May Ltd
Southampton   023 8048 0480

Ponsharden Boatyard
Penryn   01326 372215

Portsmouth Marine Engineering
Fareham   01329 232854

Priors Boatyard
Burnham-on-Crouch   01621 782160

Reeder School of Seamanship, Mike
Lymington   01590 674560

Rossiter Yachts
Christchurch   01202 483250

Seafix Boat Transfer
North Wales   0845 528 0139

Sealand Boat Deliveries Ltd
Liverpool   01254 705225

Shearwater Sailing
Southampton   01962 775213

**Shepards Wharf Boatyard
Cowes Harbour Commission**
Cowes   01983 297821

Silvers Marina Ltd
Helensburgh   01436 831222

Southcoasting Navigators
Devon   01626 335626

Waterfront Marine
Bangor   01248 352513

West Country Boat Transport
                         01566 785651

Wicor Marine
Fareham   01329 237112

Winters Marine Ltd
Salcombe   01548 843580

Wolff, David   07659 550131**Yacht
Solutions Ltd**
Portsmouth   023 9275 5155

Yarmouth Marine Service
Yarmouth, IoW   01983 760521

Youngboats
Faversham   01795 536176

BOOKS, CHARTS & PUBLISHERS

Adlard Coles Nautical
London   020 7631 5600

Brown Son & Ferguson Ltd
Glasgow   0141 429 1234

Cooke & Son Ltd, B Hull 01482 223454

Dubois Phillips & McCallum Ltd
Liverpool   0151 236 2776

Imray, Laurie, Norie & Wilson
Huntingdon   01480 462114

Kelvin Hughes
Southampton   023 8063 4911

Lilley & Gillie Ltd, John 0191 257 2217

Marine Chart Services
Wellingborough   01933 441629

Price & Co Ltd, WF
Bristol   0117 929 2229

QPC
Fareham   01329 287880

Stanford Charts
Bristol   0117 929 9966

Stanford Charts
London   020 7836 1321

Stanford Charts   0845 880 3730
Manchester   0870 890 3730

Wiley Nautical
Chichester   01243 779777

BOW THRUSTERS

ARS Anglian Diesels Ltd
Wakefield   01924 332492

Buckler's Hard Boat Builders Ltd
Beaulieu   01590 616214

JS Mouldings International
Bursledon   023 8063 4400

BREAKDOWN

BJ Marine Ltd
Bangor, Ireland   028 9127 1434

Seafit Marine Services
Falmouth   01326 313713

CHANDLERS

ABC Powermarine
Beaumaris   01248 811413

Admiral Marine Supplies
Bootle   01469 575909

Allgadgets.co.uk
Exmouth   01395 227727

Alpine Room & Yacht Equipment
Chelmsford   01245 223563

Aquatogs
Cowes   01983 295071

Arbroath Fishermen's Association
Arbroath   01241 873132

Ardfern Yacht Centre Ltd Argyll	01852 500247
Ardoran Marine Oban	01631 566123
Arthurs Chandlery Gosport	023 9252 6522
Arun Canvas and Rigging Ltd Littlehampton	01903 732561
Aruncraft Chandlers Littlehampton	01903 713327
ASAP Supplies – Equipment & Spares Worldwide Beccles	0845 1300870
Auto Marine Southsea	02392 825601
Bayside Marine Brixham	01803 856771
Bedwell and Co Walton on the Naze	01255 675873
BJ Marine Ltd Bangor	028 9127 1434
Bluecastle Chandlers Portland	01305 822298
Blue Water Marine Ltd Pwllheli	01758 614600
Boatacs Westcliffe on Sea	01702 475057
Boathouse, The Penryn	01326 374177
Boston Marina	01205 364420
Bosun's Locker, The Falmouth	01326 312212
Bosun's Locker, The Ramsgate	01843 597158
Bosuns Locker, The South Queensferry	0131 331 3875/4496
B+ St Peter Port	01481 726071
Bridger Marine, John Exeter	01392 250970
Bristol Boat Ltd Bristol	01225 872032
Brixham Yacht Supplies Ltd Brixham	01803 882290
Brunel Chandlery Ltd Neyland	01646 601667
Bucklers Hard Boat Builders Beaulieu	01590 616214
Burghead Boat Centre Findhorn	01309 690099
Bussell & Co, WL Weymouth	01305 785633
Buzzard Marine Yarmouth	01983 760707
C & M Marine Bridlington	01262 672212
Cabin Yacht Stores Rochester	01634 718020
Caley Marina Inverness	01463 236539
Cambrian Boat Centre Swansea	01792 467263
Cantell & Son Ltd Newhaven	01273 514118

Carne (Sales) Ltd, David Penryn	01326 374177
Carrickcraft Malahide	+353 1 845 5438
Caters Carrick Ltd Carrickfergus	028 93351919
CH Marine (Cork) Cork	+353 21 4315700
CH Marine Skibbereen	+353 28 23190
Charity & Taylor Ltd Lowestoft	01502 581529
Chertsey Marine Ltd Penton Hook Marina	01932 565195
Chicks Marine Ltd Guernsey	01481 723716
Christchurch Boat Shop Christchurch	01202 482751
Clapson & Son (Shipbuilders) Ltd South Ferriby Marina	01652 635620
Clarke, Albert, Marine Newtownards	028 9187 2325
Clyde Chandlers Ardrossan	01294 471444
Coastal Marine Boatbuilders Ltd (Dunbar) Eyemouth	01890 750328
Coates Marine Ltd Whitby	01947 604486
Collins Marine St Helier	01534 732415
Compass Marine Lancing	01903 761773
Cosalt International Ltd Aberdeen	01224 588327
Cosalt International Ltd Southampton	023 8063 2824
Cotter, Kieran Baltimore	+353 28 20106
Cox Yacht Charter Ltd, Nick Lymington	01590 673489
C Q Chandlers Ltd Poole	01202 682095
Crinan Boats Ltd Lochgilphead	01546 830232
CTC Marine & Leisure Middlesbrough	01642 372372
Dale Sailing Co Ltd Milford Haven	01646 603110
Danson Marine Sidcup	0208 304 5678
Dartmouth Chandlery Dartmouth	01803 839292
Dartside Quay Brixham	01803 845445
Dauntless Boatyard Ltd Canvey Island	01268 793782
Davis's Yacht Chandler Littlehampton	01903 722778
Denney & Son, EL Redcar	01642 483507
Deva Marine Conwy	01492 572777
Dickie & Sons Ltd, AM Bangor	01248 363400

Dickie & Sons Ltd, AM Pwllheli	01758 701828
Dinghy Supplies Ltd/Sutton Marine Ltd Sutton	+353 1 832 2312
Diverse Yacht Services Hamble	023 80453399
Dixon Chandlery, Peter Exmouth	01395 273248
Doling & Son, GW Barrow In Furness	01229 823708
Dovey Marine Aberdovey	01654 767581
Down Marine Co Ltd Belfast	028 9048 0247
Douglas Marine Preston	01772 812462
Dubois Phillips & McCallum Ltd Liverpool	0151 236 2776
Duncan Ltd, JS Wick	01955 602689
Duncan Yacht Chandlers Ely	01353 663095
East Anglian Sea School Ipswich	01473 659992
Eccles Marine Co Middlesbrough	01642 372600
Ely Boat Chandlers Hayling Island	023 9246 1968
Emsworth Chandlery Emsworth	01243 375500
Force 4 Chandlery Stroud	0845 1300710
Exe Leisure Exeter	01392 879055
Express Marine Services Chichester	01243 773788
Fairways Chandlery Burnham-on-Crouch	01621 782659
Fairweather Marine Fareham	01329 283500
Fal Chandlers Falmouth Marina	01326 212411
Ferrypoint Boat Co Youghal	+353 24 94232
Findhorn Marina & Boatyard Findhorn	01309 690099
Firmhelm Ltd Pwllheli	01758 612244
Fisherman's Mutual Asssociation (Eyemouth) Ltd Eyemouth	01890 750373
Floetree Ltd (Loch Lomond Marina) Balloch	01389 752069
Force 4 (Deacons) Bursledon	023 8040 2182
Force 4 Chichester	01243 773788
Force 4 Chandlery Mail order	0845 1300710
Force 4 Chandlery Plymouth	01752 252489
Force 4 (Hamble Point) Southampton	023 80455 058
Force 4 (Mercury) Southampton	023 8045 4849
Force 4 (Port Hamble) Southampton	023 8045 4858

Force 4 (Shamrock)
Southampton   023 8063 2725
Force 4 (Swanwick)
Swanwick   01489 881825
Freeport Marine
Jersey   01534 888100
French Marine Motors Ltd
Brightlingsea   01206 302133
Furneaux Riddall & Co Ltd
Portsmouth   023 9266 8621
Gallichan Marine Ltd
Jersey   01534 746387
Galway Marine Chandlers Ltd
Galway   +353 91 566568
GB Attfield & Company
Dursley   01453 547185
Gibbons Ship Chandlers Ltd
Sunderland   0191 567 2101
Goodwick Marine
Fishguard   01348 873955
Gorleston Marine Ltd
Great Yarmouth   01493 661883
GP Barnes Ltd
Shoreham   01273 591705/596680
Great Outdoors
Clarenbridge, Galway +353 87 2793821
Green Marine, Jimmy
Fore St Beer   01297 20744
Grimsby Rigging Services Ltd
Grimsby   01472 362758
Gunn Navigation Services, Thomas
Aberdeen   01224 595045
Hale Marine, Ron
Portsmouth   023 92732985
Harbour Marine Services Ltd (HMS)
Southwold   01502 724721
Hardware & Marine Supplies
Wexford   +353 53 29791
Harris Marine (1984) Ltd, Ray
Barry   01446 740924
Hartlepool Marine Supplies
Hartlepool   01429 862932
Harwich Chandlers Ltd
Harwich   01255 504061
Harwoods Yarmouth   01983 760258
Hawkins Marine Shipstores, John
Rochester   01634 840812
Hayles, Harold
Yarmouth   01983 760373
Herm Seaway Marine Ltd
St Peter Port   01481 726829
Highway Marine
Sandwich   01304 613925
Hoare Ltd, Bob, Poole   01202 736704
Hodges, T
Coleraine   028 7035 6422
Hornsey (Chandlery) Ltd, Chris
Southsea   023 9273 4728
Hunter & Combes
Cowes   01983 299599

Iron Stores Marine
St Helier   01534 877755
Isles of Scilly Steamship Co
St Mary's   01720 422710
Jackson Yacht Services
Jersey   01534 743819
Jamison and Green Ltd
Belfast   028 9032 2444
Jeckells and Son Ltd
Lowestoft   01502 565007
JF Marine Chandlery
Rhu   01436 820584
JNW Services Aberdeen 01224 594050
JNW Services Peterhead 01779 477346
JSB Ltd
Tarbert, Loch Fyne   01880 820180
Johnston Brothers
Mallaig   01687 462215
Johnstons Marine Stores
Lamlash   01770 600333
Kearon Ltd, George
Arklow   +353 402 32319
Kelpie Boats
Pembroke Dock   01646 683661
Kelvin Hughes Ltd
Southampton   023 80634911
Kildale Marine Hull   01482 227464
Kingfisher Marine
Weymouth   01305 766595
Kings Lock Chandlery
Middlewich   01606 737564
Kip Chandlery Inverkip
Greenock   01475 521485
Kirkcudbright Scallop Gear Ltd
Kirkcudbright   01557 330399
Kyle Chandlers Troon   01292 311880
Landon Marine, Reg
Truro   01872 272668
Largs Chandlers Largs   01475 686026
Lencraft Boats Ltd
Dungarvan   +353 58 68220
Lincoln Marina Lincoln   01522 526896
Looe Chandlery
West Looe   01503 264355
Lynch Ltd, PA Morpeth   01670 512291
Mackay Boatbuilders (Arbroath) Ltd
Aberdeen   01241 872879
Mackay Marine Services
Aberdeen   01224 575772
Mailspeed Marine
Burnham-on-Crouch   01342 710618
Mailspeed Marine
Essex Marina   01342 710618
Mailspeed Marine
Warrington   01342 710618
Mainbrayce Chandlers
Braye, Alderney   01481 822772
Manx Marine Ltd
Douglas   01624 674842

Marine & Leisure Europe Ltd
Plymouth   01752 268826
Marine MegaStore
Hamble   023 8045 4400
Marine MegaStore
Morpeth   01670 516151
Marine Scene
Bridgend   01656 671822
Marine Scene
Cardiff   029 2070 5780
Marine Services
Jersey   01534 626930
Marine Store Wyatts
West Mersea   01206 384745
Marine Store
Maldon   01621 854380
Marine Store
Titchmarsh Marina   01621 874495
Marine Store
Walton on the Naze   01255 679028
Marine Superstore Port Solent Chandlery
Portsmouth   023 9221 9843
MarineCo
Torpoint   01752 816005
Maryport Harbour and Marina
Maryport   01900 814431
Matchett Ltd, HC
Widnes   0151 423 4420
Matthews Ltd, D
Cork   +353 214 277633
McClean
Greenock   01475 728234
McCready Sailboats Ltd
Holywood   028 9042 1821
Moore, Kevin
Cowes   01983 289699
Moore & Son, J
Mevagissey   01726 842964
Morgan & Sons Marine, LH
Brightlingsea   01206 302003
Mount Batten Boathouse
Plymouth   01752 482666
Murphy, Nicholas
Dunmore East   +353 51 383259
Mylor Chandlery & Rigging
Falmouth   01326 375482
Nancy Black Oban   01631 562550
Nautical World Bangor   028 91460330
New World Yacht Care
Helensburgh   01436 820586
Newhaven Chandlery
Newhaven   01273 612612
Nifpo Ardglass   028 4484 2144
Norfolk Marine
Great Yarmouth   01692 670272
Norfolk Marine Chandlery Shop
Norwich   01603 783150
Northshore Sport & Leisure
Brancaster Staithe   01485 210236
Ocean Leisure Ltd
London   020 7930 5050

One Stop Chandlery Maldon	01621 853558	
O'Sullivans Marine Ltd Tralee	+353 66 7129635	
Partington Marine Ltd, William Pwllheli	01758 612808	
Pascall Atkey & Sons Ltd Isle of Wight	01983 292381	
Pennine Marine Ltd Skipton	01756 792335	
Penrhos Marine Aberdovey	01654 767478	
Penzance Marine Services Penzance	01736 361081	
Perry Marine, Rob Axminster	01297 631314	
Pepe Boatyard Hayling Island	023 9246 1968	
Performance Yachting & Chandlery Plymouth	01752 565023	
Peters PLC Chichester	01243 511033	
Pinnell & Bax Northampton	01604 592808	
Piplers of Poole Poole	01202 673056	
Pirate's Cave, The Rochester	01634 295233	
Powersail Island Chandlers Ltd East Cowes Marina	01983 299800	
Preston Marine Services Ltd Preston	01772 733595	
Price & Co Ltd, WF Bristol	0117 929 2229	
PSM Ltd Alderney	07781 106635	
Purcell Marine Clarenbridge	+353 87 279 3821	
Purple Sails & Marine Walsall	08456 435510	
Quay West Marine Poole	01202 732445	
Quayside Marine Salcombe	01548 844300	
Racecourse Yacht Basin (Windsor) Ltd Windsor	01753 851501	
Rat Rigs Water Sports Cardiff	029 2062 1309	
Reliance Marine Wirral	0151 625 5219	
Rigmarine Padstow	01841 532657	
Riversway Marine Preston	0844 879 4901	
RHP Marine Cowes	01983 290421	
RNS Marine Northam	01237 474167	
Sail Loft Bideford	01271 860001	
Sailaway St Anthony	01326 231357	
Salcombe Boatstore Salcombe	01548 843708	

Salterns Chandlery Poole	01202 701556	
Shipmate Salcombe	01548 844555	
Sandrock Marine Rye	01797 222679	
Schull Watersports Centre Schull	+353 28 28554	
Sea & Shore Ship Chandler Dundee	01382 450666	
Sea Cruisers of Rye Rye	01797 222070
Sea Span Edinburgh	0131 552 2224
Sea Teach Ltd Emsworth	01243 375774
Seafare Tobermory	01688 302277
Seahog Boats Preston	01772 633016
Seamark-Nunn & Co Felixstowe	01394 451000	
Seaquest Marine Ltd St Peter Port	01481 721773	
Seaware Ltd Penryn	01326 377948
Seaway Marine Macduff	01261 832877
Sharp & Enright Dover	01304 206295
Shearwater Engineering Services Ltd Dunoon	01369 706666	
Shipshape Marine King's Lynn	01553 764058	
Ship Shape Ramsgate	01843 597000
Shorewater Sports Chichester	01243 672315	
Simpson Marine Ltd Newhaven	01273 612612	
Simpson Marine Ltd, WA Dundee	01382 566670	
Sketrick Marine Centre Killinchy	028 9754 1400	
Smith AM (Marine) Ltd London	020 8529 6988	
Solent Marine Chandlery Ltd Gosport	023 9258 4622	
South Coast Marine Christchurch	01202 482695	
South Pier Shipyard St Helier	01534 711000	
Southampton Yacht Services Ltd Southampton	023 803 35266	
Sparkes Chandlery Hayling Island	02392 463572	
S Roberts Marine Ltd Liverpool	0151 707 8300	
SSL Marine Eastbourne	01323 47900	
Standard House Chandlery Wells-next-the-Sea	01328 710593	
Stornoway Fishermen's Co-op Stornoway	01851 702563	
Sunset Marine & Watersports Sligo	+353 71 9162792	

Sussex Marine St Leonards on Sea	01424 425882	
Sussex Yachts Lyd Shoreham	01273 605482	
Sussex Marine Centre Shoreham	01273 454737	
Sutton Marine (Dublin) Sutton	+353 1 832 2312	
SW Nets Newlyn	01736 360254
Tarbert Ltd, JSB Tarbert	01880 820180
TCS Chandlery Essex Marina	01702 258094	
TCS Chandlery Grays	01375 374702
TCS Chandlery Southend	01702 444423	
Thulecraft Ltd Lerwick	01595 693192
Torbay Boating Centre Paignton	01803 558760	
Torquay Chandlers Torquay	01803 211854	
Trafalgar Yacht Services Fareham	01329 822445	
Trident UK N Shields	0191 490 1736
Union Chandlery Cork	+353 21 4554334	
Uphill Boat Services Weston-Super-Mare	01934 418617	
Upper Deck Marine and Outriggers Fowey	01726 832287	
V Ships (Isle of Man) Douglas	01624 688886	
V F Marine Rhu	01436 820584
Viking Marine Ltd Dun Laoghaire	+353 1 280 6654	
Waterfront Marine Bangor	01248 352513	
Watersport and Leisure Kings Lynn	01485 210236	
Wayne Maddox Marine Margate	01843 297157	
Western Marine Dalkey	+353 1280 0321	
Whitstable Marine Whitstable	01227 274168	
Williams Ltd, TJ Cardiff	029 20 487676
Windjammer Marine Milford Marina	01646 699070	
Yacht & Boat Chandlery Faversham	01795 531777	
Yacht Chandlers Conwy	01492 572777
Yacht Equipment Chelmsford	01245 223563	
Yachtmail Ltd Lymington	01590 672784	
Yachtshop Holyhead	01407 760031	
You Boat Chandlery Gosport	02392 522226	

MARINE SUPPLIES AND SERVICES GUIDE

CHANDLERS

CHART AGENTS

Brown Son & Ferguson Ltd
Glasgow   0141 429 1234

Chattan Security Ltd
Edinburgh   0131 554 7527

Cooke & Son Ltd, B
Hull   01482 223454

Dubois Phillips & McCallum Ltd
Liverpool   0151 236 2776

Imray Laurie Norie and Wilson Ltd
Huntingdon   01480 462114

Kelvin Hughes
Southampton   023 8063 4911

Lilley & Gillie Ltd, John
North Shields   0191 257 2217

MARINE CHART SERVICES
Maritime House, 32 Denington Rd,
Wellingborough NN8 2QH
Tel: 01933 441629
Fax: 01933 442662
www.chartsales.co.uk
Access to many thousands of
Navigation Charts & publications in
different format.

Price & Co, WF
Bristol   0117 929 2229

Sea Chest Nautical Bookshop Plymouth
01752 222012

Seath Instruments (1992) Ltd
Lowestoft   01502 573811

Small Craft Deliveries
Woodbridge   01394 382655

Smith (Marine) Ltd, AM
London   020 8529 6988

South Bank Marine Charts Ltd Grimsby
01472 361137

Stanford Charts Bristol 0117 929 9966

Stanford Charts
London   020 7836 1321

Todd Chart Agency Ltd
County Down   028 9146 6640

UK Hydrographics Office
Taunton   01823 337900

Warsash Nautical Bookshop
Warsash   01489 572384

CLOTHING

Absolute
Gorleston on Sea   01493 442259

Aquatogs Cowes   01983 295071

Crew Clothing
London   020 8875 2300

Crewsaver
Gosport   01329 820000

Douglas Gill
Nottingham   0115 9460844

Fat Face   fatface.com

Gul International Ltd
Bodmin   01208 262400

Guy Cotten UK Ltd
Liskeard   01579 347115

Harwoods Yarmouth   01983 760258

Helly Hansen
Nottingham   0115 979 5997

Henri Lloyd
Manchester   0161 799 1212

Joules   0845 6066871

Mad Cowes Clothing Co
Cowes   0845 456 5158

Matthews Ltd, D
Cork   +353 214 277633

Mountain & Marine
Poynton   01625 859863

Musto Ltd Laindon   01268 491555

Ocean World Ltd
Cowes   01983 291744

Purple Sails & Marine
Walsall   0845 6435510

Quba Sails
Lymington   01590 689362

Quba Sails
Salcombe   01548 844599

Yacht Parts
Plymouth   01752 252489

CODE OF PRACTICE EXAMINERS

Booth Marine Surveys, Graham
Birchington-on-Sea   01843 843793

Cannell & Associates, David M
Wivenhoe   01206 823337

COMPUTERS & SOFTWARE

Dolphin Maritime Software
White Cross   01524 841946

Forum Software Ltd
Nr Haverfordwest   01646 636363

Kelvin Hughes Ltd
Southampton   023 8063 4911

Memory-Map
Aldermaston   0844 8110950

PC Maritime Plymouth   01752 254205

DECK EQUIPMENT

Aries Van Gear Spares
Penryn   01326 377467

Ronstan
Gosport   023 9252 5377

Harken UK Lymington   01590 689122

IMP Royston   01763 241300

Kearon Ltd George   +353 402 32319

Pro-Boat Ltd
Burnham-on-Crouch   01621 785455

Ryland, Kenneth
Stanton   01386 584270

Smith, EC & Son Ltd
Luton   01582 729721

Timage & Co Ltd
Braintree   01376 343087

DIESEL MARINE/ FUEL ADDITIVES

Corralls Poole   01202 674551

Cotters Marine & General Supplies
Baltimore   +353 28 20106

Expresslube Henfield   01444 254115

Gorey Marine Fuel Supplies
Gorey   07797 742384

Hammond Motorboats
Dover   01304 206809

Iron Wharf Boatyard
Faversham   01795 536296

Lallow, Clare Cowes   01983 760707

Marine Support & Towage
Cowes   01983 200716/07860 297633

Quayside Fuel
Weymouth   07747 182181

Rossiter Yachts
Christchurch   01202 483250

Sleeman & Hawken
Shaldon   01626 778266

DIVERS

Abco Divers Belfast   028 90610492

Andark Diving
Burseldon   01489 581755

Argonaut Marine
Aberdeen   01224 706526

Baltimore Diving and Watersports
Centre West Cork   +353 28 20300

C & C Marine Services
Largs   01475 687180

Cardiff Commercial Boat Operators Ltd
Cardiff   029 2037 7872

Clyde Diving Centre
Inverkip   01475 521281

Divetech UK King's Lynn 01485 572323

Diving & Marine Engineering
Barry   01446 721553

Donnelly, R South Shields 07973 119455

DV Diving   028 9146 4671

Falmouth Divers Ltd
Penryn   01326 374736

Fathoms Ltd Wick   01955 605956

Felixarc Marine Ltd
Lowestoft   01502 509215

Grampian Diving Services
New Deer   01771 644206

Higgins, Noel   +353 872027650

Hudson, Dave
Trearddur Bay   01407 860628

Hunt, Kevin Tralee   +353 6671 25979

Kaymac Diving Services
Swansea   08431 165523

Keller, Hilary
Buncrana   +353 77 62146

Kilkee Diving Centre
Kilkee   +353 6590 56707

Leask Marine Kirkwall   01856 874725

Looe Divers Hannafore   01503 262727

MacDonald, D Nairn   01667 455661

Medway Diving Contractors Ltd
Gillingham   01634 851902

MMC Diving Services
Lake, Isle of Wight   07966 579965

Mojo Maritime
Penzance   01736 762771

Murray, Alex Stornoway 01851 704978

New Dawn Dive Centre
Lymington   01590 675656

Northern Divers (Engineering) Ltd Hull
01482 227276

Offshore Marine Services Ltd
Bembridge   01983 873125

Parkinson (Sinbad Marine Services), J
Killybegs   +353 73 31417

Port of London Authority
Gravesend   01474 560311

Purcell, D – Crouch Sailing School
Burnham   01621 784140/0585 33

Salvesen UK Ltd
Liverpool   0151 933 6038

Sea-Lift Diving Dover   01304 829956

Southern Cylinder Services
Fareham   01329 221125

Sub Aqua Services
North Ormesby   01642 230209

Teign Diving Centre
Teignmouth   01626 773965

Tuskar Rock Marine
Rosslare   +353 53 33376

Underwater Services
Dyffryn Arbwy   01341 247702

Wilson Alan c/o Portrush Yacht Club
Portrush   028 2076 2225

Woolford, William
Bridlington   01262 671710

ELECTRICAL AND ELECTRONIC ENGINEERS

AAS Marine
Aberystwyth   01970 631090

Allworth Riverside Services, Adrian
Chelsea Harbour Marina 07831 574774

Baker, Keith
Brentford   07792 937790

Belson Design Ltd, Nick
Southampton   077 6835 1330

Biggs, John Weymouth Marina,
Weymouth   01305 778445

BJ Marine Ltd Bangor   028 9127 1434

Boat Electrics Troon   01292 315355

Calibra Marine
Dartmouth   01803 833094

Campbell & McHardy Lossiemouth
Marina, Lossiemouth   01343 812137

CES Sandown Sparkes Marina,
Hayling Island   023 9246 6005

Colin Coady Marine
Malahide   +353 87 265 6496

Contact Electrical
Arbroath   01241 874528

DDZ Marine Ardossan   01294 607077

EC Leisure Craft
Essex Marina   01702 568482

Energy Solutions
Rochester   01634 290772

Enterprise Marine Electronic & Technical Services Ltd
Aberdeen   01224 593281

Eurotek Marine
Eastbourne   01323 479144

Evans, Lyndon
Brentford   07795 218704

Floetree Ltd (Loch Lomond Marina)
Balloch   01389 752069

Hamble Marine
Hamble   02380 001088

HNP Engineers (Lerwick) Ltd
Lerwick   01595 692493

Jackson Yacht Services
Jersey   01534 743819

Jedynak, A Salcombe   01548 843321

Kippford Slipway Ltd
Dalbeattie   01556 620249

Lynch Ltd, PA
Morpeth   01670 512291

Lynch, John Tralee   +353 87 992 3102

Mackay Boatbuilders (Arbroath) Ltd
Aberdeen   01241 872879

Marine, AW
Gosport   023 9250 1207

Marine Electrical Repair Service
London   020 7228 1336

MB Marine Troon   01292 311944

MES Falmouth Marina,
Falmouth   01326 378497

Mount Batten Boathouse
Plymouth   01752 482666

New World Yacht Care
Rhu   01436 820586

Neyland Marine Services Ltd
Milford Haven   01646 600358

Powell, Martin Shamrock Quay,
Southampton   023 8033 2123

R & J Marine Electricians Suffolk Yacht
Harbour Ltd, Ipswich   01473 659737

Radio & Electronic Services Beaucette
Marina, Guernsey   01481 728837

Redcar Fish Company
Stockton-on-Tees   01642 633638

RHP Marine Cowes   01983 290421

Rothwell, Chris
Torquay Marina   01803 850960

Ruddy Marine
Galway   +353 87 742 7439

Rutherford, Jeff Largs 01475 568026

SM International
Plymouth   01752 662129

Sussex Fishing Services
Rye   01797 223895

Tony's Marine Service
Coleraine   028 7035 6422

Ultra Marine Systems
Mayflower International Marina,
Plymouth   07989 941020

Upham, Roger
Chichester   01243 528299

Volspec
Ipswich   01473 780144

Weyland Marine Services
Milford Haven   01646 600358

ELECTRONIC DEVICES AND EQUIPMENT

Anchorwatch UK
Edinburgh   0131 447 5057

Aquascan International Ltd
Newport   01633 841117

Atlantis Marine Power Ltd
Plymouth   01752 208810

Autosound Marine
Bradford   01274 688990

B&G Romsey   01794 518448

Brookes & Gatehouse
Romsey   01794 518448

Boat Electrics & Electronics Ltd
Troon   01292 315355

Cactus Navigation & Communication
London   020 7833 3435

CDL Aberdeen   01224 706655

Charity & Taylor Ltd
Lowestoft   01502 581529

Diverse Yacht Services
Hamble   023 8045 3399

Dyfed Electronics Ltd
Milford Haven   01646 694572

Echopilot Marine Electronics Ltd
Ringwood   01425 476211

Enterprise Marine
Aberdeen   01224 593281

Euronav Ltd
Portsmouth   023 9237 3855

Furuno UK
Fraserburgh   01346 518300

Furuno UK
Havant   023 9244 1000

MARINE SUPPLIES AND SERVICES GUIDE

CHART AGENTS – ELECTRONIC DEVICES AND EQUIPMENT

Garmin (Europe) Ltd
Romsey　　0870 850 1242

Golden Arrow Marine Ltd
Southampton　　023 8071 0371

Greenham Regis Marine Electronics
Lymington　　01590 671144

Greenham Regis Marine Electronics
Poole　　01202 676363

Greenham Regis Marine Electronics
Southampton　　023 8063 6555

ICS Electronics Arundel　01903 731101

JG Technologies Ltd
Weymouth　　0845 458 9616

KM Electronics
Lowestoft　　01502 569079

Kongsberg Simrad Ltd
Aberdeen　　01224 226500

Kongsberg Simrad Ltd
Wick　　01955 603606

Landau UK Ltd Hamble　02380 454040

Enterprise Marine
Aberdeen　　01224 593281

Marathon Leisure
Hayling Island　　023 9263 7711

Marine Instruments
Falmouth　　01326 375483

MB Marine Troon　　01292 311944

Microcustom Ltd Ipswich　01473 215777

Nasa Marine Instruments
Stevenage　　01438 354033

Navionics UK Plymouth　01752 204735

Ocean Leisure Ltd
London　　020 7930 5050

Plymouth Marine Electronics
Plymouth　　01752 227711

Radio & Electronic Services Ltd
St Peter Port　　01481 728837

Raymarine Ltd
Portsmouth　　02392 714700

Redfish Car Company
Stockton-on-Tees　　01642 633638

Robertson, MK Oban　　01631 563836

Satcom Distribution Ltd
Salisbury　　01722 410800

Seaquest Marine Ltd
Guernsey　　01481 721773

Seatronics Aberdeen　01224 853100

Selex Communications
Aberdeen　　01224 890316

Selex Communications
Bristol　　0117 931 3550

Selex Communications
Brixham　　01803 882716

Selex Communications
Fraserburgh　　01346 518187

Selex Communications
Glasgow　　0141 882 6909

Selex Communications
Hull　　01482 326144

Selex Communications
Kilkeel　　028 4176 9009

Selex Communications
Liverpool　　01268 823400

Selex Communications
Lowestoft　　01502 572365

Selex Communications
Newcastle upon Tyne　0191 265 0374

Selex Communications
Newlyn　　01736 361320

Selex Communications
Penryn　　01326 378031

Selex Communications
Plymouth　　01752 222878

Selex Communications
Rosyth　　01383 419606

Selex Communications
Southampton　　023 8051 1868

Silva Ltd Livingston　01506 419555

SM International
Plymouth　　01752 662129

Sperry Marine Ltd
Peterhead　　01779 473475

Stenmar Ltd Aberdeen　01224 827288

Transas Nautic
Portsmouth　　023 9267 4016

Veripos Precise Navigation
Fraserburgh　　01346 511411

Wema (UK) Honiton　01404 881810

Wilson & Co Ltd, DB
Glasgow　　0141 647 0161

Woodsons of Aberdeen Ltd
Aberdeen　　01224 722884

ENGINES AND ACCESSORIES

Airylea Motors
Aberdeen　　01224 872891

Amble Boat Co Ltd
Amble　　01665 710267

Anchor Marine Products
Benfleet　　01268 566666

Aquafac Ltd Luton　01582 568700

Barrus Ltd, EP Bicester　01869 363636

British Polar Engines Ltd
Glasgow　　0141 445 2455

Bukh Diesel UK Ltd
Poole　　01202 668840

CJ Marine Mechanical
Troon　　01292 313400

Cleghorn Waring Ltd
Letchworth　　01462 480380

Cook's Diesel Service Ltd
Faversham　　01795 538553

Southern Shipwright (SSL)
Brighton　　01273 601779

Southern Shipwright (SSL)
Eastbourne　　01323 479000

Fender-Fix Maidstone　01622 751518

Fettes & Rankine Engineering
Aberdeen　　01224 573343

Fleetwood & Sons Ltd, Henry
Lossiemouth　　01343 813015

Gorleston Marine Ltd
Great Yarmouth　　01493 661883

Halyard Salisbury　01722 710922

Interseals (Guernsey) Ltd
Guernsey　　01481 246364

Kelpie Boats
Pembroke Dock　　01646 683661

Keypart Watford　01923 330570

Lancing Marine Brighton 01273 410025

Lencraft Boats Ltd
Dungarvan　　+353 58 68220

Lewmar Ltd Havant　023 9247 1841

Liverpool Power Boats
Bootle　　0151 944 1163

Lynch Ltd, PA Morpeth　01670 512291

MacDonald & Co Ltd, JN
Glasgow　　0141 810 3400

Mariners Weigh
Shaldon　　01626 873698

MMS Ardrossan　01294 604831

Mooring Mate Ltd
Bournemouth　　01202 421199

Newens Marine, Chas
Putney　　020 8788 4587

Ocean Safety
Southampton　　023 8072 0800

RK Marine Ltd Hamble　01489 583585

RK Marine Ltd Swanwick　01489 583572

Sillette Sonic Ltd
Sutton　　020 8337 7543

Smith & Son Ltd, EC
Luton　　01582 729721

Sowester Simpson-Lawrence Ltd
Poole　　01202 667700

Timage & Co Ltd
Braintree　　01376 343087

Vetus Den Ouden Ltd
Totton　　023 8045 4507

Western Marine
Dublin　　+353 1 280 0321

Whitstable Marine
Whitstable　　01227 262525

Yates Marine, Martin
Galgate　　01524 751750

Ynys Marine Cardigan　01239 613179

FOUL-WEATHER GEAR

Aquatogs Cowes　01983 295071

Crew Clothing
London　　020 8875 2300

Century
Finchampstead 0118 9731616
Crewsaver Gosport 01329 820000
Douglas Gill
Nottingham 0115 946 0844
FBI
Leeds 0113 270 7000
Gul International Ltd
Bodmin 01208 262400
Helly Hansen
Nottingham 0115 979 5997
Henri Lloyd
Manchester 0161 799 1212
Musto Ltd
Laindon 01268 491555
Pro Rainer
Windsor 07752 903882

GENERAL MARINE EQUIPMENT & SPARES

Ampair
Ringwood 01425 480780
Aries Vane Gear Spares
Penryn 01326 377467
Arthurs Chandlery, R
Gosport 023 9252 6522
Atlantis Marine Power Ltd
Plymouth 01752 208810
Barden UK Ltd Fareham 01489 570770
Calibra Marine International Ltd
Southampton 08702 400358
CH Marine (Cork)
Cork +353 21 4315700
Chris Hornsey (Chandlery) Ltd
Southsea 023 9273 4728
Compass Marine
(Dartmouth) Dartmouth 01803 835915
Cox Yacht Charter Ltd, Nick
Lymington 01590 673489
CTC Marine & Leisure
Middlesbrough 01642 372600
Docksafe Ltd Bangor 028 9147 0453
Frederiksen Boat Fittings (UK) Ltd
Gosport 023 9252 5377
Furneaux Riddall & Co Ltd
Portsmouth 023 9266 8621
Hardware & Marine Supplies
Co Wexford +353 (53) 29791
Index Marine
Bournemouth 01202 470149
Kearon Ltd, George
Arklow +353 402 32319
Marathon Leisure
Hayling Island 023 9263 7711
Pro-Boat Ltd
Burnham-on-Crouch 01621 785455
Pump International Ltd
Cornwall 01209 831937
Quay West Marine
Poole 01202 732445

Rogers, Angie Bristol 0117 973 8276
Ryland, Kenneth
Stanton 01386 584270
Tiflex
Liskeard 01579 320808
Vetus Boating Equipment
Southampton 02380 454507
Whitstable Marine
Whitstable 01227 262525
Yacht Parts
Plymouth 01752 252489

HARBOUR MASTERS

Aberaeron 01545 571645
Aberdeen 01224 597000
Aberdovey 01654 767626
Aberystwyth 01970 611433
Alderney & Burhou 01481 822620
Amble 01665 710306
Anstruther 01333 310836
Appledore 01237 474569
Arbroath 01241 872166
Ardglass 028 4484 1291
Ardrossan Control Tower
01294 463972
Arinagour Piermaster 01879 230347
Arklow +353 402 32466
Baltimore +353 28 22145
Banff 01261 815544
Bantry Bay +353 27 53277
Barmouth 01341 280671
Barry 01446 732665
Beaucette 01481 245000
Beaulieu River 01590 616200
Belfast Lough 028 90 553012
Belfast River Manager 028 90 328507
Bembridge 01983 872828
Berwick-upon-Tweed 01289 307404
Bideford 01237 346131
Blyth 01670 352678
Boston 01205 362328
Bridlington 01262 670148/9
Bridport 01308 423222
Brighton 01273 819919
Bristol 0117 926 4797
Brixham 01803 853321
Buckie 01542 831700
07842 532360
Bude 01288 353111
Burghead 01343 835337
Burnham-on-Crouch 01621 783602

Burnham-on-Sea 01278 782180
Burtonport +353 075 42155
Caernarfon 01286 672118
Caernarfon 07786 730865
Camber Berthing Offices – Portsmouth
023 92297395
Campbeltown 01586 552552
07825 732862
Caledonian Canal Off.
(Inverness) 01463 725500
Cardiff 029 20400500
Carnlough Harbour 07703 606763
Castletown Bay 01624 823549
Charlestown 01726 67526
Chichester Harbour 01243 512301
Clovelly 01273 431549
07975 501380
Conwy 01492 596253
Cork +353 21 4273125
Corpach Canal Sea Lock
01397 772249
Courtmacsherry +353 8673 94299
+353 23 46311/46600
Coverack 01326 380679
Cowes 01983 293952
Crail 01333 450820
Craobh Haven 01852 502222
Crinan Canal Office 01546 603210
Cromarty Firth 01381 600479
Cromarty Harbour 01381 600493
Crookhaven +353 28 35319
Cullen 01542 831700
Dingle +353 66 9151629
Douglas 01624 686628
Dover 01304 240400 Ext 4520
Dublin +353 1 874871
Dun Laoghaire
+353 1 280 1130/8074
Dunbar 01368 863206
Dundee 01382 224121
Dunmore East +353 51 383166
East Loch Tarbert 01859 502444
Eastbourne 01323 470099
Eigg Harbour 01687 482428
Elie 01333 330051
Estuary Control -
Dumbarton 01389 726211
Exe 01392 274306
Eyemouth 01890 750223
07885 742505
Felixstowe 07803 476621

Findochty	07842 532360	Lossiemouth (Marina)	07969 213513	Portsmouth Harbour Control	
Fisherrow	0131 665 5900		07969 213521		023 92723694
Fishguard (Lower Harbour)		Lough Foyle	028 7186 0555	Portsmouth Harbour	023 92723124
01348 874726		Lowestoft	01502 572286	Preston	01772 726711
Fishguard	01348 404425	Lyme Regis	01297 442137	Pwllheli	01758 701219
Fleetwood	01253 872323	Lymington	01590 672014	Queenborough	01795 662051
Flotta	01856 701411	Lyness	01856 791387	Queens Gareloch/Rhu	01436 674321
Folkestone	01303 715354	Macduff	01261 832236	Ramsey	01624 812245
Fowey	01726 832471/2.	Maryport	01900 814431	Ramsgate	01843 572100
Fraserburgh	01346 515858	Menai Strait	01248 712312	River Bann & Coleraine	
Galway Bay	+353 91 561874	Methil	01333 462725		028 7034 2012
Garlieston	01988 600274	Mevagissey	01726 843305	River Blackwater	01621 856487
Glasson Dock	07910 315606	Milford Haven	01646 696100	River Colne	
Gorey Port Control	01534 447788	Minehead (Mon-Fri)	01643 702566	(Brightlingsea)	01206 302200
Gourdon	01569 762741	Montrose	01674 672302	River Dart	01803 832337
Great Yarmouth	01493 335501	Mousehole	01736 731511	River Deben	01473 736257
Grimsby Dockmaster	01472 359181	Mullion Cove	01326 240222	River Exe Dockmaster	01392 274306
Groomsport Bay	028 91 278040	Nairn Harbour Office	01667 452453	River Humber	01482 327171
Hamble River	01489 576387	Newhaven Harbour Admin		River Medway	01795 596593
Hayle	07500 993867		01273 612872/612926	River Orwell	01473 231010
Helford River	01326 250749	Newlyn	01736 731897	River Roach	01621 783602
Helmsdale	01431 821692	Newquay	07737 387217	River Stour	01255 243000
Holy Island	01289 389217	Newport Harbour Office	01983 525994	River Tyne/North	
Holyhead	01407 763071	North Berwick	00776 467373	Shields	0191 257 2080
Hopeman	01343 835337	Oban	01631 562892	River Yealm	01752 872533
Howth	+353 1 832 2252	Padstow	01841 532239	Rivers Alde & Ore	07528 092635
Ilfracombe	01271 862108	Peel	01624 842338	Rosslare Europort	+353 53 915 7921
Inverness	01463 715715	Penrhyn Bangor	01248 352525	Rothesay	01700 503842
Ipswich	01473 211771	Penzance	01736 366113		07799 724225
Irvine	01294 487286	Peterhead	01779 483630	Ryde	01983 613879
Johnshaven	01561 362262	Pierowall	01857 677216	Salcombe	01548 843791
Kettletoft Bay	01857 600227	Pittenweem	01333 312591	Sark	01481 832323
Killybegs	+353 73 31032	Plockton	01599 534589	Scalloway	01595 880574
Kilmore Quay	+353 53 912 9955	Polperro	01503 272809	Scarborough	01723 373530
Kinlochbervie	01971 521235	Poole	01202 440233	Scrabster	01847 892779
	07901 514350	Port Ellen Harbour Association		Seaham	07786 565205
Kinsale	+353 21 4772503		01496 302458	Sharpness, Gloucester Harbour	
Kirkcudbright	01557 331135	Port Isaac	01208 880321	Trustees	01453 811913
Kirkwall	01856 872292		07855 429422	Shoreham	01273 598100
Langstone Harbour	023 9246 3419	Port St Mary	01624 833205	Silloth	016973 31358
Larne	02828 872100	Porth Dinllaen	01758 720276	Sligo	+353 91 53819
Lerwick	01595 692991	Porthleven	01326 574207		+353 86 0870767
Littlehampton	01903 721215	Porthmadog	01766 512927	Southampton	023 8033 9733
Liverpool	0151 949 6134/5	Portknockie	01542 840833	Southend-on-Sea	01702 611889
Loch Gairloch	01445 712140	Portland	01305 824044	Southwold	01502 724712
Loch Inver	01571 844267	Portpatrick	01776 810355	St Helier	01534 447788
	07958 734610	Portree	01478 612926	St Ives	07793 515460
Looe	01503 262839	Portrush	028 70822307	St Margaret's Hope	01856 831454
	07918 728955	Portsmouth Harbour		St Mary's	01720 422768
		Commercial Docks	023 92297395	St Michael's Mount	07870 400282

St Monans (part-time)	07930 869538
St Peter Port	01481 720229
Stonehaven	01569 762741
Stornoway	01851 702688
Strangford Lough	028 44 881637
Stranraer	**07734 073421**
Stromness	07810 465825
Stronsay	01857 616317
Sullom Voe	01806 242551
Sunderland	0191 567 2626
Swale	01795 561234
Swansea	01792 653787
Tayport Hbr Trust	01382 553799
Tees & Hartlepool Port Authority	01429 277205
Teignmouth	01626 773165
Tenby	01834 842717
Thames Estuary	01474 562200
Tobermory Moorings Officer	07917 832497
Torquay	01803 292429
Troon	01292 281687
Truro	01872 272130
Ullapool	01854 612091
Waldringfield	01394 736291
Walton-on-the-Naze	01255 851899
Watchet	01643 703704
Waterford	+353 51 874907
Wells-next-the-Sea	01328 711646
West Bay (Bridport)	01308 423222
	07870 240636
Wexford	+353 53 912 2039
Weymouth	01305 206423
Whitby	01947 602354
Whitehaven	01946 692435
Whitehills	01261 861291
Whitstable	01227 274086
Wick	01955 602030
Wicklow	+353 404 67455
Workington	01900 602301
Yarmouth	01983 760321
Youghal	+353 24 92626

HARBOURS

Bristol Harbour	0117 903 1484
Clyde Marina – Ardrossan	
	01294 607077
Jersey Harbours St Helier	01534 885588

Maryport Harbour and Marina	
Maryport	01900 818447/4431
Peterhead Bay Authority	
Peterhead	01779 474020
Sark Moorings – Channel Islands	
	01481 832260

INSURANCE/FINANCE

Admiral Marine Ltd	
Salisbury	01722 416106
Bishop Skinner Boat Insurance	
London	0800 7838057
Bluefin London	0800 074 5200
Castlemain Ltd	
St Peter Port	01481 721319
Clark Insurance, Graham	
Tyneside	0191 455 8089
Craven Hodgson Associates	
Leeds	0113 243 8443
Giles Insurance Brokers	
Irvine	01294 315481
GJW Direct Liverpool	0151 473 8000
Haven Knox-Johnston	
West Malling	01732 223600
Lombard	
Southampton	023 8024 2171
Mardon Insurance	
Shrewsbury	0800 515629
Marine & General Insurance Services Ltd Maidstone	01622 201106
Mercia Marine Malvern	01684 564457
Nautical Insurance Services Ltd	
Leigh-on-Sea	01702 470811
Navigators & General	
Brighton	01273 863400
Pantaenius UK Ltd	
Plymouth	01752 223656
Porthcawl Insurance Consultants	
Porthcawl	01656 784866
Saga Boat Insurance Folkestone	
	01303 771135
St Margarets Insurances	
London	020 8778 6161

LIFERAFTS & INFLATABLES

Adec Marine Ltd	
Croydon	020 8686 9717
Avon Inflatables Llanelli	01554 882000
Cosalt International Ltd	
Aberdeen	01224 826662
Glaslyn Marine Supplies Ltd	
Porthmadog	01766 513545
Hale Marine, Ron	
Portsmouth	023 9273 2985
Guernsey Yacht Club	
St Peter Port	01481 722838
IBS Boats South Woodham Ferrers	
	01245 323211/425551
KTS Seasafety Kilkeel	028 918 28405
Nationwide Marine Hire	
Warrington	01925 245788

Norwest Marine Ltd	
Liverpool	0151 207 2860
Ocean Safety	
Southampton	023 8072 0800
Polymarine Ltd Conwy	01492 583322
Premium Liferaft Services	
Burnham-on-Crouch	0800 243673
Ribeye Dartmouth	01803 832060
South Eastern Marine Services Ltd	
Basildon	01268 534427
Suffolk Marine Safety	
Ipswich	01473 833010
Whitstable Marine	
Whitstable	01227 262525

MARINAS

Aberystwyth Marina	01970 611422
Amble Marina	01665 712168
Arbroath Harbour	01241 872166
Ardfern Yacht Centre	01852 500247
Ardglass Marina	028 44842332
Arklow Marina	+353 402 39901
Ballycastle Marina	028 2076 8525
Banff Harbour Marina	01261 815544
Bangor Marina	028 91 453297
Beaucette Marina	01481 245000
Bembridge Harbour	01983 872828
Berthon Lymington Marina	
	01590 647405
Birdham Pool Marina	01243 512310
Blackwater Marina	01621 740264
Boston Marina	01205 364420
Bradwell Marina	01621 776235
Bray Marina	01628 623654
Brentford Dock Marina	
	020 8232 8941
Bridgemarsh Marine	01621 740414
Brighton Marina	01273 819919
Bristol Marina	0117 921 3198
Brixham Marina	01803 882929
Bucklers Hard Marina	01590 616200
Burnham Yacht Harbour Marina Ltd	01621 782150
BWML Limehouse Marina	
	020 7308 9930
Cahersiveen Marina	
	+353 66 947 2777
Caley Marina	01463 236539
Cardiff Marina	02920 396078
Carlingford Marina	+353 42 9373072
Carrickfergus Marina	028 9336 6666
Castlepark Marina	+353 21 477 4959

Chatham Maritime Marina
01634 899200

Chelsea Harbour Marina
07770 542783

Chichester Marina 01243 512731

Clyde Marina Ltd 01294 607077

Cobbs Quay Marina 01202 674299

Coleraine Harbour
Town Centre Marina 028 7034 2012

Coleraine Marina 028 703 44768

Conwy Marina 01492 593000

Cowes Yacht Haven 01983 299975

Craobh Marina 01852 500222

Crinan Boatyard 01546 830232

Crosshaven Boatyard Marina
+353 21 483 1161

Dart Marina Yacht Harbour
01803 837161

Darthaven Marina 01803 752242

Dartside Quay 01803 845445

Deganwy Quays Marina
01492 576888

Dingle Marina +353 66 915 1629

Dover Marina 01304 241663

Dun Laoghaire Marina
+353 1 202 0040

Dunstaffnage Marina Ltd
01631 566555

East Cowes Marina 01983 293983

East Ferry Marina +353 21 483 1342

Emsworth Yacht Harbour
01243 377727

Endeavour Quay 02392 584200

Essex Marina 01702 258531

Falmouth Haven Marina
01326 310991

Falmouth Marina 01326 316620

Fambridge Yacht Haven
01621 740370

Fenit Harbour & Marina
+353 66 7136231

Fleetwood Haven Marina
01253 879062

Fox's Marina & Boatyard
01473 689111

Foyle Marina 02871 860555

Gallions Point Marina 0207 476 7054

Galway Harbour Marina
+353 91 561874

Gillingham Marina 01634 280022

Glasson Basin Marina 01524 751491

Gosport Marina 023 9252 4811

Hafan Pwllheli 01758 701219

Hamble Point Marina 02380 452464

Hamilton Dock 01502 580300

Harbour of Rye 01797 225225

Hartlepool Marina 01429 865744

Haslar Marina 023 9260 1201

Heybridge Basin 01621 853506

Holy Loch Marina 01369 701800

Holyhead Marina 01407 764242

Howth Marina +353 1839 2777

Hull Marina 01482 609960

Hythe Marina Village 02380 207073

Inverness Marina 01463 220501

Ipswich Haven Marina 01473 236644

Island Harbour Marina 01983 539994

James Watt Dock Marina
01475 729838

Kemps Quay 023 8063 2323

Kilmore Quay Marina +353 5391 29955

Kilrush Marina +353 65 9052072

King Point Marina 01752 424297

Kinsale Yacht Club Marina
+353 21 477 2196

Kip Marina 01475 521485

Kirkwall Marina 01856 871313

La Collette Yacht Basin 01534 885588

Lady Bee Marina 01273 593801

Lake Yard Marina 01202 674531

Largs Yacht Haven 01475 675333

Lawrence Cove Marina +353 27 75044

Littlehampton Marina 01903 713553

Liverpool Marina Bar & Grill
0151 707 6777

Lossiemouth Marina 01343 813066

Lowestoft Cruising Club
07913 391950

Lowestoft Haven Marina
01502 580300

Lymington Harbour Commission
01590 672014

Lymington Yacht Haven
01590 677071

Malahide Marina +353 1 845 4129

Maryport Harbour and Marina
01900 814431

Mayflower International Marina
01752 556633

Melfort Pier & Harbour 01852 200333

Mercury Yacht Harbour
023 8045 5994

Meridian Quay Marina 01472 268424

Milford Marina 01646 696312

Millbay Marina Village 01752 226785

Multihull Centre 01752 823900

Mylor Yacht Harbour 01326 372121

Nairn Marina 01667 456008

Neptune Marina Ltd 01473 215204

Newhaven Marina 01273 513881

Neyland Yacht Haven 01646 601601

Northney Marina 02392 466321

Noss Marina 01803 839087

Oban Marina & Yacht Services Ltd
01631 565333

Ocean Village Marina 023 8022 9385

Padstow Harbour 01841 532239

Parkstone Bay Marina 01202 747857

Parkstone Yacht Club Haven
01202 738824

Peel Marina 01624 842338

Penarth Quays Marina 02920 705021

Penton Hook 01932 568681

Peterhead Bay Marina 01779 477868

Plymouth Yacht Haven 01752 404231

Poolbeg YBC & Marina
+353 1 668 9983

Poole Quay Boat Haven
01202 649488

Poplar Dock Marina 0207 308 9930

Port Bannantyne Marina
01700 503116

Port Edgar Marina 0131 331 3330

Port Ellen Marina 01496 302458

Port Hamble Marina 023 8045 2741

Port of Poole Marina 01202 649488

Port Pendennis Marina
01326 211211

Port Solent Marina 02392 210765

Port Werburgh 01634 252107

Portaferry Marina 07703 209780

Portavadie Marina 01700 811075

Portishead Quays Marina
01275 841941

Portland Marina 08454 30 2012

Preston Marina 01772 733595

Quay Marinas Rhu 01436 820238

Queen Anne's Battery 01752 671142

Ridge Wharf Yacht Centre
01929 552650

Royal Clarence Marina 02392 523523

Royal Cork Yacht Club Marina
+353 21 483 1023

Royal Harbour Marina Ramsgate
01843 572100

Royal Harwich Yacht Club Marina
01473 780319

Royal Norfolk and Suffolk Yacht Club
01502 566726

Royal Northumberland Yacht Club
01670 353636

Royal Quays Marina 0191 272 8282

Ryde Leisure Harbour 01983 613879

Salterns Marina Ltd 01202 709971

Salve Engineering Marina
+353 21 483 1145

Sandpoint Marina (Dumbarton)
01389 762396

Saxon Wharf 023 8033 9490

Seaport Marina 01463 725500

Seaton's Marina 028 703 832086

Shamrock Quay 023 8022 9461

Sharpness Marine 01453 811476

Shepards Wharf Boatyard Ltd
01983 297821

Shotley Marina 01473 788982

South Dock Marina 020 7252 2244

South Ferriby Marina 01652 635620

Southdown Marina 01752 823084

Southsea Marina 02392 822719

Sovereign Harbour Marina
01323 470099

Sparkes Marina 023 92463572

St Helier Marina 01534 447708

St Katharine Marina Ltd
0207 264 5312

St Peter Port Marinas 01481 720229

St Peter's Marina 0191 265 4472

Stromness Marina 01856 871313

Suffolk Yacht Harbour Ltd
01473 659240

Sunderland Marina 0191 514 4721

Sunseeker International Marina
01202 381111

Sutton Harbour 01752 204702

Swansea Marina 01792 470310

Swanwick Marina 01489 884081

Tarbert Harbour 01880 820344

The Shipyard 01903 713327

Titchmarsh Marina 01255 672185

Tobermorey Harbour Association
01688 302876

Tollesbury Marina 01621 869202

Torpoint Yacht Harbour
01752 813658

Torquay Marina 01803 200210

Town Quay Marina 02380 234397

Troon Yacht Haven 01292 315553

Universal Marina 01489 574272

Victoria Dock Marina 01286 672346

Victoria Marina 01481 725987

Walton Yacht Basin 01255 675873

Waterford City Marina
+353 87 238 4944

Weymouth Harbour 01305 838423

Weymouth & Portland BC
01305 838423

Weymouth Marina 01305 767576

Whitby Marina 01947 602354

Whitehaven Marina 01946 692435

Whitehills Marina 01261 861291

Wick Marina 01955 602030

Windsor Marina 01753 853911

Wisbech Yacht Hbr 01945 588059

Woolverstone Marina 01473 780206

Yarmouth Harbour 01983 760321

MARINE ENGINEERS

AAS Marine
Aberystwyth 01970 631090

Allerton Engineering
Lowestoft 01502 537870

APAS Engineering Ltd
Southampton 023 8063 2558

Ardmair Boat Centre
Ullapool 01854 612054

Arisaig Marine
Inverness-shire 01687 450224

Arun Craft
Littlehampton 01903 723667

Atlantis Marine Power Ltd
Plymouth 01752 208810

Attrill & Sons, H
Bembridge 01983 872319

Auto & Marine Services
Botley 07836 507000

Auto Marine Southsea 023 9282 5601

Baker, Keith
Brentford 07792 937790

BJ Marine Ltd Bangor 028 9127 1434

Bristol Boat Ltd Bristol 01225 872032

Browne, Jimmy
Tralee +353 87 262 7158

Buzzard Marine Engineering
Yarmouth 01983 760707

C & B Marine Ltd
Chichester Marina 01243 511273

Caddy, Simon
Falmouth Marina
Falmouth 01326 372682

Caledonian Marine
Rhu Marina 01436 821184

Caratek Hull 07957 922301

Cardigan Outboards
Cardigan 01239 613966

Channel Islands Marine Ltd
Guernsey 01481 716880

Channel Islands Marine Ltd
Jersey 01534 767595

Cook's Diesel Service Ltd
Faversham 01795 538553

Cragie Engineering
Kirkwall 01856 874680

Wartsila
Havant 023 9240 0121

Crinan Boatyard Ltd
Crinan 01546 830232

Cutler Marine Engineering, John
Emsworth 01243 375014

Dale Sailing Co Ltd
Milford Haven 01646 603110

Davis Marine Services
Ramsgate 01843 586172

Denney & Son, EL
Redcar 01642 483507

DH Marine (Shetland) Ltd
Shetland 01595 690618

Emark Marine Ltd
Emsworth 01243 375383

Evans, Lyndon
Brentford 07795 218704

Evans Marine Engineering, Tony
Pwllheli 01758 703070

Felton Marine Engineering
Brighton 01273 601779

Felton Marine Engineering
Eastbourne 01323 470211

Ferrypoint Boat Co
Youghal +353 24 94232

Fettes & Rankine Engineering
Aberdeen 01224 573343

Fleming Engineering, J
Stornoway 01851 703488

Floetree Ltd (Loch Lomond Marina)
Balloch 01389 752069

Fowey Harbour Marine Engineers
Fowey 01726 832806

Fox Marine Services Ltd
Jersey 01534 721312

Freeport Marine Jersey 01534 888100

French Marine Motors Ltd
Colchester 01206 302133

French Marine Motors Ltd
Titchmarsh Marina 01255 850303

GH Douglas Marine Services
Fleetwood Harbour Village Marina,
Fleetwood   01253 877200

Golden Arrow Marine
Southampton   023 8071 0371

Goodchild Marine Services
Great Yarmouth   01493 782301

Goodwick Marine
Fishguard   01348 873955

Gosport Marina
Gosport   023 9252 4811

Griffins Garage Dingle Marina,
Co Kerry   +353 66 91 51178

Hale Marine, Ron
Portsmouth   023 9273 2985

Hamnavoe Engineering
Stromness   01856 850576

Harbour Engineering
Itchenor   01243 513454

Hartlepool Marine Engineering
Hartlepool   01429 867883

Hayles, Harold
Yarmouth   01983 760373

Herm Seaway Marine Ltd
St Peter Port   01481 726829

HNP Engineers (Lerwick Ltd)
Lerwick   01595 692493

Hodges, T
Coleraine   028 7035 6422

Home Marine Emsworth Yacht
Harbour, Emsworth   01243 374125

Hook Marine Ltd Troon 01292 679500

Humphrey, Chris
Teignmouth   01626 772324

Instow Marine Services
Bideford   01271 861081

Jones (Boatbuilders), David
Chester   01244 390363

Keating Marine Engineering Ltd, Bill
Jersey   01534 733977

Kingston Marine Services
Cowes   01983 299385

Kippford Slipway Ltd
Dalbeattie   01556 620249

Lansdale Pannell Marine
Chichester   01243 512374

Lencraft Boats Ltd
Dungarvan   +353 58 68220

Llyn Marine Services
Pwllheli   01758 612606

Lynx Engineering
St Helens, Isle of Wight 01983 873711

M&G Marine Services
Mayflower International Marina,
Plymouth   01752 563345

MacDonald & Co Ltd, JN
Glasgow   0141 810 3400

Mackay Marine Services
Aberdeen   01224 575772

Mainbrayce Marine
Alderney   01481 722772

Malakoff and Moore
Lerwick   01595 695544

Mallaig Boat Building and Engineering
Mallaig   01687 462304

Marindus Engineering
Kilmore Quay   +353 53 29794

Marine Engineering Looe
Brixham   01803 844777

Marine Engineering Looe
Looe   01503 263009

Marine Engineering Services
Port Dinorwic   01248 671215

Marine General Engineers Beaucette
Marina, Guernsey   01481 245808

Marine Propulsion
Hayling Island   07836 737488

Marine & General Engineers
St. Sampsons Harbour, Guernsey
                         01481 245808

Marine-Trak Engineering Mylor Yacht
Harbour, Falmouth   01326 376588

Marine Warehouse
Gosport   023 9258 0420

Marlec Marine
Ramsgate   01843 592176

Martin Outboards
Galgate   01524 751750

Meiher, Denis
Fenit   +353 87 958 4744

MES Marine Greenock   01475 744655

MMS Ardrossan   01294 604831

Mobile Marine Engineering Liverpool
Marina, Liverpool   01565 733553

Mount's Bay Engineering
Newlyn   01736 363095

MP Marine Maryport   01900 810299

New World Yacht Care
Helensburgh   01436 820586

North Western Automarine Engineers
Largs   01475 687139

Noss Marine Services
Dart Marina,
Dartmouth   01803 833343

Owen Marine, Robert
Porthmadog   01766 513435

Pace, Andy Newhaven   01273 516010

**Penzance Dry Dock and Engineering
Co Ltd** Penzance   01736 363838

Pirie & Co, John S
Fraserburgh   01346 513314

Portavon Marine
Keynsham   0117 986 1626

Power Afloat, Elkins Boatyard
Christchurch   01202 489555

Powerplus Marine Cowes Yacht Haven,
Cowes   01983 290421

Pro-Marine Queen Anne's Battery
Marina, Plymouth   01752 267984

PT Marine Engineering
Hayling Island   023 9246 9332

R & M Marine
Portsmouth   023 9273 7555

R & S Engineering Dingle Marina,
Ireland   +353 66 915 1189

Reddish Marine
Salcombe   01548 844094

RHP Marine Cowes   01983 290421

River Tees Engineering & Welding Ltd
Middlesbrough   01642 226226

RK Marine Ltd Hamble 01489 583585

RK Marine Ltd
Swanwick   01489 583572

Rossiter Yachts Ltd
Christchurch   01202 483250

Ryan & Roberts Marine Services
Askeaton   +353 61 392198

Salve Marine Ltd
Crosshaven   +353 21 4831145

Seamark-Nunn & Co
Felixstowe   01394 275327

Seapower Ipswich   01473 780090

Seaward Engineering
Glasgow   0141 632 4910

Seaway Marine
Gosport   023 9260 2722

Shearwater Engineering Services Ltd
Dunoon   01369 706666

Silvers Marina Ltd
Helensburgh   01436 831222

Starey Marine
Salcombe   01548 843655

Tarbert Marine Arbroath 01241 872879

Tollesbury Marine Engineering
Tollesbury Marina,
Tollesbury   01621 869919

Tony's Marine Service
Coleraine 028 7035 6422

Vasey Marine Engineering, Gordon
Fareham 07798 638625

Volspec Ltd
Tollesbury 01621 869756

Wallis, Peter Torquay Marina,
Torquay 01803 844777

WB Marine Chichester 01243 512857

West Coast Marine
Troon 01292 318121

West Marine
Brighton 01273 626656

Weymouth Marina Mechanical Services
Weymouth 01305 779379

Whittington, G Lady Bee Marine,
Shoreham 01273 593801

Whitewater Marine
Malahide +353 1 816 8473

Wigmore Wright Marine Services
Penarth Marina 029 2070 9983

Wright, M Manaccan 01326 231502

Wyko Industrial Services
Inverness 01463 224747

Ynys Marine
Cardigan 01239 613179

Youngboats
Faversham 01795 536176

1° West Marine Ltd
Portsmouth 023 9283 8335

MASTS, SPARS & RIGGING

JWS Marine Services
Portsmouth 02392 755155

A2 Rigging
Falmouth 01326 312209

Allspars Plymouth 01752 266766

Amble Boat Co Ltd
Morpeth 01665 710267

Arun Canvas & Rigging
Littlehampton 1903 732561

B+ St Peter Port 01481 726071

Buchanan, Keith
St Mary's 01720 422037

Bussell & Co, WL
Weymouth 01305 785633

Carbospars Ltd
Hamble 023 8045 6736

Cable & Rope Works
Bexhill-on-Sea 0101424 220112

Clarke Rigging, Niall
Coleraine 07916 083858

Coates Marine Ltd
Whitby 01947 604486

Dauntless Boatyard Ltd
Canvey Island 01268 793782

Davies Marine Services
Ramsgate 01843 586172

Eurospars Ltd
Plymouth 01752 550550

Exe Leisure
Exeter 01392 879055

Fox's Marine Ipswich Ltd
Ipswich 01473 689111

Freeland Yacht Spars Ltd
Dorchester on Thames 01865 341277

Gordon, AD Portland 01305 821569

Grimsby Rigging Services Ltd
Grimsby 01472 362758

Hamble Custom Rigging Centre
Hamble 023 8045 2000

Harris Rigging Totnes 01803 840160

Heyn Engineering
Belfast 028 9035 0022

Holman Rigging
Chichester 01243 514000

Irish Spars and Rigging
Malahide +353 86 209 5996

JWS Marine Services
Portsmouth 02392 755155

Kildale Marine Hull 01482 227464

Lowestoft Yacht Services
Lowestoft 01502 585535

Laverty, Billy Galway +353 86 3892614

Leitch, WB
Tarbert, Loch Fyne 01880 820287

Lewis, Harry
Kinsale +353 87 266 7127

Marine Resource Centre
Oban 01631 720291

Martin Leaning Masts & Rigging
Hayling 023 9237 1157

Mast & Rigging
Crosshaven +353 21 483 3878

Mast & Rigging Services
Largs 01475 670110

Mast & Rigging Services
Inverkip 01475 522700

MP Marine Maryport 01900 810299

Ocean Rigging
Lymington 01590 676292

Owen Sails Oban 01631 720485

Pro Rig S Ireland +353 87 298 3333

Ratsey, Stephen
Milford Haven 01646 601561

Riglt Ardrossan 07593 220213

Rig Magic Ipswich 01473 655089

Rig Shop Southampton 023 8033 8341

Roberts Marine Ltd, S
Liverpool 0151 707 8300

Ronstan
Gosport 023 9252 5377

Salcombe Boatstore
Salcombe 01548 843708

Seldén Mast Ltd
Gosport 01329 504000

Silvers Marina Ltd
Helensburgh 01436 831222

Silverwood Yacht Services Ltd
Portsmouth 023 9232 7067

Spencer Rigging
Cowes 01983 292022

Storrar Marine Store
Newcastle upon Tyne 0191 266 1037

Tedfords Rigging & Rafts
Belfast 028 9032 6763

TJ Rigging Conwy 07780 972411

TS Rigging Malden 01621 874861

Windjammer Marine
Milford Marina 01646 699070

Yacht Rigging Services
Plymouth 01752 226609

Yacht Shop, The
Fleetwood 01253 879238

Z Spars UK Hadleigh 01473 822130

NAVIGATION EQUIPMENT – GENERAL

Belson Design Ltd, Nick
Southampton 077 6835 1330

Brown Son & Ferguson Ltd
Glasgow 0141 429 1234

Cooke & Son Ltd, B
Hull 01482 223454

Diverse Yacht Services
Hamble 023 8045 3399

Dolphin Maritime Software Ltd
Lancaster 01524 841946

Dubois Phillips & McCallum Ltd
Liverpool 0151 236 2776

Garmin
Southampton 02380 524000

Geonav UK Ltd
Poole 0870 240 4575

Imray Laurie Norie and Wilson Ltd
St Ives, Cambs 01480 462114

Kelvin Hughes
Southampton — 023 8063 4911

Lilley & Gillie Ltd, John
North Shields — 0191 257 2217

Marine Chart Services
Wellingborough — 01933 441629

Navico UK Romsey — 01794 510010

PC Maritime
Plymouth — 01752 254205

Price & Co, WF Bristol — 0117 929 2229

Raymarine Ltd
Portsmouth — 023 9269 3611

Royal Institute of Navigation
London — 020 7591 3130

Sea Chest Nautical Bookshop
Plymouth — 01752 222012

Seath Instruments (1992) Ltd
Lowestoft — 01502 573811

Smith (Marine) Ltd, AM
London — 020 8529 6988

South Bank Marine Charts Ltd
Grimsby — 01472 361137

Southcoasting Navigators
Devon — 01626 335626

Stanford Charts
Bristol — 0117 929 9966
London — 020 7836 1321
Manchester — 0870 890 3730

Todd Chart Agency Ltd
County Down — 028 9146 6640

UK Hydrographic Office
Taunton — 01823 337900

Warsash Nautical Bookshop
Warsash — 01489 572384

Yachting Instruments Ltd
Sturminster Newton — 01258 817662

PAINT & OSMOSIS

Advanced Blast Cleaning Paint
Tavistock — 01822 617192/07970 407911

Herm Seaway Marine Ltd
St Peter Port — 01481 726829

Gillingham Marina — 01634 280022

Hempel Paints
Southampton — 02380 232000

International Coatings Ltd
Southampton — 023 8022 6722

Marineware Ltd
Southampton — 023 8033 0208

NLB Marine
Ardrossan — 01563 521509

Pro-Boat Ltd
Burnham on Crouch — 01621 785455

Rustbuster Ltd
Peterborough — 0870 9090093

Smith & Son Ltd, EC
Luton — 01582 729721

SP Systems
Isle of Wight — 01983 828000

PROPELLERS & STERGEAR/REPAIRS

CJR Propulsion Ltd
Southampton — 023 8063 9366

Darglow Engineering Ltd
Wareham — 01929 556512

Propeller Revolutions
Poole — 01202 671226

Sillette – Sonic Ltd
Sutton — 020 8337 7543

Vetus Den Ouden Ltd
Southampton — 02380 454507

RADIO COURSES / SCHOOLS

Bisham Abbey Sailing & Navigation School Bisham — 01628 474960

East Coast Offshore Yachting – Les Rant Perry — 01480 861381

Hamble School of Yachting
Hamble — 023 8045 6687

Pembrokeshire Cruising
Neyland — 01646 602500

Plymouth Sailing School
Plymouth — 01752 493377

Southern Sailing
Swanwick — 01489 575511

Start Point Sailing
Kingsbridge — 01548 810917

REEFING SYSTEMS

Atlantic Spars Ltd
Brixham — 01803 843322

Calibra Marine International Ltd
Southampton — 08702 400358

Eurospars Ltd
Plymouth — 01752 550550

Holman Rigging
Chichester — 01243 514000

Navimo UK Ltd
Hedge End — 01489 778850

Sea Teach Ltd
Emsworth — 01243 375774

Southern Spar Services
Northam — 023 8033 1714

Wragg, Chris
Lymington — 01590 677052

Z Spars UK Hadleigh — 01473 822130

REPAIR MATERIALS & ACCESSORIES

Akeron Ltd
Southend on Sea — 01702 297101

Howells & Son, KJ
Poole — 01202 665724

JB Timber Ltd
North Ferriby — 01482 631765

Robbins Timber Bristol — 0117 9633136

Sika Ltd
Welwyn Garden City — 01707 394444

Solent Composite Systems
East Cowes — 01983 292602

Technix Rubber & Plastics Ltd
Southampton — 01489 789944

Tiflex Liskeard — 01579 320808

Timage & Co Ltd
Braintree — 01376 343087

Trade Grade Products Ltd
Poole — 01202 820177

Wessex Resins & Adhesives Ltd
Romsey — 01794 521111

ROPE & WIRE

Cable & Rope Works
Bexhill-on-Sea — 01424 220112

Euro Rope Ltd
Scunthorpe — 01724 280480

Marlow Ropes Hailsham — 01323 444444

Mr Splice Leicester — 0800 1697178

Spinlock Ltd Cowes — 01983 295555

TJ Rigging Conwy — 07780 972411

SAFETY EQUIPMENT

AB Marine Ltd
St Peter Port — 01481 722378

Adec Marine Ltd
Croydon — 020 8686 9717

Anchorwatch UK
Edinburgh — 0131 447 5057

Avon Inflatables
Llanelli — 01554 882000

Cosalt International Ltd
Aberdeen — 01224 588327

Crewsaver Gosport — 01329 820000

Glaslyn Marine Supplies Ltd
Porthmadog — 01766 513545

Guardian Fire Protection
Manchester   0800 358 7522

Hale Marine, Ron
Portsmouth   023 9273 2985

Herm Seaway Marine Ltd
St Peter Port   01481 722838

IBS Boats South Woodham Ferrers
                   01245 323211/425551

KTS Seasafety Kilkeel   028 41762655

McMurdo Pains Wessex
Portsmouth   023 9262 3900

Met Office Bracknell   0845 300 0300

Nationwide Marine Hire
Warrington   01925 245788

Norwest Marine Ltd
Liverpool   0151 207 2860

Ocean Safety So'ton   023 8072 0800

Navimo UK Ltd
Romsey   01794 526800

Polymarine Ltd Conwy   01492 583322

Premium Liferaft Services
Burnham-on-Crouch   0800 243673

Ribeye Dartmouth   01803 832060

South Eastern Marine Services Ltd
Basildon   01268 534427

Suffolk Sailing
Ipswich   01473 604678

Whitstable Marine
Whitstable   01227 262525

Winters Marine Ltd
Salcombe   01548 843580

SAILMAKERS & REPAIRS

Allison-Gray Dundee   01382 505888

Alsop Sailmakers, John
Salcombe   01548 843702

AM Trimming Windsor   01932 821090

Arun Canvas & Rigging
Littlehampton   01903 732561

Arun Sails Chichester 01243 573185

Bank Sails, Bruce
Southampton   01489 582444

Barrett, Katy
St Peter Port   07781 404299

Batt Sails Bosham   01243 575505

Bissett and Ross
Aberdeen   01224 580659

Boatshed, The
Felinheli, Bangor   01248 679939

Breaksea Sails Barry   01446 730785

Bristol Sails Bristol 0117 922 5080

Buchanan, Keith
St Mary's   01720 422037

C&J Marine Textiles
Chichester   01243 782629

Calibra Sails
Dartmouth   01803 833094

Clarke Rigging, Niall
Coleraine   07916 083858

Coastal Covers
Portsmouth   023 9252 0200

Covercare Fareham   01329 311878

Crawford, Margaret
Kirkwall   01856 875692

Crusader Sails Poole   01202 670580

Crystal Covers
Portsmouth   023 9238 0143

Cullen Sailmakers
Galway   +353 91 771991

Dolphin Sails Harwich 01255 243366

Doyle Sails
Southampton   023 8033 2622

Downer International Sails & Chandlery
Dun Laoghaire   +353 1 280 0231

Duthie Marine Safety, Arthur
Glasgow   0141 429 4553

Dynamic Sails
Emsworth   01243 374495

Flew Sailmakers
Portchester   01329 822676

Fylde Coast Sailmaking Co
Fleetwood   01253 873476

Freeman Sails
Padstow   07771 610053

Garland Sails Bristol 01275 393473

Goacher Sails
Cumbria   01539 488686

Gowen Ocean Sailmakers
West Mersea   01206 384412

Green Sailmakers, Paul
Plymouth   01752 660317

Henderson Sails & Covers
Southsea   023 9229 4700

Hood Sailmakers
Lymington   01590 675011

Hooper, A Plymouth   01752 830411

Hyde Sails
Southampton   0845 543 8945

Jackson Yacht Services
Jersey   01534 743819

Jeckells and Son Ltd (Wroxham)
Wroxham   01603 782223

Jessail Ardrossan   01294 467311

JKA Sailmakers
Pwllheli   01758 613266

Kemp Sails Ltd
Wareham   01929 554308/554378

Kildale Marine
Hull   01482 227464

Lawrence Sailmakers, J
Brightlingsea   01206 302863

Leitch, WB
Tarbert, Loch Fyne   01880 820287

Leith UK
Berwick on Tweed   01289 307264

Le Monnier, Yannick
Galway   +353 87 628 9854

Lodey Sails Newlyn   01736 719359

Lossie Sails
Lossiemouth   07989 956698

Lucas Sails Portchester 023 9237 3699

Malakoff and Moore
Lerwick   01595 695544

McCready and Co Ltd, J
Belfast   028 90232842

McKillop Sails, John
Kingsbridge   01548 852343

McNamara Sails, Michael
Great Yarmouth   01692 584186

McWilliam Sailmaker (Crosshaven)
Crosshaven   +353 21 4831505

Sail Shape
Fowey   01726 833731

Montrose Rope and Sails
Montrose   01674 672657

Mountfield Sails
Hayling Island   023 9246 3720

Mouse Sails Holyhead   01407 763636

Nicholson Hughes Sails
Rosneath   01436 831356

North Sea Sails
Tollesbury   01621 869367

North West Sails
Keighley   01535 652949

Northrop Sails
Ramsgate   01843 851665

O'Mahony Sailmakers
Kinsale   +353 86 326 0018

O'Sullivans Marine Ltd
Tralee   +353 66 7129635

Owen Sails Benderloch 01631 720485

Parker & Kay Sailmakers –
East Ipswich   01473 659878

Parker & Kay Sailmakers –
South Hamble   023 8045 8213

Penrose Sailmakers
Falmouth   01326 312705

Pinnell & Bax
Northampton   01604 592808

Pollard Marine
Port St Mary 01624 835831

Quantum Sails
Ipswich Haven Marina 01473 659878

Quantum-Parker & Kay Sailmakers
Hamble 023 8045 8213

Quay Sails (Poole) Ltd
Poole 01202 681128

Ratsey & Lapthorn
Isle of Wight 01983 294051

Ratsey Sailmakers, Stephen
Milford Haven 01646 601561

Relling One Design
Portland 01305 826555

SO31 Bags
Southampton 023 8045 5106

Rig Shop, The
Southampton 023 8033 8341

Rockall Sails
Chichester 01243 573185

Sail Locker
Woolverstone Marina 01473 780206

Sail Style
Hayling Island 023 9246 3720

Sails & Canvas Exeter 01392 877527

Sail Register
Ulceby 01469 589444

Saltern Sail Co
West Cowes 01983 280014

Saltern Sail Company
Yarmouth 01983 760120

Sanders Sails
Lymington 01590 673981

Saturn Sails Largs 01475 689933

Scott & Co, Graham
St Peter Port 01481 259380

Shore Sailmakers
Swanwick 01489 589450

SKB Sails Falmouth 01326 372107

Sketrick Sailmakers Ltd
Killinchy 028 9754 1400

Solo Sails
Penzance 01736 366004

Storrar Marine Store
Newcastle upon Tyne 0191 266 1037

Suffolk Sails
Woodbridge 01394 386323

Sunset Sails Sligo +353 71 62792

Torquay Marina Sails and Canvas
Exeter 01392 877527

Trident UK
Gateshead 0191 490 1736

UK McWilliam Cowes 01983 281100

Underwood Sails Queen Anne's
Battery, Plymouth 01752 229661

W Sails Leigh-on-Sea 01702 714550

Warren Hall
Beaucette, Guernsey 07781 444280

Watson Sails
Dublin 13 +353 1 846 2206

WB Leitch and Son
Tarbert 01880 820287

Westaway Sails
Plymouth Yacht Haven 01752 892560

Wilkinson Sails
Burnham-on-Crouch 01621 786770

Wilkinson Sails
Teynham 01795 521503

Yacht Shop, The
Fleetwood 01253 879238

SOLAR POWER

Ampair Ringwood 01425 480780

Barden UK Ltd Fareham 01489 570770

Marlec Engineering Co Ltd
Corby 01536 201588

SPRAYHOODS & DODGERS

A & B Textiles
Gillingham 01634 579686

Allison–Gray Dundee 01382 505888

Arton, Charles
Milford-on-Sea 01590 644682

Arun Canvas and Rigging Ltd
Littlehampton 01903 732561

Boatshed, The
Felinheli, Bangor 01248 679939

Buchanan, Keith
St Mary's 01720 422037

C & J Marine Textiles
Chichester 01243 785485

Covercare Fareham 01329 311878

Covercraft
Southampton 023 8033 8286

Crystal Covers
Portsmouth 023 9238 0143

Jeckells and Son Ltd
Wroxham 01603 782223

Jessail Ardrossan 01294 467311

Lomond Boat Covers
Alexandria 01389 602734

Lucas Sails
Portchester 023 9237 3699

Poole Canvas Co Ltd
Poole 01202 677477

Sail Register
Ulceby 01469 589444

Saundersfoot Auto Marine
Saundersfoot 01834 812115

Trident UK
Gateshead 0191 490 1736

SURVEYORS AND NAVAL ARCHITECTS

Amble Boat Company Ltd
Amble 01665 710267

Ark Surveys East Anglia/South Coast
01621 857065/01794 521957

Atkin & Associates
Lymington 01590 688633

Barbican Yacht Agency Ltd
Plymouth 01752 228855

Battick, Lee St Helier 01534 611143

Booth Marine Surveys, Graham
Birchington-on-Sea 01843 843793

Byrde & Associates
Kimmeridge 01929 480064

Bureau Maritime Ltd
Maldon 01621 859181

Byrde & Associates
Kimmeridge 01929 480064

Cannell & Associates, David M
Wivenhoe 01206 823337

Cardiff Commercial Boat Operators Ltd
Cardiff 029 2037 7872

Clarke Designs LLP, Owen
Dartmouth 01803 770495

Cox, David Penryn 01326 340808

Davies, Peter N
Wivenhoe 01206 823289

Down Marine Co Ltd
Belfast 028 90480247

Evans, Martin
Kirby le Soken 07887 724055

Goodall, JL Whitby 01947 604791

Green, James Plymouth 01752 660516

Greening Naval Architect Ltd, David
Salcombe 01548 842000

Hansing & Associates
North Wales/Midlands   01248 671291

JP Services – Marine Safety & Training
Chichester   01243 537552

MacGregor, WA
Felixstowe   01394 676034

Mahoney & Co, KPO
Co Cork   +353 21 477 6150

Marinte Surveys UK
Emsworth   07798 554535

Marintec Lymington   01590 683414

Norwood Marine
Margate   01843 835711

Quay Consultants Ltd
West Wittering   01243 673056

Scott Marine Surveyors & Consultants
Conwy   01492 573001

S Roberts Marine Ltd
Liverpool   0151 707 8300

Staton-Bevan, Tony
Lymington   01590 645755/
07850 315744

Swanwick Yacht Surveyors
Southampton   01489 564822

Thomas, Stephen
Southampton   023 8048 6273

Towler, Perrin
Lymington   01590 718087

Victoria Yacht Surveys
Cornwall   0800 083 2113

Ward & McKenzie
Woodbridge   01394 383222

Ward & McKenzie (North East)
Pocklington   01759 304322

YDSA Yacht Designers & Surveyors Association
Bordon   0845 0900162

TAPE TECHNOLOGY

CC Marine Services (Rubbaweld) Ltd
London   020 7402 4009

Trade Grade Products Ltd
Poole   01202 820177

UK Epoxy Resins
Burscough   01704 892364

3M United Kingdom plc
Bracknell   01344 858315

TRANSPORT/YACHT DELIVERIES

Boat Shifters
07733 344018/01326 210548

Convoi Exceptionnel Ltd
Hamble   023 8045 3045

Debbage Yachting
Ipswich   01473 601169

East Coast Offshore Yachting
01480 861381

Forrest Marine Exeter   08452 308335

Hainsworth's UK and Continental
Bingley   01274 565925

Houghton Boat Transport
Tewkesbury   07831 486710

MCL Transboat   08455 201900

Moonfleet Sailing
Poole   01202 682269

Performance Yachting
Plymouth   01752 565023

Peters & May Ltd
Southampton   023 8048 0480

Reeder School of Seamanship, Mike
Lymington   01590 674560

Seafix Boat Transfer
North Wales   01766 514507

Sealand Boat Deliveries Ltd
Liverpool   01254 705225

Shearwater Sailing
Southampton   01962 775213

Southcoasting Navigators
Devon   01626 335626

West Country Boat Transport
01566 785651

Wolff, David   07659 550131

TUITION/SAILING SCHOOLS

Association of Scottish Yacht Charterers Argyll   07787 363562
01852 200258

Bisham Abbey Sailing & Navigation School Bisham   01628 474960

Blue Baker Yachts
Ipswich   01473 780008

Britannia Sailing (East Coast)
Ipswich   01473 787019

British Offshore Sailing School
Hamble   023 8045 7733

Coastal Sea School
Weymouth   0870 321 3271

Conwy School of Yachting
Conwy   01492 572999

Tiller School of Navigation and Seamanship,
Banstead   0845 6123466

Dart Harbour Sea School
Dartmouth   01803 839339

Dartmouth Sailing
Dartmouth   01803 833399

Drake Sailing School
Plymouth   01635 253009

East Anglian Sea School
Ipswich   01473 659992

East Coast Offshore Yachting – Les Rant Perry   01480 861381

Gibraltar Sailing Centre
Gibraltar   +350 78554

Glenans Irish Sailing School
Baltimore   +353 28 20154

Hamble School of Yachting
Hamble   023 8045 6687

Haslar Sea School
Gosport   023 9252 0099

Hobo Yachting
Southampton   023 8033 4574

Hoylake Sailing School
Wirral   0151 632 4664

Ibiza Sailing School   07092 235 853

International Yachtmaster Academy
Southampton   0800 515439

Island Sea School
Port Dinorwic   01248 352330

JP Services – Marine Safety & Training
Chichester   01243 537552

Lymington Cruising School
Lymington   01590 677478

Marine Leisure Association (MLA)
Southampton   023 8029 3822

Menorca Cruising School
01995 679240

Moncur Sailing School, Bob
Newcastle upon Tyne   0191 265 4472

Moonfleet Sailing
Poole   01202 682269

National Marine Correspondence School Macclesfield   01625 262365

Northshore King's Lynn   01485 210236

On Deck Sailing
Southampton   023 8063 9997

Pembrokeshire Cruising
Neyland   01646 602500

Performance Yachting & Chandlery
Plymouth   01752 565023

Plain Sailing
Dartmouth   01803 853843

Plymouth Sailing School
Plymouth   01752 493377

Port Edgar Marina & Sailing School		
Port Edgar	0131 331 3330	

Portsmouth Outdoor Centre
Portsmouth 023 9266 3873

Portugal Sail & Power 01473 833001

Reeder School of Seamanship, Mike
Lymington 01590 674560

Safe Water Training Sea School Ltd
Wirral 0151 630 0466

Sail East
Felixstowe 01255 502887

Sail East
River Crouch 07860 271954

Sail East
River Medway 07932 157027

Sail East Harwich 01473 689344

Sally Water Training
East Cowes 01983 299033

Sea-N-Shore
Salcombe 01548 842276

Seafever
East Grinstead 01342 316293

Solaris Mediterranean Sea School
01925 642909

Solent School of Yachting
Southampton 023 8045 7733

Southcoasting Navigators
Devon 01626 335626

Southern Sailing
Southampton 01489 575511

Start Point Sailing
Dartmouth 01548 810917

Sunsail
Port Solent/Largs 0870 770 6314

Team Sailing
Gosport 023 9252 4370

Tiller School of Navigation
Banstead 01737 211466

Workman Marine School
Portishead 01275 845844

Wride School of Sailing, Bob
North Ferriby 01482 635623

WATERSIDE ACCOMMODATION & RESTAURANTS

Abbey, The
Penzance 01736 366906

Arun View Inn, The
Littlehampton 01903 722335

Baywatch on the Beach
Bembridge 01983 873259

Beaucette Marina Restaurant
Guernsey 01481 247066

Bella Napoli
Brighton Marina 01273 818577

Bembridge Coast Hotel
Bembridge 01983 873931

Budock Vean Hotel
Porth Navas Creek 01326 252100

Café Mozart Cowes 01983 293681

Caffè Uno Port Solent 023 9237 5227

Chandlers Bar & Bistro Queen Anne's
Battery Marina, Plymouth 01752 257772

Chiquito Port Solent 02392 205070

Cruzzo Malahide Marina, Co Dublin
+353 1 845 0599

Cullins Yard Bistro
Dover 01304 211666

Custom House, The
Poole 01202 676767

Dart Marina River Lounge
Dartmouth 01803 832580

Deer Leap, The
Exmouth 01395 265030

Doghouse Swanwick Marina,
Hamble 01489 571602

Dolphin Restaurant
Gorey 01534 853370

Doune Knoydart 01687 462667

El Puertos
Penarth Marina 029 2070 5551

**Falmouth Marina Marine Bar and
Restaurant** Falmouth 01326 313481

Ferry Boat Inn West Wick Marina,
Nr Chelmsford 01621 740208

Ferry Inn, The (restaurant)
Pembroke Dock 01646 682947

First and Last, The Braye,
Alderney 01481 823162

Fisherman's Wharf
Sandwich 01304 613636

Folly Inn Cowes 01983 297171

Gaffs Restaurant Fenit Harbour
Marina, County Kerry +353 66 71 36666

Godleys Hotel Fenit,
County Kerry +353 66 71 36108

Harbour Lights Restaurant
Walton on the Naze 01255 851887

Haven Bar and Bistro, The
Lymington Yacht Haven 01590 679971

Haven Hotel Poole 08453 371550

HMS Ganges Restaurant
Mylor Yacht Harbour 01326 374320

Jolly Sailor, The
Bursledon 023 8040 5557

Kames Hotel Argyll 01700 811489

Ketch Rigger, The Hamble Point
Marina Hamble 023 8045 5601

Kota Restaurant
Porthleven 01326 562407

La Cala Lady Bee Marina,
Shoreham 01273 597422

Le Nautique
St Peter Port 01481 721714

Lighter Inn, The
Topsham 01392 875439

Mariners Bistro Sparkes Marina,
Hayling Island 023 9246 9459

Mary Mouse II Haslar Marina,
Gosport 023 9252 5200

Martha's Vineyard
Milford Haven 01646 697083

Master Builder's House Hotel Buckler's
Hard 01590 616253

Millstream Hotel
Bosham 01243 573234

Montagu Arms Hotel
Beaulieu 01590 612324

Oyster Quay Mercury Yacht Harbour,
Hamble 023 8045 7220

Paris Hotel Coverack 01326 280258

Pebble Beach, The
Gosport 023 9251 0789

Petit Champ Sark 01481 832046

Philip Leisure Group
Dartmouth 01803 833351

Priory Bay Hotel
Seaview, Isle of Wight 01983 613146

Quayside Hotel Brixham 01803 855751

Queen's Hotel Kirkwall 01856 872200

Sails Dartmouth 01803 839281

Shell Bay Seafood Restaurant
Poole Harbour 01929 450363

Simply Italian Sovereign Harbour,
Eastbourne 01323 470911

Spinnaker, The
Chichester Marina 01243 511032

Spit Sand Fort
The Solent 01329 242077

Steamboat Inn Lossiemouth Marina,
Lossiemouth 01343 812066

Tayvallich Inn, The
Argyll 01546 870282

Villa Adriana Newhaven Marina
Newhaven 01273 513976

Warehouse Brasserie, The
Poole 01202 677238

36 on the Quay
Emsworth 01243 375592

WEATHER INFORMATION

Met Office Exeter 0870 900 0100

WOOD FITTINGS

Howells & Son, KJ
Poole 01202 665724

Onward Trading Co Ltd
Southampton 01489 885250

Robbins Timber
Bristol 0117 963 3136

Sheraton Marine Cabinet
Witney 01993 868275

YACHT BROKERS

ABC Powermarine
Beaumaris   01248 811413

ABYA Association of Brokers & Yacht
Agents Bordon   0845 0900162

Adur Boat Sales
Southwick   01273 596680

Ancasta International Boat Sales
Southampton   023 8045 0000

Anglia Yacht Brokerage
Bury St Edmunds   01359 271747

Ardmair Boat Centre
Ullapool   01854 612054

Barbican Yacht Agency, The
Plymouth   01752 228855

Bates Wharf Marine Sales Ltd
                                   01932 571141

BJ Marine Bangor   028 9127 1434

Boatworks + Ltd
St Peter Port   01481 726071

Caley Marina Inverness   01463 236539

Calibra Marine International Ltd
Southampton   08702 400358

Camper & Nicholsons International
London   020 7009 1950

Clarke & Carter Interyacht Ltd Ipswich/
Burnham on Crouch
                    01473 659681/01621 785600

Coastal Leisure Ltd
Southampton   023 8033 2222

Dale Sailing Brokerage
Neyland   01646 603105

Deacons
Southampton   023 8040 2253

Exe Leisure
Topsham   001392 879055

Ferrypoint Boat Co
Youghal   +353 24 94232

Gweek Quay Boatyard
Helston   01326 221657

International Barge & Yacht Brokers
Southampton   023 8045 5205

Iron Wharf Boatyard
Faversham   01795 537122

Jackson Yacht Services
Jersey   01534 743819

Kings Yacht Agency
Beaulieu   01590 616316

Kippford Slipway Ltd
Dalbeattie   01556 620249

Lencraft Boats Ltd
Dungarvan   +353 58 68220

Liberty Yachts Ltd
Plymouth   01752 227911

Lucas Yachting, Mike
Torquay   01803 212840

Network Yacht Brokers
Dartmouth   01803 834864

Network Yacht Brokers
Plymouth   01752 605377

New Horizon Yacht Agency
Guernsey   01481 726335

Oyster Brokerage Ltd
Ipswich   01473 602263

Pearn and Co, Norman
(Looe Boatyard) Looe   01503 262244

Performance Boat Company
Maidenhead   07768 464717

Peters Chandlery
Chichester   01243 511033

Portavon Marina
Keynsham   0117 986 1626

Prosser Marine Sales Ltd
Glasgow   0141 552 2005

Retreat Boatyard
Topsham   01392 874720

SD Marine Ltd
Southampton   023 8045 7278

Sea & Shore Ship Chandler
Dundee   01382 202666

South Pier Shipyard
St Helier   01534 711000

South West Yacht Brokers Group
Plymouth   01752 401421

Sunbird Marine Services
Fareham   01329 842613

Trafalgar Yacht Services
Fareham   01329 823577

Transworld Yachts
Hamble   023 8045 7704

Walton Marine Sales
Brighton   01273 670707
Portishead   01275 840132

Walton Marine Sales
Wroxham   01603 781178

Watson Marine, Charles
Hamble   023 8045 6505

Western Marine
Dublin   +353 1280 0321

Woodrolfe Brokerage
Maldon   01621 868494

Youngboats
Faversham   01795 536176

YACHT CHARTERS & HOLIDAYS

Ardmair Boat Centre
Ullapool   01854 612054

Association of Scottish Yacht
Charterers Argyll   01880 820012

Blue Baker Yachts
Ipswich   01473 780111/780008

Camper & Nicholsons International
London   020 7009 1950

Coastal Leisure Ltd
Southampton   023 8033 2222

Crusader Yachting
Turkey   01732 867321

Dartmouth Sailing
Dartmouth   01803 833399

Dartmouth Yacht Charters
Kingswear   01803 752935

Doune Marine Mallaig   01687 462667

Four Seasons Yacht Charter
Gosport   023 9251 1789

Golden Black Sailing
Cornwall   01209 715757

Hamble Point Yacht Charters
Hamble   023 8045 7110

Haslar Marina & Victory Yacht Charters
Gosport   023 9252 0099

Indulgence Charters
Wendover   01296 696006

Liberty Yachts West Country, Greece,
Mallorca & Italy   01752 227911

Nautilus Yachting Mediterranean
& Caribbean   01732 867445

On Deck Sailing
Southampton   023 8063 9997

Patriot Charters & Sail School
Milford Haven   01437 741202

West Country Yachts
Plymouth   01752 606999
Falmouth   01326 212320

Puffin Yachts
Port Solent   01483 420728

Sailing Holidays Ltd
Mediterranean   020 8459 8787

Sailing Holidays in Ireland
Kinsale   +353 21 477 2927

Setsail Holidays Greece, Turkey,
Croatia, Majorca   01787 310445

Shannon Sailing Ltd
Tipperary   +353 67 24499

Sleat Marine Services
Isle of Skye   01471 844216

Smart Yachts
Mediterranean   01425 614804

South West Marine Training
Dartmouth   01803 853843

Sovereign Sailingl
Kinsale   +353 87 6172555

Sunsail
Worldwide   0870 770 0102

Templecraft Yacht Charters
Lewes   01273 812333

TJ Sailing Gosport   07803 499691

Top Yacht Sailing Ltd
Havant   02392 347655

Victory Yacht Charters
Gosport   023 9252 0099

West Wales Yacht Charter
Pwllheli   07748 634869

39 North (Mediterranean)
Kingskerwell   07071 393939

YACHT CLUBS

Aberaeron YC
Aberdovey   01545 570077

Aberdeen and Stonehaven SC
Nr Inverurie   01569 764006

Aberdour BC   01383 860029

Abersoch Power BC
Abersoch   01758 712027

Aberystwyth BC
Aberystwyth   01970 624575

Aldeburgh YC   01728 452562

Alderney SC   01481 822959

Alexandra YC
Southend-on-Sea   01702 340363

Arklow SC   +353 402 33100

Arun YC Littlehampton 01903 716016

Axe YC Axemouth   01297 20043

Ayr Yacht and CC   01292 476034

Ballyholme YC Bangor 028 91271467

Baltimore SC   +353 28 20426

Banff SC   01464 820308

Bantry Bay SC   +353 27 51724

Barry YC   01446 735511

Beaulieu River SC
Brockenhurst   01590 616273

Bembridge SC
Isle of Wight   01983 872237

Benfleet YC
Canvey Island   01268 792278

**Blackpool and
Fleetwood YC**   01253 884205

Blackwater SC Maldon 01621 853923

Blundellsands SC   0151 929 2101

Bosham SC Chichester 01243 572341

Brading Haven YC
Isle of Wight   01983 872289

Bradwell CC   01621 892970

Bradwell Quay YC
Wickford   01268 890173

Brancaster Staithe SC 01485 210249

Brandy Hole YC
Hullbridge   01702 230320

Brightlingsea SC   01206 303275

Brighton Marina YC
Peacehaven   01273 818711

Bristol Avon SC   01225 873472

Bristol Channel YC
Swansea   01792 366000

Bristol Corinthian YC
Axbridge   01934 732033

Brixham YC   01803 853332

**Burnham Overy
Staithe SC**   01328 730961

Burnham-on-Crouch SC
                       01621 782812

Burnham-on-Sea SC
Bridgwater   01278 792911

Burry Port YC   01554 833635

Cabot CC   01275 855207

Caernarfon SC (Menai Strait)
Caernarfon   01286 672861

Campbeltown SC   01586 552488

Island YC Canvey Island 01702 510360

Cardiff YC   029 2046 3697

Cardiff Bay YC   029 20226575

Carlingford Lough YC
Rostrevor   028 4173 8604

Carrickfergus SC
Whitehead   028 93 351402

Castle Cove SC
Weymouth   01305 783708

Castlegate Marine Club
Stockton on Tees   01642 583299

Chanonry SC Fortrose 01463 221415

Chichester Cruiser and Racing Club
                       01483 770391

Chichester YC   01243 512918

Christchurch SC   01202 483150

Clyde CC Glasgow   0141 221 2774

Co Antrim YC
Carrickfergus   028 9337 2322

Cobnor Activities Centre Trust
                       01243 572791

Coleraine YC   028 703 44503

Colne YC Brightlingsea 01206 302594

Conwy YC Deganwy   01492 583690

Coquet YC   01665 710367

Corrib Rowing & YC
Galway City   +353 91 564560

Cowes Combined Clubs
                       01983 295744

Cowes Corinthian YC
Isle of Wight   01983 296333

Cowes Yachting   01983 280770

Cramond BC   0131 336 1356

Creeksea SC
Burnham-on-Crouch   01245 320578

Crookhaven SC   087 2379997 mobile

Crouch YC
Burnham-on-Crouch   01621 782252

Dale YC   01646 636362

Dartmouth YC   01803 832305

Deben YC Woodbridge   01394 384440

Dell Quay SC Chichester 01243 514639

Dingle SC   +353 66 51984

Douglas Bay YC   01624 673965

Dovey YC Aberdovey   01213 600008

Dun Laoghaire MYC   +353 1 288 938

Dunbar SC
Cockburnspath   01368 86287

East Antrim BC   028 28 277204

East Belfast YC   028 9065 6283

East Cowes SC   01983 531687

East Dorset SC Poole 01202 706111

East Lothian YC   01620 892698

Eastney Cruising Association
Portsmouth   023 92734103

Eling SC   023 80863987

Emsworth SC   01243 372850

Emsworth Slipper SC 01243 378881

Essex YC Southend   01702 478404

Exe SC (River Exe)
Exmouth   01395 264607

Eyott SC Mayland   01245 320703

Fairlie YC   01294 213940

Falmouth Town SC   01326 373915

Falmouth Watersports Association
Falmouth   01326 211223

Fareham Sailing & Motor BC
Fareham   01329 280738

Felixstowe Ferry SC 01394 283785

Findhorn YC Findhorn 01309 690247

Fishguard Bay YC
Lower Fishguard   01348 872866

Flushing SC Falmouth 01326 374043

Folkestone Yacht and Motor BC
Folkestone   01303 251574

Forth Corinthian YC
Haddington   0131 552 5939

Forth YCs Association
Edinburgh   0131 552 3006

Fowey Gallants SC   01726 832335

Foynes YC Foynes   +353 69 91201

Galway Bay SC   +353 91 794527

Glasson SC
Lancaster   01524 751089

Glenans Irish Sailing School
                       +353 1 6611481

Glenans Irish SC (Westport)
+353 98 26046

Gosport CC Gosport — 02392 586838

Gravesend SC — 07538 326623

Greenwich YC London — 020 8858 7339

Grimsby and Cleethorpes YC
Grimsby — 01472 356678

Guernsey YC
St Peter Port — 01481 725342

Hamble River SC
Southampton — 023 80452070

Hampton Pier YC
Herne Bay — 01227 364749

Hardway SC Gosport — 023 9258 1875

Hartlepool YC — 01429 233423

Harwich Town SC — 01255 503200

Hastings and St Leonards YC
Hastings — 01424 420656

Haven Ports YC
Woodbridge — 01473 659658

Hayling Ferry SC; Locks SC
Hayling Island — 023 80829833

Hayling Island SC — 023 92463768

Helensburgh SC Rhu — 01436 672778

Helensburgh — 01436 821234

Helford River SC
Helston — 01326 231006

Herne Bay SC — 01227 375650

Highcliffe SC
Christchurch — 01425 274874

Holyhead SC — 01407 762526

Holywood YC — 028 90423355

Hoo Ness YC Sidcup — 01634 250052

Hornet SC Gosport — 023 9258 0403

Howth YC — +353 1 832 2141

Hoylake SC Wirral — 0151 632 2616

Hullbridge YC — 01702 231797

Humber Yawl Club — 01482 667224

Hundred of Hoo SC — 01634 250102

Hurlingham YC London — 020 8788 5547

Hurst Castle SC — 01590 645589

Hythe SC Southampton — 02380 846563

Hythe & Saltwood SC — 01303 265178

Ilfracombe YC — 01271 863969

Iniscealtra SC
Limerick — +353 61 338347

Invergordon BC — 01349 893772

Irish CC — +353 214870031

Island CC Salcombe — 01548 531176

Island SC Isle of Wight — 01983 296621

Island YC Canvey Island — 01268 510360

Isle of Bute SC
Rothesay — 01700 502819

Isle of Man YC
Port St Mary — 01624 832088

Itchenor SC Chichester — 01243 512400

Keyhaven YC — 01590 642165

Killyleagh YC — 028 4482 8250

Kircubbin SC — 028 4273 8422

Kirkcudbright SC — 01557 331727

Langstone SC Havant — 023 9248 4577

Largs SC Largs — 01475 670000

Larne Rowing & SC — 028 2827 4573

Lawrenny YC — 01646 651212

Leigh-on-Sea SC — 01702 476788

Lerwick BC — 01595 696954

Lilliput SC Poole — 01202 740319

Littlehampton Yacht Club
Littlehampton — 01903 713990

Loch Ryan SC Stranraer — 01776 706322

Lochaber YC Fort William 01397 772361

Locks SC Portsmouth — 023 9282 9833

Looe SC — 01503 262559

Lossiemouth CC
Fochabers — 01348 812121

Lough Swilly YC Fahn — +353 74 22377

Lowestoft CC — 01502 574376

Lyme Regis Power BC — 01297 443788

Lyme Regis SC — 01297 442373

Lymington Town SC — 0159 674514

Lympstone SC Exeter — 01395 278792

Madoc YC Porthmadog — 01766 512976

Malahide YC — +353 1 845 3372

Maldon Little Ship Club
01621 854139

Manx Sailing & CC
Ramsey — 01624 813494

Marchwood YC — 023 80666141

Margate YC — 01843 292602

Marina BC Pwllheli — 01758 612271

Maryport YC — 01228 560865

Mayflower SC Plymouth 01752 662526

Mayo SC (Rosmoney)
Rosmoney — +353 98 27772

Medway YC Rochester — 01634 718399

Menai Bridge BC
Beaumaris — 01248 810583

Mengham Rythe SC
Hayling Island — 023 92463337

Merioneth YC
Barmouth — 01341 280000

Monkstone Cruising and SC
Swansea — 01792 812229

Montrose SC Montrose — 01674 672554

Mumbles YC Swansea — 01792 369321

Mylor YC Falmouth — 01326 374391

Nairn SC — 01667 453897

National YC
Dun Laoghaire — +353 1 280 5725

Netley SC Netley — 023 80454272

New Quay YC
Aberdovey — 01545 560516

Newhaven & Seaford SC
Seaford — 01323 890077

Newport and Uskmouth SC
Cardiff — 01633 271417

Newtownards SC — 028 9181 3426

Neyland YC — 01646 600267

North Devon YC
Bideford — 01271 861390

North Fambridge Yacht Centre
01621 740370

North Haven YC Poole — 01202 708830

North of England Yachting Association
Kirkwall — 01856 872331

North Sunderland Marine Club
Sunderland — 01665 721231

North Wales CC
Conwy — 01492 593481

North West Venturers YC (Beaumaris)
Beaumaris — 0161 2921943

Oban SC Ledaig by Oban
01631 563999

Orford SC Woodbridge — 01394 450997

Orkney SC Kirkwall — 01856 872331

Orwell YC Ipswich — 01473 602288

Oulton Broad Yacht Station
01502 574946

Ouse Amateur SC
Kings Lynn — 01553 772239

Paignton SC Paignton — 01803 525817

Parkstone YC Poole — 01202 743610

Peel Sailing and CC
Peel — 01624 842390

Pembroke Haven YC — 01646 684403

Pembrokeshire YC
Milford Haven — 01646 692799

Penarth YC — 029 20708196

Pentland Firth YC
Thurso — 01847 891803

Penzance YC — 01736 364989

Peterhead SC Ellon — 01779 75527

Pin Mill SC Woodbridge — 01394 780271

Plym YC Plymouth — 01752 404991

Poolbeg YC — +353 1 660 4681

Poole YC	01202 672687	
Porlock Weir SC		
Watchet	01643 862702	
Port Edgar YC Penicuik	0131 657 2854	
Port Navas YC		
Falmouth	01326 340065	
Port of Falmouth Sailing Association		
Falmouth	01326 372927	
Portchester SC		
Portchester	023 9237 6375	
Porthcawl Harbour BC		
Swansea	01656 655935	
Porthmadog SC		
Porthmadog	01766 513546	
Portrush YC Portrush	028 7082 3932	
Portsmouth SC	02392 820596	
Prestwick SC Prestwick	01292 671117	
Pwllheli SC Pwllheli	01758 613343	
Queenborough YC		
Queenborough	01795 663955	
Quoile YC Downpatrick	028 44 612266	
R Towy BC Tenby	01267 241755	
RAFYC	023 80452208	
Redclyffe YC Poole	01929 557227	
Restronguet SC		
Falmouth	01326 374536	
Ribble CC		
Lytham St Anne's	01253 739983	
River Wyre YC	01253 811948	
RNSA (Plymouth)	01752 55123/83	
Rochester CC	01634 841350	
Rock Sailing and Water Ski Club		
Wadebridge	01208 862431	
Royal Dart YC		
Dartmouth	01803 752496	
Royal Motor YC Poole	01202 707227	
Royal Anglesey YC (Beaumaris)		
Anglesey	01248 810295	
Royal Burnham YC		
Burnham-on-Crouch	01621 782044	
Royal Channel Islands YC (Jersey)		
St Aubin	01534 745783	
Royal Cinque Ports YC		
Dover	01304 206262	
Royal Corinthian YC (Burnham-on-Crouch)		
Burnham-on-Crouch	01621 782105	
Royal Corinthian YC (Cowes)		
Cowes	01983 293581	
Royal Cork YC		
Crosshaven	+353 214 831023	
Royal Cornwall YC (RCYC)		
Falmouth	01326 312126	

Royal Dorset YC		
Weymouth	01305 786258	
Royal Forth YC		
Edinburgh	0131 552 3006	
Royal Fowey YC		
Fowey	01726 833573	
Royal Gourock YC		
Gourock	01475 632983	
Royal Highland YC		
Connel	01852 300460	
Royal Irish YC		
Dun Laoghaire	+353 1 280 9452	
Royal London YC		
Isle of Wight	019 83299727	
Royal Lymington YC	01590 672677	
Royal Mersey YC		
Birkenhead	0151 645 3204	
Royal Motor YC Poole	01202 707227	
Royal Naval Club and Royal Albert YC		
Portsmouth	023 9282 5924	
Royal Naval Sailing Association		
Gosport	023 9252 1100	
Royal Norfolk & Suffolk YC		
Lowestoft	01502 566726	
Royal North of Ireland YC		
	028 90 428041	
Royal Northern and Clyde YC		
Rhu	01436 820322	
Royal Northumberland YC		
Blyth	01670 353636	
Royal Plymouth Corinthian YC		
Plymouth	01752 664327	
Royal Scottish Motor YC		
	0141 881 1024	
Royal Solent YC		
Yarmouth	01983 760256	
Royal Southampton YC		
Southampton	023 8022 3352	
Royal Southern YC		
Southampton	023 8045 0300	
Royal St George YC		
Dun Laoghaire	+353 1 280 1811	
Royal Tay YC Dundee	01382 477133	
Royal Temple YC		
Ramsgate	01843 591766	
Royal Torbay YC		
Torquay	01803 292006	
Royal Ulster YC		
Bangor	028 91 270568	
Royal Victoria YC		
Fishbourne	01983 882325	

Royal Welsh YC (Caernarfon)		
Caernarfon	01286 672599	
Royal Welsh YC		
Aernarfon	01286 672599	
Royal Western YC		
Plymouth	01752 226299	
Royal Yacht Squadron		
Isle of Wight	01983 292191	
Royal Yorkshire YC		
Bridlington	01262 672041	
Rye Harbour SC	01797 223136	
Salcombe YC	01548 842593	
Saltash SC	01752 845988	
Scalloway BC Lerwick	01595 880409	
Scarborough YC	01723 373821	
Schull SC	+353 28 37352	
Scillonian Sailing and BC		
St Mary's	01720 277229	
Seasalter SC		
Whitstable	07773 189943	
Seaview YC		
Isle of Wight	01983 613268	
Shoreham SC Henfield	01273 453078	
Skerries SC		
Carlingdford Lough	+353 1 849 1233	
Slaughden SC Duxford	01728 689036	
Sligo YC Sligo	+353 71 77168	
Solva Boat Owners Association		
Fishguard	01437 721538	
Solway YC		
Kirkdudbright	01556 620312	
South Caernavonshire YC		
Abersoch	01758 712338	
South Cork SC	+353 28 36383	
South Devon Sailing School		
Newton Abbot	01626 52352	
South Gare Marine Club - Sail Section		
Middlesbrough	01642 505630	
South Shields SC	0191 456 5821	
South Woodham Ferrers YC		
Chelmsford	01245 325391	
Southampton SC	023 8044 6575	
Southwold SC	01986 784225	
Sovereign Harbour YC		
Eastbourne	01323 470888	
St Helier YC	01534 721307/32229	
St Mawes SC	01326 270686	
Starcross Fishing & CC (River Exe)		
Starcross	01626 891996	

Starcross YC
Exeter   01626 890470

Stoke SC Ipswich   01473 624989

Stornoway SC   01851 705412

Stour SC   01206 393924

Strangford Lough YC
Newtownards   028 97 541202

Strangford SC
Downpatrick   028 4488 1404

Strood YC
Aylesford   01634 718261

Sunderland YC   0191 567 5133

Sunsail Portsmouth   023 92222224

Sussex YC
Shoreham-by-Sea   01273 464868

Swanage SC   01929 422987

Swansea Yacht & Sub-Aqua Club
Swansea   01792 469096

Tamar River SC
Plymouth   01752 362741

Tarbert Lochfyne YC   01880 820376

Tay Corinthian BC
Dundee   01382 553534

Tay YCs Association   01738 621860

Tees & Hartlepool YC   01429 233423

Tees SC
Aycliffe Village   01429 265400

Teifi BC - Cardigan Bay
Fishguard   01239 613846

Teign Corinthian YC
Teignmouth   01626 777699

Tenby SC   01834 842762

Tenby YC   01834 842762

Thames Estuary YC   01702 345967

Thorney Island SC   01243 371731

Thorpe Bay YC   01702 587563

Thurrock YC Grays   01375 373720

Tollesbury CC   01621 869561

Topsham SC   01392 877524

Torpoint Mosquito SC -
Plymouth   01752 812508

Tralee SC   +353 66 7136119

Troon CC   01292 311190

Troon YC   01292 315315 **Tudor SC**
Portsmouth   023 92662002

Tynemouth SC
Newcastle upon Tyne   0191 2572167

Up River YC
Hullbridge   01702 231654

Upnor SC   01634 718043

Vanguard SC
Workington   01228 674238

Wakering YC
Rochford   01702 530926

Waldringfield SC
Woodbridge   01394 283347

Walls Regatta Club
Lerwick   01595 809273

Walton & Frinton YC
Walton-on-the-Naze   01255 675526

Warrenpoint BC   028 4175 2137

Warsash SC
Southampton   01489 583575

Watchet Boat Owner Association
Watchet   01984 633736

Waterford Harbour SC
Dunmore East   +353 51 383389

Watermouth YC
Watchet   01271 865048

Wear Boating Association
                                   0191 567 5313

Wells SC
Wells-next-the-sea   01328 711190

West Kirby SC   0151 625 5579

West Mersea YC
Colchester   01206 382947

Western Isles YC   01688 302371

Western YC
Kilrush   +353 87 2262885

Weston Bay YC
Portishead   07867 966429

Weston CC
Southampton   02380 466790

Weston SC
Southampton   02380 452527

Wexford HBC   +353 53 22039

Weymouth SC
Weymouth   01305 785481

Whitby YC   07786 289393

Whitstable YC   01227 272942

Wicklow SC   +353 404 67526

Witham SC
Boston, Lincs   01205 363598

Wivenhoe SC
Colchester   01206 822132

Woodbridge CC   01394 386737

Wormit BC   01382 553878

Yarmouth SC   01983 760270

Yealm YC
Newton Ferrers   01752 872291

Youghal Sailing Club   +353 24 92447

YACHT DESIGNERS

Cannell & Associates, David M
Wivenhoe   01206 823337

Clarke Designs LLP, Owen
Dartmouth   01803 770495

Giles Naval Architects, Laurent
Lymington   01590 641777

Harvey Design, Ray
Barton on Sea   01425 613492

Jones Yacht Design, Stephen
Warsash   01489 576439

Wharram Designs, James
Truro   01872 864792

Wolstenholme Yacht Design
Coltishall   01603 737024

YACHT MANAGEMENT

Barbican Yacht Agency Ltd
Plymouth   01752 228855

Coastal Leisure Ltd
Southampton   023 8033 2222

O'Sullivan Boat Management
Dun Laoghaire   +353 86 829 6625

Swanwick Yacht Surveyors
Swanwick   01489 564822

Amble Boat Company Ltd
Amble   01665 710267

YACHT VALETING

Autogleam
Lymington   0800 074 4672

Blackwell, Craig
Co Meath   +353 87 677 9605

Bright 'N' Clean
South Coast   07789 494430

Clean It All
Nr Brixham   01803 844564

Kip Marina
Inverkip   01475 521485

Mainstay Yacht Maintenance
Dartmouth   01803 839076

Mobile Yacht Maintenance
                                   07900 148806

Shipshape
Hayling Is   023 9232 4500